Practicing Feminisms, Reconstructing Psychology

Critical Perspectives on Women and Gender

Critical Perspectives on Women and Gender brings books on timely issues and controversies to an interdisciplinary audience. The series explores gender-related topics and illuminates the issues involved in current debates in feminist scholarship and across the disciplines.

Titles in the series

Michelle Fine
Disruptive Voices: The Possibilities of Feminist Research

Susan D. Clayton and Faye J. Crosby
Justice, Gender, and Affirmative Action

Janice Doane and Devon Hodges
From Klein to Kristeva: Psychoanalytic Feminism and the Search for the "Good Enough" Mother

Jill Dolan
Presence and Desire: Essays on Gender, Sexuality, Performance

Judith Newton
Starting Over: Feminism and the Politics of Cultural Critique

Jill G. Morawski
Practicing Feminisms, Reconstructing Psychology: Notes on a Liminal Science

Practicing Feminisms, Reconstructing Psychology

Notes on a Liminal Science

Jill G. Morawski

Ann Arbor

The University of Michigan Press

Published in the United States of America by
The University of Michigan Press
Manufactured in the United States of America
♾ Printed on acid-free paper

1997 1996 1995 1994 4 3 2 1

A CIP catalogue record for this book is available from the British Library.

Library of Congress Cataloging-in-Publication Data

Morawski, Jill Gladys.
Practicing feminisms, reconstructing psychology : notes on a liminal science / Jill G. Morawski.
p. cm.—(Critical perspectives on women and gender)
Includes bibliographical references and index.
ISBN 0-472-09481-5 (alk. paper).—ISBN 0-472-06481-9 (pbk. : alk. paper)
1. Feminist psychology. I. Title. II. Series.
BF201.4.M67 1994
150'.82—dc20 94-10786
CIP

To the memory of Janet Bushman Morawski,
and to the future she dreamed for all of us.

Contents

Introduction

A great deal of our tacit understanding of science would suggest, indeed, would insist, that the meshing of feminism and psychology is unimaginable, impossible, antithetical, and at last, undesirable. Yet there exists a hearty and ambitious (if loosely joined) collective of psychologists who define their work as just such a meshing. Many of these feminist psychologists go about their daily scientific duties without regard for the looming contradiction: For them, feminism, like democracy, is taken to be wholly compatible with science. Yet other psychologists stumble across difficulties in the pairing of the two missions. Given the presence of this collective force and the relatively stable conditions under which most of its members produce their feminist science, it would seem that the most difficult task lying ahead is to convince those psychologists who take feminist psychology as a set of problematic if not contradictory terms that it really is a feasible, desirable, and important scientific enterprise.

Such persuasion is not the subject of the present book. In fact, this project reflects a wariness toward exerting too much energy in what often become defensive programs. In psychology, as in other sciences, efforts from the margin to convince the center are rarely successful. But it is not the bleak prospects of victory that cause my reluctance about a reparative program aimed primarily at a separate and sometimes resistant audience. Rather, it is my sense that such argumentative writings and related border debates have deflected attention from far more interesting and vastly more auspicious events in feminist psychology. Thus my project embraces these more promising actions and strives to elucidate them. Instead of depicting the field of feminist psychology merely as marred by internally generated controversies and externally motivated oppressions, all of which do exist at times, I propose that we perceive that terrain as being richly fertilized by promising actions of *disobedience.* Feminist psychology is rapidly outgrowing its self-images as a remedial movement or an oppositional field and is successfully replacing ill-suited investigative practices with innovative and transformative ones.

This extended, multifocal essay is intended to delineate the new, evolving contours of feminist psychology. It proceeds by recollecting how feminist ventures are altering the dearest of scientific tenets, notably objectivity, subjectivity, and validity. And it is, indeed, a venture in recollecting, for I try to assemble the strategical actions that are enabling feminist psychologists not simply to exist in what is sometimes an unfriendly ecosystem but, more important, to restructure and revitalize that system. Through such gathering of research from both inside and outside the discipline of psychology, I propose that feminist psychologists are becoming involved in making a new and different science, one that takes gender far beyond its conceptualization as a psychological attribute or individual difference. It is a science that is cognitive and rational, but differently so because it involves self-conscious thinking about and rethinking the very nature of those cognitions and rational judgments. This science, however, is in process, and for that reason is situated somewhere betwixt and between the old scientific order and some yet to be settled one.

If my project has been born of a resistance against sinking back into old negotiations and treacherously stacked debates about the feasibility of feminist psychology, then it is one conceived with optimism: a belief that something is becoming of feminist researchers' efforts, enduring as long as there has been a discipline of psychology, to transform their science as well as the gendered relations of everyday life. But the project also derives from a more personal concern. As a member of that feminist minority of psychologists who have not been comfortable with the reigning methods of psychology, who see the routine investigative practices as being saturated with dubitable representations of human capacities—including those representations of race and economic status as well as gender—I have too often found myself caught between that same old rock and a hard place. In the company of more conventional feminist psychologists, I somehow inherit the garb of the "the critic," and while I am graciously received, there often seems to be no space where my work and words connect with theirs, no middle place to meet. I am the critic, and although the critic is almost always granted a position, it is usually on the outskirts. In the company of feminists in the wider academy, I again often find myself situated at the edge, although at these times I become a "feminist psychologist," a representative of a profession that is perceived, sometimes wrongly, as unrelentingly empiricist, scientistic, and inattentive to other modalities of feminist thought.

In these professional relations, and in the awkward identities that I find figuring me, I have begun not simply to resist the labelling and refuse the stereotyping, but to try to comprehend what boundaries are forming me thusly. The uncomfortable positions in which many feminist psychologists find themselves are the effect of certain structuring of social relations in psychology and across the academy generally, and it is those arrangements, I believe, that further hinder acknowledgement of what feminist psychology is becoming. Therefore, an auxiliary aim of my project is to test and push those boundaries, finding where they are merely false dividers or one-way mirrors that shorten our sight and diminish our conversations—in other words, to find where the boundaries can be moved or eliminated.

Sketching some details about the specific locale in which I stand intimates the larger objectives that frame this essay. One aim of the project is to generate a more clearly cultural study of one specific scientific enterprise—feminist psychology—in order to comprehend the historical, rhetorical, material, and regulative forces that both sustain and constrain that enterprise. Such cultural analysis serves to interrupt some of the mythic conceptions of science that may becloud researchers' self-understandings and replace them with a more comprehensive, if more complex, perspective on how scientific knowledge is produced, revised, and transmitted. To accomplish this aim, I elected not to stand apart from the ongoing scientific practices, assessing them afar with a set of analytic tools for registering the cultural dimensions of science, but instead to enter into the nuanced strategies constituting these practices in order to see and report on how researchers are using available resources—methods, epistemologies, and language. What can be seen through this approach, and what is reported in the following account, is a rather different feminist psychology than the one portrayed as simply a deviant (and defensive) field. Once no longer described in the conventional language about what science is, a language that aspires to some acontextual and philosophically neutral account of the true essence of science, feminist psychology can be seen as a distinct and dynamic scientific practice motivated by forces originating both inside and outside the profession of psychology. More importantly, feminist psychology can be appreciated as a transformative science, one in which many of its practitioners are reflexively embracing a cultural analysis of science to produce new psychological knowledge.

Among these new and different productions are reconfigurations of some of the classic working categories of psychological research: objectivity, subjectivity, and validity. These alterations are most often local, specific, intermittent, and partial and only by aggregating and reanalyzing them can we recognize their broader consequences. Chapter 1 introduces the domain of feminist psychology by contrasting the story of its origins and development with a narrative situating the field both in the shadow of its host discipline, psychology, and within the cultural horizon of changing social practices, economies, and gender behaviors. The ensuing three main chapters—concerning objectivity, subjectivity, and validity respectively—articulate the various innovations and conceptual trespassings that are altering those core categories of psychological research.

The central chapters of this book report provocative transformations, noting the various strategies and experimental cases through which such changes are being accomplished. Running through these accounts, although often implicitly, is evidence of feminist psychologists' working assumptions of scientific knowledge as power and of scientific accomplishments as more than merely rendering representations of the world. Science, in these works, is refigured as (or returned to) morality and politics. Thus, realized in these practices and rehearsed in these chapters is a critical engagement with science—one in which its practitioners are aware of their own cultural and moral involvement. In this sense, the chapters do not offer a dispassionate social study of scientific activity but rather, as Donna Haraway suggests, simultaneously document the social contingency of scientific knowing and maintain a deep commitment to understanding the world.

Throughout the chapters, this new feminist inquiry is illustrated by innovative investigations of gender, primarily of research on women. The portrait of gender that emerges cannot cohere, however, without representing the dynamics of race, class, ethnicity, and sexual preference. Making gender a central category of psychological analysis is not sufficient, for the experiences of being a woman (or man) are constituted differently, depending on other salient markers and conditions of personhood. North American psychology has long been criticized for its construction of an abstracted human mind, one supposedly universal in form but in actuality framed by the social experiences of white, middle-class Americans, usually males. Feminist psychology is one of the few psychological domains to challenge such cultural myopia and is beginning, perhaps not as ambitiously as it could, to develop more inclusive investigative practices. Chapter 3, "Subjectivity," gives special attention to the possibilities as well as to the difficulties of forging a culturally diverse psychology.

The organization of the book maps onto three prominent action-arenas of psychological investigation, transmuting those arenas into practices that are at once more fitting to actual investigative activities and to feminist commitments. What in psychology has been traditionally configured as scientific acts of objectivity, subjectivity, and validity are briefly introduced and then set against or, rather, replaced by descriptions of transformations, sometimes subtle and sometimes striking, of these actions through feminist-guided inquiry. Each of these three mainstay chapters incorporates exemplars of transformative actions that are drawn from recent research; the case examples thus supply descriptive as well as normative grounds for revised scientific practice. Understanding the movement from older to newer modes of scientific practices is critical to the way we think about science and our engagements in science. In order to introduce the fundamental and yet complex implications of such changes in scientific activities, I have created interchapters that explore to varying degrees some of the requisite intricacies and challenges. The interchapters, then, probe further into possibilities, problems, and unanswered questions, sometimes posing open quandaries and rarely delivering cognitive closure; yet they do not address all the questions and opportunities ensuing from new practices. The first interchapter takes up the question of what resources are available to guide feminist psychological inquiry once we see that our longstanding partnership with or reliance upon empiricism (as peculiarly defined by psychology) restricts our moves, curtails innovation, and sometimes forces repetition of age-old problems. Drawing on the resources of varied intellectual projects, that interchapter aims to summarize a new foundation for inquiry, a view that can be termed social epistemology. The second and third interchapters, succeeding the chapters on objectivity and subjectivity respectively, address some implications of reflexive practices, the primary one being the ways in which psychological investigations are altered by acknowledging the observer, the subject, and the relations between observer and subject as conscious and self-conscious agents in the making of science. These interchapters maintain no pretense of linear progression or closure for they aim simply to elucidate some of the implications of altering the social relations and objectives of our research, including our own standpoints and subjectivities. Following from this structure, the main chapters of the book can be read on their own, but the interchapters are requisite to apprehending the complications and wayward possibilities of investigative practices.

The portrait of feminist psychology that I am attempting to compile cannot be comprehensively featured in a single text. The unimagined transformations of feminist psychology encompass every move in our investigative practices. The book focuses on three major action-arenas (objectivity, subjectivity, and validity) because they figure so prominently in our investigative discourse, but gives little attention to other arenas. Matters pertaining to the social relations among investigators, systems (formal and informal) of communicating scientific findings, and political activism, for example, are only briefly discussed, yet are matters central to scientific life. Immersion in the chosen action-arenas also bypasses evaluation of particular theories, although such analysis remains crucial to feminist projects. The book concentrates on North American feminist psychology, only occasionally drawing on materials produced by British investigators, yet it is important to feminist psychology that its international scope and variations be explored.

As a practice in optimism and possibility, this project sometimes slides over nuances and fine-lined differences in the conversations about feminist psychology. And in order to bring to the foreground this vibrant program in the making, I decided to omit footnotes and limit the references—both decisions represent digressions from my usual bibliographic preoccupations. These omissions do not mean that we need not attend to detail, to varied opinions, and to contests over one idea or another. I hope that this style of writing will be taken in good faith and understood as an almost unavoidable consequence of trying to sketch out the flickering contours of a larger picture.

In the pages that follow, I repeatedly insist on viewing science as a *social practice* whose products are the effects of complex social relations sustained over time and shaped by a continually changing culture. As a form of science, albeit an anomalous one, this project is no exception and, therefore, my indebtedness extends to many cultural workers whose practices have influenced my own over the years. Those individuals who have been of more immediate inspiration I can mention by name. I thank Abigail Stewart and LeAnn Fields for their continued faith in the project; Laurel Furumoto, Anne Louise Shapiro, and Lloyd Strickland for their ongoing support of my work; and Gail Agronick, Betty Bayer, Mary Gergen, Kareen Ror Malone, Robert Steele, and Ruth Striegel-Moore for sharing their creative senses. For their conversations, analyses, and technical assistance, I thank Rebekah Bradley, Heather Brown, Sarah Carney, Jaclyn Friedman, Elizabeth Gilbert, David Lilly, Sherri Nass, Santina Scalia, Dena Silberstein, Susan Walker, and Julie Zaidler. As always, I am indebted to the library staff at Wesleyan and, in particular, to Steve Lebergott and his colleagues who searched the world for my often eccentric requests. And as typically seems to be the case, last but not least, I thank Thomas Palley for his support, and Davia and Sophie Palley for their patience, a quality that in preschoolers is too often misappreciated.

Chapter 1

Feminisms and Psychologies

Recently I addressed a group of physicians who are investigating and treating infertility. As a feminist aware of sexism in medicine, and in reproductive technologies in particular, I became interested in the practices of this medical specialty. Yet as a feminist who believes that science and technology need not and can no longer be loathed or feared, I tried to contemplate how science, including medical science, might yield the potential to empower women (and how women have the potential to transform science). When faced with the physicians' questions about how infertility clinics can better meet the needs of their patients, I offered several suggestions, including the employment of feminist psychologists in the clinics. My recommendation received an immediate response, but not, in this instance, from any skeptical or defensive physician. Rather, a psychologist in the room leapt up to identify the wrongness of my proposal, pronouncing feminist psychology to be an unacceptable contradiction, a dangerous merging of the political (hence biased) and the scientific (hence objective). At that moment, years of thinking and reading and forming a feminist psychology urgently sought a place in my voice. And my distress over psychology's residual positivism—its oppositional ridges of fact and value that still mark our roadways—interrupted my surely unsatisfactory response. For, to express a lack of faith in positivist science would certainly have curtailed any attempt to persuade that psychologist that feminist psychology is a reasonable scientific enterprise.

Feminist psychology, to many researchers situated outside that intellectual domain, is indeed a contradiction in terms. Feminist psychologists are hardly exonerated from this oppositional bind for many work and speak with two identities: the scientific voice of steady reason and the feminist voice of passionate commitment. To complicate matters further, as we labor to change the world and to transform reality, that reality is often turned against us. Like Madonna's staged performances with their subversive depiction of social life, our work is readily available to be recuperated into undesirable if not oppressive representations of that life (Bordo 1990b). Like Virginia Woolf's criticisms of sexist regimes, our writings can, at any time, be reinterpreted or ignored (Silver 1991). Feminist psychologists are sometimes unpleasingly dressed in garbs stereotypically associated with feminists, and more importantly, with the conceptual oppositions and juxtapositions just described—with the multiple realities of the culture in which we live. Feminist psychologists do wear these oppositions and multiplicities; they are inescapable features of trying to accommodate the complexities of science and of women's lives, all the while struggling to see wonderland. Feminist work is subject to reinterpretation and reclamation by the force of traditional paradigms within which and against which we work. Feminist psychologists' labor is marked—and challenged—by what has been described as the "dual crises" (Unger 1983) or "internal tensions" (Yllö 1988) of meshing feminism and psychology.

This chapter cleaves two approaches to assisting feminist psychology: the philosophical and the historical. Its departure from psychology's traditional uses of philosophy and history warrants prefatory comment. With that preliminary sketch, the remainder of the chapter reexamines the heritage of feminist work in psychology, comparing the more-or-less standard story with one that amplifies the social texture and culture of that scientific enterprise.

Regarding "Science"

Whether seen as an impossible impediment or as a necessary predicament, the contradictions of feminist psychology take their acute form only when viewed through the interpretive lens of a particular model of science, albeit the privileged model. Within psychology this conventional perspective, generally called empiricist, takes science to be an intellectual venture demarcated by unique rules of inquiry and presumes the existence of a knowable external reality and the availability of investigative procedures that ensure against contamination of that knowledge by human interests or prejudices. (From this platform, feminism, even in its generic dictionary definition as "advocacy" of the claims of women, represents a potential contaminant.) For instance, psychology's extended commitment to positivism and its own rendition of operationism have had implications for the rules of inquiry even long after positivism and operationism were purportedly abandoned. Among the rules guiding research are the views that theoretical statements must be empirically verifiable, that central constructs must be defined in terms of the concrete operations used to observe them, that "controlled" experiments are highly desirable if not necessary, and that theories should have universal applicability (Koch and Leary 1985; Toulmin and Leary 1985). In addition to such guiding instructions, research has for the most part proceeded with the premise that psychologists' observations represent the world in an accurate and literal way, that, using the example of developmental research, "Neither the infant nor the psychologist needs to struggle with ambiguity or develop its own unique meaning. The meaning is simply *there,* "written on the rocks," (Bradley 1993, 7–8). In other words, psychologists (not unlike some other social scientists) have selected and grafted a hypothetically descriptive philosophy of science, making it a prescriptive model for practice. This model has constituted, in the words of Stephen Toulmin and David Leary (1985), a "cult of empiricism." Taken in their sum, these regulative instructions supposedly ensure against the contamination of metaphysics and personal biases.

This empiricist program, melded with positivism, is neither monolithic nor static, and over the course of the twentieth century these empiricist perspectives have made space for moral and political commitments. The beliefs in reductionism, in objectivity freed of personal bias, and the assertion that objective claims, in principle, can be verified by anyone, were merged with a liberal political theory. As described by Allison Jaggar, according to this positivist view,

> good scientists are detached observers and manipulators of nature who follow strict methodological rules, which enable them to separate themselves from the special values, interests and emotions generated by their class, race, sex or unique situation. (1983, 356)

Revitalized by a normative moral philosophy, social scientists reconfected objectivity to mean "independence from the value judgments of any particular individual." Yet it nevertheless may contain consensual moral or political values (357). What has been termed "liberal feminism" is one version of this philosophical turn (although it distinguishes between the empirical and normative components of theory, the latter are identified as universal human values). As Jaggar observed, "In short, liberal feminists assume that their view reflects the impartial perspective of the rational, detached observer and consequently constitutes the most unbiased and objective feminist theory" (358).

However, science alternatively may be defined not as a set of formal rules (attempts to document these rules have been largely unsuccessful), but instead, as a practice that entails no unique activities or cognitions and that, therefore, requires no distinctive categories or rules to be understood (Fuller 1988; Latour 1987; Longino 1990; Woolgar 1988a). Rather than assuming that science constitutes a special or distinctive form of knowledge, it is suggested that "the practices of scientific investigation, its products, and its norms are historically variant" (Rouse 1992, 7). In this alternative view, revered concepts such as objectivity, reality, and representation are taken as the result of scientific work and not as unproblematic preconditions. That is, science is constituted through practical activities including those of designating what reality is and deciding what counts as objectivity. This view, emerging in diverse forms from new social studies of science and from feminist studies of science, does not take science to be independent of its practitioners and their actions. The new analyses of science as practice are developing this epistemological position in various ways, but for our present purposes, I will refer to them collectively as the "social epistemology" of science. I do so realizing that a social epistemology of science can mean many things, especially since scholars from diverse vantage points have begun developing ideas about the cultural dimensions of science in opposition to or as an amendment to the common understanding of science as a rational or cognitive enterprise.

The first interchapter visits the jumble of resources that inform my working concept of social epistemology. It describes this epistemic stance as a recognition of science as a constitutively cultural practice, that is, as a practice wherein cognitive processes and pursuits are not independent of the social relations of doing science. In this sense we cannot presume that science has essential qualities that unconditionally distinguish it from other human activities. Likewise we can no longer assume that methodological norms reflect what is actually practiced or that published accounts of experiments are sufficient records of what actually transpired in experimental work. We must look behind what is taken as consensus and conformity in scientific outcomes and reappraise tacit distinctions between descriptive and normative, fact and value, discovery and justification. When seen as a web of social practices ever undergoing modification, science cannot be talked about in terms of the classical domains of "epistemology," "theory," "method," "empirical findings," and "politics." Although such terms pervade our every thought about the doing of science, a social epistemological perspective calls them into question, and invites us to reconsider each of them through the practical functions they have in abetting the overarching objectives of science, in getting the work done. More specifically, we need to elucidate the consequences of some feminist psychologists' adherence to, and often resolute belief in, the conventional ideas of psychological science as predominantly cognitive enterprise, one whose artifacts (texts and articles) more or less accurately represent its practices and whose divisions of the world and scientific work are appropriate.

Using this overarching perspective ignores or, more appropriately, discards the common distinction between descriptive and prescriptive analyses of science: It invites openly political and moral questions about what versions of science best serve feminist psychology. How would a feminist psychology benefit from replacing psychology's canonical view of science with another one? Can this replacement be made? Is it being made and, if so, what are its effects? These questions move away from the matter of simply trying to determine what conditions (whether they be cultural, material, conceptual) are relevant to establishing truths about the world and begin to critically entertain how these conditions cohere in various practices—aiming finally to be engaged with the science. In this sense, the questions fit with what Joseph Rouse has called "cultural studies of science" that find "normative issues inevitably at stake in both science and cultural studies of science, but see them as arising both locally and reflexively. One cannot not be politically and epistemologically engaged" (1992, 20).

Until recently, most feminist research undertaken within the discipline of psychology has adhered to empiricism (Peplau and Conrad 1989; Parlee 1979; Walsh 1989; Lykes and Stewart 1986), the formula most commonly followed by North American social science in this century (Furner 1975). Empiricism, as defined by its psychological practitioners, entails several core assumptions: that universally valid knowledge of reality is possible; and that knowledge is attainable by anyone who employs empirical means—the use of sensory apparatuses and certain rational procedures. The attainment of such knowledge further presumes the existence of independent or autonomous knowers who are capable, at least in theory, of employing these rational and empirical procedures. For many psychologists who locate their research programs within a domain known as "feminist psychology," or feminist-grounded science, the question of replacing the epistemological canon with another formula would undoubtedly appear either unnecessary or premature. Two such advocates of maintaining psychology's empiricist tradition, Letitia Peplau and Eva Conrad (1989), have argued that although they take value neutrality to be an "illusion" and are skeptical of the possibility of "universal facts or laws about human behavior," feminist psychology nevertheless should subscribe to an empiricist program (384–85). In their endorsement, the empiricist position is not elucidated but is equated with "the methods of science" (398). Empiricism works, and the fruits of their research are the best measures of that success. (A closer look at this position, its assumptions about the world and knowledge, and its relation to various feminist theories is addressed in later chapters, particularly chapter 2).

For other researchers, both within and outside psychology, empiricism is itself taken to be a key subject for feminist analysis. For them, the classic empiricist concept of knowledge, along with the scientific methods and resultant theories of human performance, retain marks of sexist or androcentric thought (Bleier 1986a; Bordo 1987; Hare-Mustin and Marecek 1990a, 1990b; Keller 1985a; Merchant 1980; Morawski 1990; Unger 1983). Still other researchers, skeptical about the appropriateness of empiricist programs but reluctant to abandon them altogether, often perceive an impasse in feminist psychology as it is currently practiced. They find themselves in something of a no-win situation (Morawski 1988a). Despite the coalescence of these varied but related responses to empiricist psychology, there exists no tabulation of the costs and benefits of allying feminist psychology with empiricist metatheory and method. Yet, such an assessment is needed in order to evaluate the suitability of an empiricist philosophy of science to feminist commitments, the risks of impasse or stuckness, and the comparative practicability of alternative models for advancing feminist work.

Regarding "History"

An appraisal of those feminist efforts rooted firmly in the epistemic and methodological traditions of North American psychology, I believe, will reveal their limits and indicate the benefits—practical and political—of articulating a social epistemology of the science. Thus, a similar appraisal needs to be made of alternative feminist efforts, increasingly common in their appearance but generally unrecognized for their departure from the guidelines set by empiricist research. Just as conventional research marks the limits of rule abiding and canonical procedures, so, too, daring transgressions of these procedures signal viable alternatives to those limited practices. The remainder of this chapter reconsiders the last century of feminist work in psychology, contrasting the popular legacy of repair and progress with a less linear, or coherent, narrative. A review of the techniques of the predominant feminist orientation, an empiricism equated with the scientific methods of psychology, is followed by a historical reexamination and case illustrations of the consequences of embracing that orientation. By heeding their history, feminist psychologists can move to refashion both their sense-making narratives and their investigative practices. Self-reflection may well lead us to find ourselves not quite anywhere, yet en route to somewhere exciting, but that story of our liminal space is entertained in the proceeding interchapter.

The history recounted here cannot trace all the routes taken by feminist psychologists—the blind alleys as well as expansive wildernesses they sometimes have traveled. Rather, the story tells of some of the efforts—and the consequences of those efforts—toward a feminist psychology that were accommodated to the understanding of empiricist science as it evolved in psychology. Empiricism, as it is considered here, represents a set of norms to govern practice, however idealized, that when located in the writings of many feminist psychologists, has been held as a superordinate guide to scientific work and a support for liberal political values. Of course, as intimated in a social epistemological perspective, psychologists (including feminist psychologists) have not always believed that these ideals corresponded in a one-to-one relation with science as it was actually practiced. They have not always believed, for instance, that a golden rule for methods were pregiven in empiricist epistemology. Nor can it be claimed that their personal standpoints always corresponded with their adherence to strict normative conventions about doing science. Although the history to be recounted concentrates on the visible effects of assimilating a dominant episteme, another version is needed to chronicle personal beliefs and commitments. The present history illuminates how many of the products of feminist-guided psychology in the twentieth century bear significant traces of an aspiration to correct and follow certain empiricist ideals, and how insofar as these objectives were sought or articulated, certain knowledge about science and mental life was ignored or forfeited. Depending on the standpoint of a retrospective observer, these objectives can be counted as either errors in logic or as essential strategies for survival. The historical narrative presented here does not adjudicate between these two interpretations of feminist work. Rather the following account tries to locate some of the *consequences* of the routes that were taken, and does so by tracing the avowed aims of a visible feminist psychology and locating particular historical conditions and social relations that affected the realization of these aims.

Following the Rules

Most psychologists whose research has been guided by feminist interests have subscribed to an epistemological position that is commonly known as empiricism. Sandra Harding (1986b) has identified the coupling of this epistemology with feminist objectives as "feminist empiricism." She named it as one of the three predominant epistemological positions that feminists in science have engaged in order to resolve the noted paradox of attempting to derive objective knowledge claims from a stance of political commitment ("feminist standpoint" and "feminist postmodernism" being the other two available epistemologies).

Feminist empiricism takes sexist biases to be an unfortunate but removable feature of scientific inquiry. The remediation of science basically requires the eradication of bias through doing *better* science; better in this case means stricter adherence to the methodological rules governing research. Feminist science, then, is simply *good* science as it is ideally defined. Feminist empiricists also generally claim that social movements (such as feminism) make it possible to correct systematic distortions of science (such as androcentrism and sexism), and that women scientists, in particular, are more likely to detect these biases and work toward their removal. Both claims are evident in the feminist empiricist research done in psychology. However, Harding noted that this dual-faceted program, the removal of bias and inclusion of more women scientists, actually "subverts" empiricism because "the social identity of the inquirer is supposed to be irrelevant to the 'goodness' of the results of research" (1986b, 25). Another and related subversive claim often made in feminist-empiricist psychology is that "science can never be fully 'objective' or value-neutral" (Peplau and Conrad 1989, 382; Lott 1985; Unger 1983; Wallston 1981), and, thus, that personal values play a constructive role in the conduct of politically useful research. These challenges to or subversions of the rules are among a number of epistemological slippages in feminist empiricist research. Such slippages from the basic tenets of empiricism are hardly insignificant and will be discussed in detail later.

Setting aside questions about the logical coherence of the feminist empiricist model, much can be said about actual research ensuing from it. Just twenty years ago an empirically minded researcher motivated by feminist interests could easily compile a comprehensive (and not too lengthy) bibliography of relevant research; today such an undertaking would require volumes in which to record the published work. Within psychology, feminist-empiricist research burgeoned into three genres of inquiry. The first genre consists of *critical analyses* of the male-biased methods and content of psychological research. Critical investigations from a feminist-empiricist stance have appeared with such speed and acuteness in methods that they now represent some of the most astute critiques of contemporary experimental psychology (Lott 1985). Through this genre, psychology's methodological practices have been found faulty due to misrepresentative sampling of subjects, neglect of gender of the experimenter, use of sex-biased instruments and stimuli, inaccurate analyses of data, unsound inferences and generalizations, and failure to systematically report certain experimental outcomes, among other defects (Grady 1981; McHugh, Koeske, and Frieze 1986). This long list of methodological improprieties is matched by equally impressive assessments of biased content and androcentric theories. To compile a full compendium of deficient theories would practically comprise an undoing of the introductory psychology textbook: Feminist scholars have reported sex bias in theories of intelligence, cognition, social influence, perception, attribution, learning, memory, clinical disorders, identity, language, and so on.

These critical studies demonstrate technical skill, adroit empiricist logic, and philosophical perspicacity. They also have employed diverse methodologies. Janice Haaken's (1988) study of the biases inherent in field-dependence research combined careful historical examination of actual laboratory activities with conceptual analyses of the overarching psychological assumptions embedded in the entire project. Mary Parlee's (1982) multi-stage experiments have helped locate biases in the psychology of the menstrual cycle and exemplify how feminist critics have used experimental methods to debunk conventional scientific knowledge. Given the sophisticated modes of analysis and the substantial implications of these studies, their relative obscurity among psychologists outside the subcommunity of feminist psychology is regrettable—but telling.

A second genre of feminist empiricist correctives has entailed more careful investigation of *sex/gender differences*. This work weaves two strands of critical inspection: It proceeds with skepticism about or refusal to trust previous, nonfeminist studies of sex or gender difference, and it pays special attention to the possible *environmental* causes of difference (and hence, identifies sources of gender discrimination). Again, a list of the areas in which this research has been done would nearly exhaust the stock of contemporary psychological concerns. Alice Eagly's (1987b) long-term project to untangle and identify sex differences in social influence exemplifies the durability of these research programs. The work of Kay Deaux and Brenda Major (1987) elucidates the complex analyses underlying the seemingly simple matter of examining sex/gender differences. With these conceptual and methodological advances, the questions of what it means to study differences, and what differences should be studied, become more pressing. As Rachel Hare-Mustin and Jean Marecek

(1990a) note, the very inquiry into how the sexes differ is part of the legacy of androcentric psychology whose "research program is reactive rather than proactive. The energies of feminists are deflected from questions of their own choosing in order to counter exaggerated claims of difference, refute claims of female deficiency, and oppose policies and practices based on those claims" (14). Conventional difference models elide the occasional parodoxical meanings of difference. At times such as establishing maternity leaves or divorce settlements, the assertion of "no difference" between genders makes a difference for women's lives and vice versa (Hare-Mustin and Marecek 1990c; Jaggar 1990, Minow 1990).

A third avenue taken in feminist empiricism consists of investigating *women's experiences*. These studies include psychological processes related to female reproduction (menarche, menstruation, pregnancy, lactation, and menopause), yet range far beyond reproductive experiences to encompass women's experiences that androcentric theories either omit, deny, or misrepresent. Carol Gilligan's (1982) studies of a form of moral decision making that was discounted in earlier research on the topic, and Mary Belenky and colleagues' (1986) studies of women's relational modes of learning, are now familiar examples. Research on battered women (Yllö 1988), and eating disorders (Striegel-Moore, Silberstein, and Rodin 1986) illustrates studies of phenomena unique to women or experienced largely by women. Research conducted by Abigail Stewart and her colleagues (Stewart and Healey 1986; Stewart and Malley 1989; Stewart and Gold-Steinberg 1990) on female development across the lifespan, along with work on math avoidance (Eccles 1989) and women's midlife experiences (M. Gergen 1990) explore the implications specific to women of experiences sometimes shared by men and women alike. Although many researchers investigating women's experience claim an empiricist framework, they rarely adopt orthodox experimental techniques. Experimentation at once strips away the context that is necessary to understand lived experience (Mies 1983; Mishler 1979; Parlee 1979) and demands a relationship between researcher and subject that constrains or distorts the outcome (Sherif 1979; Unger 1983; Walsh 1989).

Whereas the feminist empiricist employing conventional methods eschews serious analysis of context and must invoke hypotheticals like "culture," "ideology," and "context" to account for women's experiences, the feminist empiricist who examines context by employing less canonical methods, like open-ended interviewing, diaries, or participant observation, risks her "empiricist" status by transgressing usual scientific understandings of "objectivity" and the autonomous individual. The risks of pursuing women's experiences are especially salient once we agree that understanding another's experience requires extended analysis (beyond the immediate confines of the specific research setting) and a special relationship with research participants. Here the dangers become at least twofold: the consequential failure to follow the usual scientific guidelines for control and assessment, and violation of the research ethic of observer "detachment" from the objects (persons) being studied. Thus, as Michelle Fine and Susan Gordon have claimed

> If you really want to know either of us, don't put us in a laboratory, or hand us a survey, or even interview us separately alone in our homes. Watch me (MF) with women friends, my son, his father, my niece or my mother and you will see what feels most authentic to me. These very moments, which construct who I am when I am most me, remain remote from psychological studies of individuals or even groups. (1989, 23)

Through varied resolutions of these dilemmas, studies of women's experience have uncovered unexamined, hidden, suppressed, and taken-for-granted features of human action and have, to varying degrees, found connections linking psychological experience to material and social conditions.

The feminist empiricist project in psychology takes its ultimate form as a narrative of *restoration*. It is a story wherein the empiricist tradition is represented as a search for veridical and objective knowledge that eventually is restored to its democratic and good-science status by the infusion of feminist ideals. Ruby Riemer (1986) has described feminists' commitment to this story—and to the canonical epistemology—as a "philosophical seduction" of the daughter. The seduction amounts to women's adoption of male rules that somehow contain "a promise of selfhood and inclusion in some philosophical community which, as women alone, they fail to fully achieve" (58). The three basic directions of the feminist empiricist program in psychology display some of the implications of this seduction.

Somehow, however, in restoring a natural story of scientific ethos and progress, feminist empiricists get stuck. Either their work evaporates in the text of the master narrative, becoming subsumed in that story rather than altering it, or, intentionally or not, it is taken to be inordinately disruptive of the seamless coherence of the epistemological story.

The underrepresentation or sheer disregard of feminist empiricist research in mainstream-malestream psychology intimates that there is more to scientific practice than the familiar rules suggest. Two recent studies of publication practices reveal the failure of feminist psychology to be received by the broader psychology community and corroborate suspicions that science is not always democratic (Fine and Gordon 1989; Lykes and Stewart 1986). The feminist psychology or psychology of gender that does break this barrier tends to be of a particular kind (i.e., that which maximizes gender differences), and then is often misrepresented (Kahn and Yoder 1989; Mednick 1989).

The narrative of restoration guiding feminist empiricism, then, seems to offer an insufficient guidebook for correcting or altering the master plan of psychology. In addition to its mythic representation of scientific practices, this story comes packaged with certain tacit assumptions about human nature and the appropriate means to describe and inscribe that nature. Feminist projects have bumped against at least two of these: Assumptions about *difference* along with its centrality to the study of humans, and meta-methodological assumptions about *forms of individual control*. Assumptions about difference, especially difference between men and women, are entrenched in the language, methods, and cognitive orientations of psychology. Even when these notions of difference are critically questioned, they seem to lead to a quagmire of damned if you do, damned if you don't. For instance, numerous ongoing debates involve indicting the researcher who seeks to locate gender differences as well as the one who doesn't (Baumeister 1988; Eagly 1987a, 1990; Kahn and Yoder 1989; Hare-Mustin and Marecek 1988, 1990a, 1990b). Likewise, the construction of particular difference models, like agency and communion, invites charges of dualist thinking (Crawford 1989; Morawski 1987; Peplau and Conrad 1989). Assumptions about the control of individuals and about difference are deeply embedded in both methods and theories. Attempts to study women's experiences that take seriously the transindividual, contextually embedded, or socially constructed nature of those experiences risk using methodologies that are appropriate to their mandate but that fail to meet orthodox standards of the science (Fine and Gordon 1989; Yllö 1988). Analysis beyond the individual is de facto suspect, yet those theories and methods that bracket or defy individualist assumptions are necessary for identifying social power in social structures and interactions (Fine 1985; Kahn and Yoder 1989; Sampson 1977). In the end, the scientific practices adopted in feminist empiricism come as a tightly wrapped package of premises—about the structure of mental life and the attributes of human performance—that are difficult to unwrap and separate without significantly altering those research practices.

The exclusion or neglect of certain avenues of research, the paradoxes or double binds of difference research, and the assumptions constraining theory development might be described as posing an impasse to feminist empiricist work in psychology. Add to these conditions the epistemological problematics (paradoxes?) of feminist empiricism described earlier. If feminist empiricists claim an essentially normative feature of scientific inquiry but equate those values with liberal political theory, they find themselves, as Jaggar (1983) has discussed, endorsing a politics that basically reconfirms the idea of rational, detached observers and harbors other gendered assumptions about the world that warrant careful analysis, but not immediate acceptance. Further, as Harding (1986b) noted, if feminist empiricists posit that observers' identity, specifically their gender, and their personal values matter in the conduct of research, then they upset a basic understanding of empiricism. In sum, the varieties of empiricism "are as androcentered as the liberal moral-political theories that they inform. A woman can claim space within them only to the extent that she is prepared and able to be 'more like a man'—usually a privileged white man" (Code 1993, 712). On close inspection these barriers appear formidable, complete with roots and sprouting branches as well as a visible trunk. Thus, a fuller appreciation of the current problematics in feminist empiricist psychology is necessary if we are to comprehend the options that are actually available. This appreciation requires a longer field of vision in order to see the narrative of restoration in its historical context, and to ascertain more precisely how we have fared with that story.

Having Followed the Rules

Ruby Riemer's (1986) image of the philosophical seduction of women scholars takes tangible form in the history of North American psychology in the twentieth century. That history is a paradigmatic story of women's attempts to become full-fledged members of an intellectual community. Traditional histories of psychology, à la E. G. Boring, omit or underrepresent the presence of women workers, but recent revisions have catalogued the multiple contributions that women have made to the science (O'Connell and Russo 1983; Rosenberg 1982; Rossiter 1982; Russo and Denmark 1987; Scarborough and Furumoto 1987; Shields 1975; Shields and Mallory 1987; Stevens and Gardner 1982). With this historical reconstruction of women's participation well underway, a place is made for asking more difficult questions about women's experiences once they do become scientific psychologists (Scarborough and Furumoto 1987) and, in particular, about the experiences of those women psychologists who are, or were, committed to feminist ideals (Morawski and Agronick 1991). The questions call for inquiry into the sorts of contributions women have made and the forms of discrimination as well as opportunities they faced—an inquiry that takes these factors not as incidental, personal life events but as important features of their scientific lives. These questions also invite exploration of the *strategies* used by women to gain entrance into, and maintain a position within, the scientific community, on the one hand, and examination of particular efforts made by feminists to change the world as well as to construct a psychological understanding of that world, on the other hand. Wending through this series of questions takes us well beyond the regulative guidelines of psychological inquiry and the necessary violations of these regulations: It brings us closer to comprehending how our science is comprised of nonexceptional practices yet how it takes diverse forms in particular locations and times (Rouse 1992).

Women psychologists, especially those with feminist-reform interests, had to advance their feminist visions through a sustained allegiance to the norms of the scientific community, and they had to do so while positioned at the margins of that community. Upon closer inspection, feminist-oriented women psychologists often lived the implications of their philosophical seclusion: The epistemological world to which they strove to belong did not fully accommodate them or their politics. Some of these psychologists (actually a small number of those who were formally trained) became successful participants in their science, yet the intellectual, political, and personal costs were often high. By revisiting the tensions of disciplinary adherence and social marginality, we can begin to broaden our understanding of the costs of that precarious relationship between feminism and the dominant epistemological framework of psychology.

Marginality

Asked to write a commentary on a series of autobiographies by "modern women," John B. Watson ([1927], 1978) assessed these women's work in behavioral terms, an evaluation in keeping with the theoretical orientation for which he became an instrumental leader. Watson explained that the modern women have never been trained to work like men: "Women's customs have changed so rapidly that work traditions have never had a chance to soak in . . . not being trained from infancy to the tradition of incessant manipulative work, they drop out of the race as soon as they get comfortable" (142). What does it mean when such a prominent scientist, one who collaborated with women scientists, maintained—and to some extent did so with scientific language—a discriminatory ideology (Harris 1984; Harris and Morawski 1979)? What is the effect when a founding father of the discipline, G. Stanley Hall, simultaneously mentored women psychologists in training, and developed theories that identified the unsuitability of women in the workplace and defended their place in the domestic sphere (Diehl 1986)? What did it mean when influential researchers engaged evolutionary theory, implicit in much early psychological research, to confirm taken-for-granted gender differences (Shields 1975)? What did it mean when five notable psychologists published utopias that outline the centrality of psychology to the promotion of human improvement, while advocating traditional roles for women (Morawski 1984)? Given these implicit and explicit accounts of the psychological handicaps of females, the actual social marginality of women in psychology is understandable. And given the contradictory messages of a democratic science that seems receptive to female students but which conveys an ideology of their inferiority, it is also understandable that marginality had complicated consequences, including perhaps, anxiety and paranoia.

Women of the early twentieth century, whose education was often inspired by feminist visions, and who successfully acquired the skills and credentials of the new psychology, nevertheless were marginalized (Rosenberg 1982). Articulation of these contradictory and crippling social relations has been hindered by the avowed democratic ethos of science, the very epistemic stance that attracted these women to science in the first place. Women entering science at the time

> banked so heavily on merit—the belief that if only they were good enough, trained enough, committed enough, their achievement of superior performance would be rewarded—because it seemed so incontestable. Merit and achievement were, presumably, a matter of personal control and volition, and therefore, protected them from political manipulation by others. (Glazer and Slater 1987, 22)

Recent historical studies document how the lives of women entering psychology early in the century were marked by exclusions, conflicts, and compromises. These histories also tell of the ways in which women navigated their marginal status. By tracing the lives of a number of investigators who were among the first generation of women in psychology, Elizabeth Scarborough and Laurel Furumoto (1987) identified two persistent issues: the *conflict between personal attachments and career autonomy*, and the *denial of opportunity*. Their study convincingly details the ways in which these women confronted professional barriers, from the case of Margaret Floy Washburn's reluctant realization that meritocracy in science was a myth, to the difficult and unsuccessful efforts of Ethel Puffer and Milicent Shinn to reconcile the demands of family and career. Women's exclusion was often overt as well as indirect, and Furumoto (1988) has traced the official exclusion of women from at least one prestigious society, the Experimentalists, between 1904 and 1929.

Historical studies of women in psychology and related professions indicate that women participants had to use special strategies to compensate for marginality and exclusion (Furumoto 1992).

Margaret Rossiter (1982) has documented some of the common patterns of women's careers within laboratory science: Whereas the early generation of women often ended up in low-status areas designated as women's work, later generations found employment as associates to well-known researchers or as workers engaged in their spouses' projects. As in the case of Christine Ladd-Franklin, some women psychologists enhanced their chances of successful participation by developing research interests that were not dependent on laboratory facilities from which they were often excluded (Furumoto 1992). From their historical investigations, Penina Glazer and Miriam Slater (1987) identified specific choices that women made to acquire and retain professional positions. Women succeeded in their careers by undertaking innovative ventures for which there was no existing expertise; taking subordinate posts; superforming in a field; or choosing isolated, separate occupations—that is, working in women's colleges or in distinctly women's fields such as nursing. The result of these tactics, however, was double-edged; Glazer and Slater found that the women scientists survived successfully, but they did so at the cost of forfeiting or limiting the education of intellectual progeny who would carry on their research ventures.

Thus far, marginalization has been discussed in terms of how it affected the position of individual researchers and their strategies to ensure survival and relative success, even when success did not encompass the production of knowledge or the training (reproduction) of a future generation of workers. For many women social scientists of that era, it seems, *survival* meant success; the production and reproduction of intellectual ideas were luxuries. However, marginalization does need to be understood in terms of the consequential fate of intellectual visions and ventures. Just as women's secondary roles regulated and restricted individual careers, so they have influenced the scientific work resulting from those careers. More historical investigation needs to be done to fully appreciate these consequences, for at present we have only glimpses into the livelihood of the intellectual and political projects that were undertaken by women psychologists. Women in the first half of this century for whom feminism informed their scientific agenda, and for whom marginalization seemed a taken-for-granted feature of life, appear to have channeled their science and feminism into one of three career paths: Careers that required or facilitated adherence to the norm of science, as understood at the time; careers in which science served higher goals of social reform; and careers that were situated outside scientific and political institutions, and thus, least influenced by the normative expectations of these institutions. The first career path, one regulated by the norms and social relations of science, is discussed in the following section. The other two are nearly invisible given our narrow conception of science and its proper history; however, they were viable options—and sometimes the only ones—available to women who sought in science a means to promote social change. As such, they deserve attention.

As Rossiter (1982) and Glazer and Slater (1987) have documented, women entering science often found work in less prestigious areas, or in areas requiring intensive labor. Within social science, women's work came to be associated with applied science—in government, schools, and welfare agencies (Deegan 1988; Fitzpatrick 1990). Within psychology, women frequently found employment in the areas of mental testing, evaluation, and counseling (Capshew and Lazlo 1986). Such scientific work is held to be derivative and, hence, restricts the extent to which creative input can be made, or even appreciated. More importantly, as Barrie Thorne (1990) has noted, this career path posed difficult contradictions for reform-motivated women during the early part of the century:

> Their commitment to "scientific" and expert knowledge led them in anti-democratic and even coercive directions. Their reform efforts depended on their entrepreneurial skills, bringing a dependence on the wealthy and powerful that undermined their concern for the oppressed. Their belief in the salutary possibilities of state intervention obscured ways in which the state maintains inequalities of gender, race and class. (22)

Many reform activities eventually merged with movements toward professionalization, and political motivations became mediated by professional goals, regulations, and boundary making. Thus, for instance, social work and the child-guidance movement became further distanced from reform and charity and more clearly identified with providing welfare assistance to individuals, rather than with promoting social reform or community action (Lubove 1965).

Women who entered into these applied fields, these targeted

opportunities for professional employment of women, were not simply do-gooders or workers without intellectual convictions. Yet their careers contained contradictions and their work often served ideologies that countered or conflicted with their initial political ideals. The psychologist Leta Hollingworth participated actively in the development and delivery of psychological tests, but she was not blind to the problems of that enterprise. Hollingworth (1940) described the "scientific 'ghost'" created by testing methods that distanced the investigator from the children being tested, ultimately ensuring "that the investigator himself never see a child" (47). Grace Adams, who received her Ph.D. with E. B. Titchener, discovered that her work in applied psychology both victimized the children involved and abused the purported scientific status of psychology. Disillusioned, Adams quit, and eventually wrote articles about this and other "scams" that she ridiculed as "popular" psychology. Her failure to find employment as an experimental psychologist in academe thus indirectly led her to a career in journalism (Morawski and Hornstein 1991).

Hollingworth and Adams are exceptional cases in several senses: They succeeded in securing and completing doctoral work in psychology and they were able to publish commentaries on psychology. Many women whose career trajectory brought them to applied or auxiliary services in psychology had neither of these opportunities. For instance, Annie Fisher graduated from Wesleyan University in 1904, (just eight years before it terminated its first "experiment" with coeducation and returned to being an all-male institution) and received her M.A. from New York University. Her education fostered a devotion to science, and her experiences in an immigrant community fed a life-long belief in acknowledging the similarities between people of different backgrounds. Unlike Hollingworth and Adams, but like most politically motivated women who gained access to higher education, Fisher's lengthy career in education provided no substantial audience beyond local educators, and left unrecorded her struggles between her vision of "one world family" and her reluctant use of individual-centered and biased mental tests in the classroom (Rose 1982).

The historical lacuna created by overlooking the struggles and contradictions of this group of women workers—as marginals and incidentals in the canonical history of science—also leaves unrecorded the lives of those women who followed careers that moved them outside the discipline completely. These women's drift away from psychology and, sometimes, from professional careers altogether, was undoubtedly connected with their marginalism and exclusion. Yet their failures to obtain a proper place in psychology sometimes was connected with their politics and active resistance. Beatrice Hinkle ([1927], 1978), whose own interest in psychological processes led her to a medical degree and a psychoanalytic career, observed that "modern women are engaged in a real creative effort, even though it may not be realized, for behind their stridency and revolt lies the great inner meaning of woman's struggle with the forces of conservativism and inertia" (141). Leta Hollingworth (1940), who fought to be an insider, nonetheless did recognize multiple options for feminists. Her lecture notes include the seeds of two proposals: "We can find out only by the living of hundreds of experimental lives, and the study of these lives in the living" and "The New Woman, consciously experimenting with her own life, to find the Good Life" (60).

We know little about those women excluded (or excluding themselves) from the experiment of finding a life within or at the margins of psychology. In a study of feminist psychologists working in the 1920s, Gail Agronick (1988; Morawski and Agronick 1991) investigated the lives of several women who sought to study psychological issues, both inside and outside psychology, and who engaged diverse strategies for realizing employment, feminist goals, and personal well-being. Beatrice Hinkle's interest in psychology was developed through her position as a physician, not a psychologist. Within this role, Hinkle advanced distinctly feminist criticisms of Freud, criticisms that were not being produced within psychology, despite the discipline's anti-Freudian stance. Hinkle also rejected the very project of the experimental study of sex differences on the grounds that such differentiation could not be ascertained until discriminatory practices within society and psychology were eliminated. She did not frame women as passive recipients of sexism but as participants, and she anticipated the need for women to become self-conscious of their disadvantaged position (Hinkle 1920, 1978). Lorine Pruette, who had had undergraduate training in chemistry, dedicated her graduate work to psychological studies at Clark University, eventually completing a doctorate in sociology in 1924. She taught both psychology and sociology, and received extensive postdoctoral training in psychoanalysis. Pruette held that women's psychological nature is determined by social and political conditions, and her research suggested that women's work, both in paid labor and unpaid domestic activities, distorted their lives and minds. Pruette's economic theory of gender, her critiques of motherhood and capitalism, coupled with her sarcastic writings on Freud, would not have been received well, if at all, within the annals of psychology. For someone who claimed that "there can be no lasting success for women in a capitalistic society" (Pruette quoted in Trigg 1987, 16), and subverted her mentor's (G. Stanley Hall) view of women as the civilizing forces in an uncivil, masculinist society, psychology would have been an unhappy home.

Feminist and economic-based theories of human functioning, psychoanalytic models twisted into something of a feminist form, or claims that experimental studies of gender difference are fundamentally and inescapably biased, were not ideas that typically were given voice in the field of psychology at the time. Pruette and Hinkle found a forum for these ideas in other disciplines, albeit still at the margins of those fields. And although able to develop and publish these ideas, they, like those women who did adhere to the disciplinary rules of psychology, had little opportunity to train a future generation of researchers to continue their feminist projects.

With exclusion and marginalization in mind, the story of women's participation in psychology becomes even more curious when their growing numbers in the science's work force are considered. Although there were no women present at the founding meeting of the American Psychological Association (APA) in 1892, by 1928 women constituted 34 percent of its membership (Rossiter 1982). By the outset of World War II, well over one thousand women held graduate degrees, and were granted nearly 20 percent of the doctorates. Contemporary data are even more impressive: Between 1976 and 1988 the proportion of women receiving baccalaureate degrees increased from 54 to 70 percent, and the proportion of women obtaining master's degrees rose from over 50 to approximately 66 percent. Whereas women were awarded 17 percent of psychology doctorates granted in 1960, they earned 58 percent of those degrees in 1990 (Kohout 1991; National Science Foundation 1992).

These increases are due to the increase in the numbers of women and to decreases in the numbers of men obtaining doctoral degrees with the figures varying significantly across subfields: Clinical psychology, a subfield with considerable need for "women's work" (Philipson, 1992), has had the greatest proportionate gains (Kohout, 1991). If these increases in representation have affected marginalization and exclusion, they have not eliminated them. In a sample of articles appearing in the prestigious *Journal of Personality and Social Psychology*, only 13 percent of first authors in 1968 were women and 15 percent in 1988, and in neither 1968 nor 1988 were there any female editors or associate editors (West, Newsom, and Fenaughty 1992). Concerning employment opportunities, the situation is similar: Women psychologists in academic psychology receive approximately 88 percent of men's pay (National Science Foundation 1992), and they represent only 19 percent of tenured psychology faculty and 14 percent of its full professors (Kohout 1991). As one study indicated, the "world" of women psychologists differs from that of men not only in salary but in other areas including career mobility and publication productivity (Cohen and Gutek 1991). Clearly numbers of women alone, even the most impressive numbers, cannot completely end the processes of marginalization and exclusion.

In her comprehensive history of the first generation of feminist-inspired psychologists Rosalind Rosenberg found an unfortunate story

> of lives of these exceptional women, of the frustration felt by those whose work was celebrated in graduate school but who could find no academic position in which to carry on their research; of the regret felt by those for whom sexual expression and intellectual achievement proved irreconcilable; and of the strain felt by those who clung to an image of themselves as committed reformers even while they were trying to prove themselves as objective, detached scientists. It is a story, in many ways, of failure—of women restricted by simple prejudice to the periphery of academe, who never had access to the professional chairs of the major universities, who never commanded the funds to direct large-scale research, who never trained the graduate students who might have spread their influence, and who, by the 1920s, no longer had the galvanizing support of a woman's movement to give political effect to their ideas. (1982, xxi)

The stories of feminist psychologists of later generations are not always so catastrophic, yet they often share the tragedy of exclusion and discrimination. Throughout this century the career directions newly available to women interested in psychology along with gains in women's rights at once afforded greater chances for meaningful work, yet in different ways limited the integrity and/or viability of that work. Those individuals who ended up doing the women's work of science, notably applied psychology, faced multiple contradictions between that work and their political commitments, and those who abandoned the discipline ultimately had no power to alter it.

Those individuals who were able to work more centrally in the discipline faced other challenges. The conditions and consequences of feminist empiricists who worked within psychology make no simple history, yet their heritage illumines some of the current dynamics of feminist empiricism. For those with marginal status, adherence to the norms of the scientific community had varied consequences. Regardless of their particular epistemic commitments or idiosyncratic career opportunities, these workers had to grapple with the implications of both their personal identity and their political interests; to do so they often invented styles and directives of work, some of which were considerably more successful than others.

Costs of Adherence?

Feminist empiricists have taken several approaches to restoring the norms of scientific empiricism to psychology—to freeing empiricism of apparent sexist biases. In addition to these feminist-empiricist criticisms and correctives, other feminists in psychology have suggested that empiricism itself—its model of knowledge and of human nature—are implicated in the production of sexist science. Heeding these other researchers, several core features of that empiricist psychology can be found responsible for a biased understanding of sex/gender. These features include, first, the desirability and privileging of abstract and universal knowledge—an epistemic aspiration that dissolves distinct features of history, culture, class, race, and ethnicity and their relations to human action. Second, both conceptually and methodologically, the orthodox epistemology incorporates notions of autonomous or self-contained agents. The presumption of and preoccupation with individualism, at best, collapse social relations into discrete social exchanges between individuals and denies the complex relational aspects of everyday experiences, including those within the experimental laboratory. Third, assumptions about objectivity as good and also possible depend on eschewing the reflexive properties of human science—the ways in which investigators are constituting forces in scientific practices and products and are constituted through those practices. Finally, the normative epistemology takes science and society, like facts and values, to be discrete and separate entities. This posited separateness is at odds with the tangible and diverse ways in which science is a cultural practice—simultaneously a product and producer of society. It forecloses consideration of how science and society, and facts and values, are made into separate or distinct spheres of the world.

This feminist analysis is neither ubiquitous nor rare, although it is more common outside the United States than within (Parlee 1991; Unger 1983), and more often produced by those who do not use conventional research methods than by those who do. Setting aside questions of its origins and possibilities, both of which will be taken up in the next section, this post-empirical feminist analysis provides a vehicle for revisiting earlier feminist empiricist work without restricting our return solely to an excavation of discriminatory, or sexist, practices. Along with an appreciation of marginality and exclusion, this countertext likewise aids us in seeing what sorts of science feminist empiricists were able to construct and how it transformed the understanding of gender. Employing the countertext likewise enables us to see how three moments in the history of feminist-empiricist psychologists' study of gender actually highlight empiricism's limitations and contradictions (which paradoxically accompanied its emancipatory possibilities). These moments also show how women's situated status in psychology has been as consequential to their work as has been their dedication to scientific norms. It is through a reviewing of such moments that we can begin to configure science not as a system of abstract rules but as local practices structured through relations of order and power.

Endless Search of Difference?

Among the ambitions of the fledging discipline at the dawn of the twentieth century, the hope to establish uncontestable scientific knowledge about sex was a significant one. With the tools of open-minded empirical inquiry, psychologists set out to investigate the true causes, whether nature or nurture, of sex-related differences (Lewin 1984; Morawski 1985; Rosenberg 1982; Shields 1975). A substantial amount of this early research was undertaken by researchers, mainly women, who assessed sex differences in every conceivable psychological capacity. Devoting substantial time to studying these differences, Helen Thompson Woolley and Leta Hollingworth eventually announced the results to be something of a toss-up. Measures of motor, affective, sensory and intellectual abilities, combined with assessments of association of ideas, memory, stammering, attention, nervous behavior, fear, reading speech, reasoning, and the like, proved to be equivocal. Most studies found minimal or no differences, and some of the results favored male while others favored female performances. With such equivocal findings, the question of differences seemed to wane. As Hollingworth (1918) noted in her final review of sex-differences research, any researcher intent on reporting sex differences regarding mental traits would "automatically do himself out of his review. He would have very little to report" (428).

These findings, however, did not deter psychologists who were convinced of the existence of real sex differences. To these psychologists, the failure to find sex differences meant either that researchers were looking in the wrong place or that the research was faulty. What's more, understanding sex differences remained especially crucial to psychologists who linked the project of scientific psychology with aims of social control and welfare. After all, marriage and the family, institutions where issues of sex and gender seemed to be most relevant, were primary sources of socialization and individual well-being (Morawski 1985). The solution was straightforward: Sex differences lay at a deeper recess of mental life and hence needed to be studied by means other than the testing of mental or behavioral functions. A search then began to locate and name the causal origins of sex differences. After extended efforts to successfully design an intelligence test that would produce no sex differences (Minton 1988), Lewis Terman, along with his research associate Catherine Cox Miles, turned to the design of an instrument that would measure masculinity and femininity (Terman and Miles 1936). Their successful M-F test, and the many M-F tests that were modeled after it, demonstrated the existence of meaningful sex differences. The tests shared three core assumptions: that substantial psychological sex differences existed, but at a level that could not be readily detected by ordinary observers; that these attributes were so psychologically charged that subjects had to be deceived about the purpose of the test lest they "fake" their response; and that masculinity and femininity were somehow intimately linked with psychological stability and deviance—with individual well-being. Florence Goodenough (1946) described this psychologically difficult search for difference:

> when we come to deal with what is often called the "private world" of the individual, comprising as it does, the feelings, urges, beliefs, attitudes, and desires of which he may be only dimly aware and which he is often reluctant to admit even to himself, much less to others, the problems of measurement are of a very different nature. Here the universe which we wish to assay is no longer overt and accessible but covert and jealously guarded. (456)

For some researchers, the early research results indicating the equivocality or absence of sex differences were sufficient. However, for other researchers, those outcomes were unsatisfactory and signalled the need to modify the scientific search, essentially to design new methods and concepts such as masculinity-femininity. The commitment to an empiricist epistemology did not (and still does not) *fix* the course for the study of sex difference; nor did it or does it *determine* when the game is over—when results are to be taken as final. But perhaps what is more important is that the empiricist project, as it has evolved in psychology, facilitates an insistence on such differences. Masculinity and femininity research illustrates psychology's sustained reliance on the idea of bounded individuals whose mental life is independent of historical circumstance and is available to measurement. That research, in presuming an accessible "reality," must ever rely on what we already know about that otherwise invisible mental reality. In this case, presuppositions and everyday understandings about male and female differences have fueled recurrent efforts to locate them. The inscription devices (tests, batteries, and inventories) give tangible and recursive form to that prior, tacit knowledge. Thus, the polarities of masculine and feminine, retaining presupposed qualities of the "instrumental" and "expressive," or "agentic" and "communal," become always available to empirical detection. The commitment to individual-centered theories and the minimization of historical factors further guide the narrow search for differences within the individual and mask cultural constructions as psychological ones. Psychological masculinity and femininity, then, became both symbolic *signifiers* of some inner real stuff and the *signified,* once they were operationalized and measured.

The empiricist program has also relied on a presumed set of social relations in experimental research. Experimental subjects do not really know *themselves* or their crucial inner workings, and they have reasons (incentives or desires) to evade scrutiny—to deceive *others.* Researchers are held to be capable of discerning such intrapsychic features of subjects: Apparently they neither lack self knowledge nor need to be constrained from deception, as do subjects. A number of consequences arise from these normative social relations inside the laboratory. On one level, wariness toward subjects' reports further distances psychological theory from consideration of the workings of everyday life. On another level, these technical arrangements structure or reduce the experimenter's interaction with subjects, and this controlled assessment of the subjects further functions to produce results that confirm both the experimenter's suspicions and the very social relations that have been constructed in the research. In aspiring to develop a psychological language for talking about gender and in designing means to inscribe (to detect, measure, and assess) gender, the empiricist project ultimately fashioned a relatively enduring conception of sex and gender, and established something of an intellectual monopoly on speaking about it. However, the indexical, recursive, and reflexive processes in that undertaking have remained undetectable to most empiricist observers' eyes. If investigators resist acknowledging those dimensions of scientific practice, then the search for differences proceeds without certain forms of reappraisal.

It might be argued that this tale of unending pursuit, and the consequent perpetuation of a certain reality, merely documents a case of bad science, not a shortcoming of empiricist psychology. Researchers, according to this argument, simply went about their work incorrectly—particularly in their understandings of what that reality looked like, how it contained masculine and feminine forms. However, given their beliefs in universal knowledge, in the ability to abstract features of the world that transcend history and culture, and in the detached position of the observer, it is difficult to imagine how they could have proceeded otherwise. How else could researchers record and analyze gender experiences without either abandoning the aspirations to abstraction and universality or dramatically revising notions of the detached, objective observer? The challenge of such a mission is only magnified when we recall that the reality being investigated has been one that is not directly observable but, rather, resides in the recesses of the human mind.

The particular reality of sex differences that was at first challenged and eventually reclaimed, in this research program, although not by the same group of investigators, gained renewed interest in the late 1960s as psychologists participated in the larger cultural conversations about women's rights. However, the psychological reality defined during the earlier period did not develop without criticism, and it is informative to consider how some of its early critics fared in the decades prior to the cultural negotiations that feminism later impelled.

Science as Social Order

If the scientific search for sex differences was uncovering a reality, however obscure, of a psychological gender, a dichotomous psychic realm of masculine and feminine, then the contours of this psychological reality had to be, and could be, documented through conventional norms of inquiry: logical statements, proper methodological procedures, and the generation of reliable data. For the most part, the research went uncontested during the 1930s and 1940s as numerous studies documented stable psychological gender attributes in males and females along with gender-relevant behavioral tendencies. The metatheoretical framework being sustained in and through these studies was a culturally normative one: gender was an "ascribed" attribute; psychological gender should be consistent with one's biological sex; and gender-related behaviors should correspond with gender-related social roles such as mating, parenting, fighting, emoting, and working in the paid-labor force.

Among psychologists studying issues of sex and gender, there was little controversy, and in general, the field gave the appearance of normal paradigm development marked by the accumulation of data, identification of relevant variables, and the refinement of theory. Although notable controversy was absent from this science-as-usual, there is evidence of occasional, but substantive, dissent. As evidenced in the two episodes to be described, disagreement with the normative metatheory was difficult to demonstrate and even more difficult to voice. Regardless of the grounds for, or degree of, dissent, and regardless of which procedures for scientific argument were deployed, the critics failed to persuade the research community, or even to sustain a productive dialogue.

The first example of dissent from the accepted science entails a critique of research methodology (Morawski 1988b). Ruth Herschberger, a trained sociologist, attempted to engage an eminent psychologist, Robert Yerkes, in a discussion of the adequacy of certain experimental techniques being utilized in the study of sex, on the one hand, and the adequacy of the scientific language, on the other hand. In particular, Herschberger challenged a set of Yerkes' experiments that assayed the social relations between male and female chimpanzees. The experiments reported in the *Journal of Comparative Psychology* (Yerkes 1940) and later in the book *Chimpanzees, a Laboratory Colony* (Yerkes 1943), revealed sex-specific social hierarchies of dominance-subordination and rights-privileges. Male chimpanzees were found to be the "naturally" dominant members of mixed-sex pairings, controlling the rights and privileges of food-getting. The study reported two additional findings. First, on the rare occasions when male chimpanzees were not dominant, it was reported to be due to an aberrational personality trait of one of the pair, e.g., "exceptional aggressiveness" of the female or inordinate "sexual selectiveness" of a male. Second, the results indicated that male and female chimpanzees react differently to being socially controlled; for instance, whereas on certain occasions the male commands, demands and "physically imposes his will," the female "cajoles, requests, begs" and uses sexual allure (Yerkes 1940, 186).

Herschberger initially expressed her concerns about the study in a personal communication with Yerkes. In that letter, she questioned the semantics of the study, particularly the use of the term *natural* for male but not female dominance. Herschberger then noted a possible breach in objective methods, even intimating that a "matriarchal scientist" might reach different conclusions about the observed behavior. Yerkes' reply capitulated on several points but, in the end, reaffirmed his general conclusions. Although admitting that the word *naturally* was unsatisfactory, he nevertheless defended its use on the grounds that a lengthier and more accurate description would have been boring to the readers. He further admitted that the research was "scientifically crude and tentative" but made no gesture toward amending a report of his findings.

There is no record of further communication between Herschberger and Yerkes. After an unsuccessful attempt to persuade the experimenter of gender bias, Herschberger adopted a dramatic mode of persuasion for what can only be assumed to be a different audience. Her book, *Adam's Rib* (1948), contains a chapter devoted to the chimpanzee experiments and ostensibly addressed to Yerkes and his experimental colleagues. In contrast to usual forms of scientific communication, the response is presented in the subject's voice: Josie, a female chimpanzee in the experiment, criticizes the methodology, findings, and language of the journal article in which her behavior is reported. Josie's account is not just an anthropomorphic tale of a chimpanzee's perspective on food chutes and narrow-minded observers, but blends this monkey talk with a learned exposé on methodology and human androcentrism. Josie reanalyzes the quantitative data by including those scores of successful food acquisition by the female chimpanzees that the researchers dropped from their analysis on the grounds that behavior during the days of estrus should be discounted. She finds the experimenters' omissions to be sexist and suggests that "the period of sexual interest is, by implication, an extra-natural phase in women (for it makes us *act* dominant when we're really *naturally* subordinate), it looks like we girl chimps spend about 14 days out of every 32 in the toils of Satan" (Herschberger 1948, 8-9). The researchers were further reminded of experimental errors, including the unmentioned availability of food in addition to that delivered and monitored through a food chute, the relative inequity in body weights of the male and female subjects, and the use of only male experimenters. Taken separately or together, these methodological flaws reflect systematic gender bias in the experimental design.

Just as Josie speaks as a skilled methodologist, so she appears to be an astute student of semantics as well as a critic of human sexual relations. She finds that terms used to describe chimpanzee behavior signal implicit assumptions about female passivity and male dominance; Josie especially criticizes the use of the expression "sexually receptive" to refer to the female chimpanzee's participation in sexual activity, and "prostitution" to refer to social relations between male and female chimpanzees. Josie expresses pity for human females not just because their reality is seen through a distorting "screen of language" but also because they seem to live in a harsher, sexist social world.

By employing a fictional genre, Herschberger documented some ways in which primatology simply mirrored the patriarchal and corporate world of humans, a claim that is now being substantiated in empirical and historical studies (Haraway 1990; Small 1984). Her efforts to engage in a conventional form of scientific conversation were as unsuccessful as her choice of an alternative form is revealing. If her methodological criticisms adhered to scientific norms, why then did she need to borrow another's voice, a subject and animal's voice at that? While the recent discoveries of pervasive sex bias in primate research supports the credibility of Herschberger's analysis, her final decision to adopt such a distanced and problematic, if humorous, form of communication is a telling indicator of perceived resistance within the research community.

The second example, the reception of Georgene Seward's efforts to reformulate the paradigmatic perspective on sex and gender, entails not resistance but rather silence. Unlike Herschberger's case, where adherence to conventional scientific practices, when confronted by resistance, ultimately culminated in a notable departure from those practices, Seward's project consistently subscribed to those norms. Shortly after World War II, Seward compiled an extensive and meticulous review of the psychological studies of sex, a survey ranging from research on hormones in rats and chicks to adolescents' emotions and adult marriage satisfaction. Her objective was not to challenge the validity of the experimentation but to appraise the overall interpretations and extrapolations drawn from them. Drawing loosely upon an evolutionary model, Seward suggested that the research indicated variability and change in the psychology of sex and gender. Whereas under primitive conditions sex roles are directed by biological differences, under modern conditions, those roles are not so simply determined. That is, within elaborate social systems, physical modes of interaction give way to inherently social modes, and the research indicated that "since individual differences in ability outweigh sex differences, men and women should be given equal opportunities to achieve as individuals without regard to sex" (Seward 1946, 249-50). Just as the research literature suggested that psychological sex differences had social, not biological origins, so it also showed that social roles had been arbitrarily determined on the basis of biologically assigned sex—an assignment that contributes to, if not creates, psychological distress. From these data, it was apparent to Seward that "the emotional conflict in which woman finds herself is of social rather than biological origin" (248). Seward thus extended this interpretation of the existing research to formulate compatible social policy. Her policy recommendations not only accorded with the research but also with the democratic ethos of contemporary science, for Seward advocated "a democratic reformulation of sex roles" (Seward 1946, 249). Women should be allowed to contribute "to building the new society" in postwar America (249), and men should be permitted to contribute to emotional life, for "just as women may learn from men how to achieve, so men may learn from women how to cherish," and hence, to revalue feminine characteristics. Social roles ascribed by sex would then give way to patterns whereby individuals, men and women, would blend roles and cooperate "in the tremendous adventure of reconstructing Western culture" (252).

The decades following Seward's systematic appraisal, however, produced a quite different understanding of sex and gender, realizing not hers, but another's, postwar agenda. Psychological research continued with the usual practice of documenting psychological sex differences without evaluating their social malleability or pathological consequences. Seward's comprehensive and cautious analysis of over seven hundred studies had no noticeable or even momentary impact on that research trajectory.

These two episodes show how adherence to canonical practices is not sufficient for scientific persuasion. Leaving aside the issue of the two investigators' marginal professional status (which, after all, was not atypical for women researchers), it is evident that their scientific projects, especially their contestations of existing knowledge, which remained grounded by the current understandings of rational inquiry, nevertheless went nearly unacknowledged. Both projects shared assumptions that diverged from the dominant cultural ones about gender. Although these two cases of dissent are by no means consequential projects in the history of the psychology of sex, they are by no means anomalous. They serve as historically specific examples of how psychological science embraces the governing assumptions of social order—how its research reflects and accounts for that social order—and how these assumptions defy questioning, even if the questions follow proper scientific etiquette. As cultural conditions changed, so did the psychology of gender, and twenty-five years after Herschberger's and Seward's challenges, the science moved on an ironic plane toward discovery and incorporation of some of their chief ideas.

Androgyny and the Professional Woman

By the early 1970s, the psychological study of sex and gender was inextricably bound up with the new feminist movement in North America. This second-wave of feminism, while neither politically nor intellectually unified, took form in the academy through a liberal feminism that sought to identify the forces of women's oppression and to grant women equal treatment in the private and public realm. This women's movement, in proclaiming that the "personal is political" also claimed the significance, indeed the necessity, of systematically reexamining our understanding of the individual, including the psychological features of the gender system. The effectiveness and longevity of this revived feminism notwithstanding, its impact on the academy was attenuated by other events of the period. A liberalization of intellectual activities across the disciplines during the late 1960s coincided with an ongoing critique of American culture; the resultant critical reflections were especially notable in the social sciences, where researchers self-consciously questioned the validity, meaning, and social relevance of their work (Bernstein 1983; Rabinow and Sullivan 1979). Within this climate of self-reflection, critical psychologists challenged some of the discipline's central epistemological tenets, reexamined the validity and ethics of their investigations, and questioned whether psychological research actually promoted human welfare. However, the liberalization of social thought did not have a lasting effect on most areas of psychological research. The predominant theoretical perspective taking shape during this period, the cognitive "turn" if not "revolution," incorporated little of the self-criticism and politicization that transpired during the 1960s and 1970s.

A visible exception to this apparent ideological resilience of psychology has been research on sex and gender. The feminism emerging during the 1960s made way for new scholarship across the disciplines: feminist researchers worked to recover the untold past of women's lives, to debunk sexual myths, to identify vectors of oppression, and to devise theories that at once incorporated women's experiences and took gender as a meaningful—if not essential—category for explanation. Within psychology, feminist researchers' foremost efforts entailed an empiricist debunking of the masculine assumptions embedded in theory, methods, and interpretations of research. Naomi Weisstein's (1971) unsettling exposure of sexist assumptions pervading psychology, Eleanor Maccoby and Carol Jacklin's (1974) comprehensive synthesis of (developmental) sex-difference research, Anne Constantinopole's (1973) analysis of the faulty premises of masculinity and femininity research, and Mary Parlee's (1973) methodological critique and empirical correctives of the biases of menstrual-cycle research are stellar examples of how empiricist logic and rules could be used to reveal the biases that saturated empiricist-based psychology. Feminist investigators deployed the governing empiricist framework not just to debunk sexist practices and ideals but also to document experimentally the different experiences of males and females, along with those aspects of women's experiences that had been neglected or suppressed by androcentric theories. Historical reassessments of women's accomplishments in psychology (despite sustained discrimination), as discussed earlier in this chapter, also fueled this recovery program, as did studies attending to gender roles across the life span, gender prejudice and discrimination, and gender-related cognitive capacities.

These feminist-empiricist reassessments shared a general (if unarticulated) suspicion that the classic representations of psychological attributes of gender, masculinity and femininity, were inaccurate representations. While Constantinopole (1973) was preparing her indictment of these constructs as the product of a simplistic dualist model and a constrictive, circular methodology, Sandra Bem (1974) was designing a new psychometric instrument to provide greater empirical accuracy in representing masculinity and femininity as it exists within individuals. The Bem Sex Role Inventory (BSRI) was free from the classic presuppositions that gender attributes are bipolar and mutually exclusive. The BSRI also did not assume that some sort of identity or suitability between biological sex (assigned sex) and psychological gender characteristics is necessary for mental adjustment.

In other words, the BSRI was constructed to scientifically and politically displace longstanding notions about gender *difference,* about the existence of some *essential* qualities of what it means to be male or female and, thus, about what should count as *normal gender identity.* The BSRI offered a corrective to these unwarranted precepts by furnishing a new gender category: androgyny. By combining masculine and feminine attributes, the androgyny construct disrupted assumptions of gender dualism that had long served as markers for some set of obscure, yet presumably real, gender differences. This concept also supplied a new model for social policy: Whereas the classical conceptions of psychological gender contain norms of female and male subjectivity, models incorporating androgyny afford a vision of flexible, successful human agents operating in a complex, nongender-structured social world. In fact, Bem (1974) explicitly stated that the androgyny concept is consistent with feminist values, and many other researchers have adopted the concept for its emancipatory potential.

To judge by the wide use of masculinity-femininity scales that have incorporated androgyny, the concept appealed to many psychologists seeking to remedy bias in gender studies. This emerging research area hosted worrisome problems, however, and the literature on androgyny soon indicated that the new measurement devices held both theoretical and psychometric complications. There was little understanding of precisely how femininity and masculinity combined to form this newly recognized type of social agency: Is androgyny the result of additive processes, that is, so much femininity plus so much masculinity; is it the interaction of some particular set of attributes from each sex; or is it the result of reaching some threshold of these two gender attributes? Related to these conceptual uncertainties was the fact that the androgyny model acknowledges and, in fact, is constituted by conventional images of femininity and masculinity. In spite of its emancipatory promise, the model retains the classic gender dualisms and, hence, the latent notion of some real gender difference. The revised psychometric tests objectify these dualisms and claim to represent some real inner psychological entities: Like their prototypes, these tests yielded psychological images that served as signifiers and the signified, marking out the real nature of gender.

Another problematic feature of androgyny emerged from both empirical studies and critical analyses (Morawski 1985, 1987). What was introduced as the possibility of a flexible, enabling, and even gender-free personhood revealed an uncomfortable resemblance to conventional masculinity: Just as quantitative analysis suggested that masculinity scores alone were good predictors of androgynous behavior, so qualitative analyses illuminated individualist, male-centered ideals underlying the concept. Androgyny appeared at once to maintain gender dualisms and to perpetuate a state of cultural ideals favoring a particular type of social agency: that of a cognitively flexible, independent, and self-contained individual (Sampson 1977). Seen with regard to the feminist-empiricist goals of removing sexist bias, androgyny research is particularly revealing: The correction of biases resulted in a model that apparently is weighted toward masculine attributes and is consistent with the assumptions about an independent and instrumental social agent. Androgyny research thus embodies several ironic features of feminist empiricism. The removal of biased ideas was realized through replacement by other gender-linked values, and relatedly, the complicated process of eliminating those biases resulted in a model that apparently privileges masculinity. This is not the first time in recent history that feminists' use of androgynous imagery has backfired (Gubar 1981; Smith-Rosenberg 1985).

From another perspective, androgyny symbolizes a culture-specific dilemma: It represents the identity plight of individuals desiring to undertake *instrumental* tasks, which are marked as masculine by society, while retaining *expressive* qualities, marked as feminine. In the 1970s and 1980s many American women who had had the privilege of access to higher education experienced such a dilemma of identity. For them, the idea of androgyny promised a resolution of, or at least the possibility that there was an alternative to the double bind ensuing from the restrictive psychological order of a sexist society. Androgyny offered a new psychological identity based on a long-standing cultural ideal of self-contained individualism (Sampson 1977). Androgyny also shifted the boundaries of mental well-being not simply by removing sexual orientation and biological sex from the equation of psychological normality, but perhaps more importantly, by embracing the flexibility or mobility of identity. Thus, in the spirit of liberal feminism, the scientific discovery of androgyny buttressed the beliefs that many reputed sex differences were superficial and that their elimination would facilitate equal treatment of women and men. In the spirit of American democratic liberalism, this scientific concept served the ongoing mission of dismantling barriers that prevented individuals from achieving their potential. In keeping with the tradition of scientific psychology, the androgyny model locates these barriers largely within the individual and proffers an individual-centered recipe for their elimination. Also in keeping with psychology's traditions, androgyny was discovered and investigated primarily by women researchers: Gender has largely been a women's problem within the science just as sexism has been a personal concern primarily of women. Not the least, the study of androgyny was in keeping with recent theoretical moves, at once cultural and scientific, to represent the self as mobile, multiple, flexible, fractured, and fragmented (Cushman 1990; Fraser and Nicholson 1990; Gergen 1991; Kihlstrom and Cantor 1983; Rosenberg and Gara 1985).

The notion of androgyny, then, is a scientific *and* a cultural accomplishment, but it is more than a surface reflection of the investigators' own psychological desires and utopian ideals. Close analysis of the androgyny concept reveals its containment of governing notions of subjectivity; in the end, the case of androgyny shows how psychology often proceeds with inadequate notions of subjectivity (sometimes *through* and sometimes *against* implicit concepts of the subjectivity of psychologists themselves). In modern psychological theory the individual is taken as an autonomous and rational agent who is best understood through study of his or her internal mental processes (Rose 1985, 1990a, 1990b; Sampson 1981; Venn 1984). This subjectivity, however, is investigated and theorized through supposedly context-independent procedures. What is produced in experimental investigations is an abstracted subjectivity existing independent of its social and historical context. Just as context-stripping in our methods has been the object of critical analyses (Mishler 1979; Mies 1983; Parlee 1979; Westkott 1979), so must be our reigning models of subjectivity, for they fail to indicate how subjectivity is constructed through social structures and processes (including material conditions, power relations, and historical circumstances). Features of subjectivity such as gender identity, for instance, should be seen not as freely available resources or choices, but as products of particular social arrangements.

Although a similar sort of abstracted subjectivity is posited for the psychological scientist, it is generally assumed that, given the rational rules of scientific practice, the definition of the researcher's subjectivity requires even less consideration. Yet, psychologists have worked to define a scientific identity that bifurcates their subjective selves, one that separates their scientific from their nonscientific subjectivities (Morawski 1992). This separation is becoming less tenable as science is being found, for instance, to be practiced by gendered subjectivities, by transmitters of cultural (biased) values regarding gender. The case of androgyny research illustrates both the attempts and failure to bifurcate psychologists' subjectivity. Just as researchers cannot remove the cultural clothing of their subjects (Cushman 1990) and, in fact, must rely on cultural identities in their investigative practices (Danziger 1990), so must they proceed with—and be motivated by—the cultural understandings contained in their own research (Fine 1989; Berg and Smith 1988) and writing (Lopes 1991; Morawski and Steele 1991).

In exploring androgyny, then, women scientists not only have engaged struggles with their own identities, but also have transmitted constructions and contradictions of cultural practices of gender—constructions and contradictions that cohere in science as well as in other domains of social life. If androgyny concepts were science fiction, then their investigators have ultimately uncovered both the fact and the fantasy of the liberal claims of women's rights and have attempted the earnest enlistment of science to realize those claims. Feminist psychologists aspiring to wed their experimental science to a political vision, to couple the scientific and the fictional, find themselves to be a part of that new relationship, and yet to remain outside it. Their kinship with both enterprises affects the social complexity of the arrangement. Their social marginality as scientists and as feminists operates alongside and within a double bind resulting from the efforts to construct a subjectivity compatible with both science and feminism. The double consciousness described by feminist scholars in various disciplines thus surfaces in feminist psychology as both the *object and the subject* of that inquiry; it is produced in the subjectivities of the investigators and their subjects alike.

Special Histories, Common Positions

Feminist-empiricist psychologists, like other scientists (Brush 1974; Samelson 1978), have created a history that simultaneously reaffirms and regulates scientific practices. Their primary historical narrative is a story of restoration functioning to protect particular epistemic commitments, however mythic they might be, while at the same time, functioning to mobilize a significant departure from that epistemic tradition that has privileged certain agents, subjectivities, and experiences at the expense of excluding others. Yet, however imaginary the narrative of restoration may be, and despite evidence suggesting that adherence to its traditions is problematic, that narrative has enabled some measurable success in the scientific construal of sex and gender. Donna Haraway (1986) refers to such feminist operations as altering the "narrative field" of a science. If it is acknowledged that feminist science is not an unbiased science but, rather, a better science in the sense of giving a fuller, more coherent version, then feminist science alters "a 'field' of stories or possible accounts by raising the cost of some accounts, by destabilizing the plausibility of some strategies of explanation" (81). Feminist science operates to change the possibilities for understanding and leading lives.

Psychologists who have fostered the coalition of empiricist science and feminist objectives have, for the most part, favored conventional scientific practice once cleansed of its sexist biases, but have not embraced the entirety of empiricism's dominant narrative. Feminist-empiricist psychologists have adhered strategically to the normative practices of that science as a way to reform the procedures and products of those practices, notably by objective assessment and removal of sexist techniques. When they have done so, the consequences have not always been positive or consistent, but have sometimes been unexpected, partial, contradictory, and contrary. Insofar as feminist-empiricist psychologists have succeeded in increasing the participation of women in science, and in identifying androcentric methods, there has been a payoff in this extended policy of overall adherence. When the accomplishments are configured within a matrix of gains and losses, however, the situation becomes even more complicated. Marginalization of women psychologists, despite their increase in number and visibility, persists in multiple forms, along with minimization—if not dismissal—of the outcomes of feminist-empiricist research. As noted earlier, various assessments of methodological practices indicate that the gains in nonsexist methods are local and scattered. Finally, feminist-empiricist work has been accompanied by epistemological problems arising from contradictions between classical empiricist thought and feminist revisions of that epistemology. These epistemological inconsistencies parallel practical problems that occur when feminist empiricists locate and remedy some aspects of an androcentric science and not others. Not infrequently, these contradictions and inconsistencies yield paradoxes. The case of androgyny illustrates one paradoxical consequence of this partial awareness: Critical regard for certain sexist presumptions of psychological theorizing motivated substantial alterations in this theoretical model, but resulted in a construal of psychological subjectivity that nevertheless continued to reflect cultural patterns of gender. Not only does the psychological subject inscribed in the androgyny model represent the life trajectories and dilemmas of a specific class of women, but that subject remains peculiarly marked as masculine.

The paradoxical play, and ongoing resistance accompanying feminist empiricism—the very slippery slope of its achievements—are more readily identified by contrasting that systematic program with more radical, albeit less successful, feminist epistemologies. However, having regularly interjected that comparison throughout the chapter *forces* a conflict, and presupposes alternatives that are themselves somewhat mythical. Feminist scientists may be well aware of epistemological alternatives, especially as they make contact with feminist studies in other disciplines and newer philosophies of science. Yet their options to experiment with alternative perspectives and, hence, to enact new practices of investigation are constrained by the formidable machinery of the discipline. North American psychology, a discipline whose knowledge is produced wholly within universities and professional schools, operates within shifting yet well-demarcated boundaries that determine what counts as legitimate scientific practice.

The case of operationism in psychological practice illustrates how even flawed understandings of scientific procedure, once integrated into routine research activities, are resilient to modification or elimination (Green 1992; Koch 1992; Leahey 1980). Another case, the contents of social psychology reports, illustrates how investigative standards shift: What are taken as legitimate and appropriate methods of inquiry do change over time, notably in terms of what counts as a sufficient procedural information, statistical analyses, citations, graphic illustrations, and number of subjects and even in terms of what constitutes a publishable unit of experimentation (Reis and

Stiller 1992; West, Newsom, and Fenaughty 1992). What is perhaps most interesting about these alterations in scientific practice, is that although they appear to be adopted wholesale, with rare deviations and near hegemonic utilization, they are not the result of public and deliberate decision making, but rather evolve more or less silently with mixed reactions to their appropriateness or meaningfulness as scientific procedures (Funder 1992; Higgins 1992; Reis and Stiller 1992; Schneider 1992; Wegner 1992; West, Newsom, and Fenaughty 1992; Zanna 1992). These cases offer evidence of how psychology as science is constituted through decisive though not always deliberate actions (Latour 1987) and how boundaries of legitimate conduct, however variable over time, delimit an investigator's range of investigative choices. The feminist-empiricist researcher can survive within this bounded social institution, although her actions may be paradoxical and her achievements may be indirect and fragile. She is especially challenged to work within the dominant guidelines of scientific practice, confronting their idiosyncrasies and shifts yet all the while negotiating acceptance of even her minor investigative innovations and transgressions. Historical reassessments of feminist-empiricist work document the constraints and liabilities of being positioned both within and between current science and the unrealized.

Consideration of science as action, with shifting, not always logical rules; participants with varied interests (i.e., feminist and nonfeminist); and differences of opinion over even retrospective events suggests that the history retold in this chapter is, at best, a partial portrayal. Most historical accounts—whether uplifting narratives of restoration that hearten feminist empiricists or critical narratives of constraint and paradox that are less reassuring—reconstruct past science using a model of linear progression or stability. Except for the occurrence of rare and retrospectively revered "paradigm" revolutions, the historiography of modern science retains its own tidy narrative of the transhistorical and universal nature of inquiry. Everyday histories of science, especially of psychology, presume that empiricism means much the same thing as it did fifty, or one hundred fifty, years ago. Although this chapter departs from such normative storytelling, it merely begins to incorporate the messiness of practices, agents, and products that *is* science. Once the more popular metanarrative is bracketed (Lyotard 1984), and empiricism, along with its attendant scientific norms and practices, is again considered to be (to some degree) historically contingent, then the more local, multivocal, and historically recent narratives of feminist empiricism can be reexamined, reappreciated, and perhaps, reconstructed. Some routes to the reconsideration of scientific practices and reappraisal of feminist psychology are charted in the ensuing interchapter.

Interchapter

Betwixt and Between

The previous chapter nests, in somewhat awkward juxtaposition, divergent stories about the heritage of women psychologists, and more specifically, feminist-inspired psychologists. As a member of that allied group of feminist psychologists, I have pondered over its life course, alternately calculating its potentials and speculating on its fate. This book grew from those ponderings: The resulting theses, sometimes audacious and at other times more sensible, draw upon diverse intellectual enterprises. The explorations of this book are indebted to those studies; thus it is relevant to introduce some of the resources, as well as some conceptual problems, that have motivated my thinking just as they have modified my own sense of self and place as an intellectual worker.

Borrowed Images

The historical narrative generally associated with feminist-empiricist psychology contrasts with, and is complicated by, another story, also mentioned in the previous chapter, that is more paradoxical than progressive. Both accounts position feminist research as marginal: One plot foretells the eventual end of marginality in science through corrective measures, and the other forecasts feminist psychology's continuation in an unfriendly if not oppressive scientific system. While retaining the shared sense of marginalism, a third telling is imaginable. In this story, the idea of liminality describes the situation of marginals and, at the same time, outlines the contours of an action-based, transformative science. As introduced by the anthropologist Victor Turner, the concept "liminality" refers to a particular space/time in rituals, a phase in a rite of passage between the ritual separation of the initiates from the community and their eventual reaggregation in their new place in society. Liminality is the threshold, the betwixt and between of established social states in which "the most characteristic midliminal symbolism is that of paradox, or being *both* this and *that*" (Turner 1977, 37). In exploring the fate of liminality in posttribal societies (modern cultures), Turner ventured to examine how this betwixt-and-between state, this marginality, furnishes a place not just for momentary inversion, or reversal, of mundane social reality, but also for its ultimate subversion, or replacement. Liminal phases can give rise to the production of metalanguages that are "devised for the purpose of talking *about* the various languages of everyday, and in which mundane axioms become problematic, up for speculative grabs"—perhaps for taking new and unexpected purchases on the social world (Turner 1977, 45). In these transitory metalanguages lay unique opportunities for substantive change in existing social arrangements.

Science has escaped neither anthropologists' observations nor their taxonomical analyses; insofar as it constitutes a culture or subculture, science has been found to retain practices akin to tribal customs, ever regulating its participants through rites, symbols, and collective social meanings. But the introduction of liminality and liminal time/space is not intended here as an invitation to read psychological science as a "culture of the other," as a distinctly different social order. On the contrary, many of the historical accounts of the psychology created over the last chapter portray the mundane or indigenous character of psychological practices in Western, usually North American, culture. There is a more important sense in which science should *not* be viewed as a separate culture. Donna Haraway (1986) and Bruno Latour (1983), for example, have countered the myths of science as other, as outside the rest of culture, particularly as outside of politics, by questioning the very function of such mystifying boundaries—between science and politics, and between science and society more generally. While retaining relatively common tools of cultural analysis, researchers like Haraway and Latour investigate specific techniques used in and through science to accomplish larger cultural projects. One instrumental means by which science manages to move culture is the very representation of science as separate, as outside culture. By bracketing science from other cultural activities, especially by dividing it from politics and ethics, scientific knowledge gains a distinctive status as disinterested and, therefore, more powerful knowledge. By comparison with this example, the notion of liminality is not evoked to intimate any paranormal qualities of psychology, but simply to help identify social practices. With the location of a liminal science, we are better able to see how such practices are constitutive of the particular cultural ambitions of psychology, and how feminist psychology, in particular, does or does not fit those dominant culture ambitions.

Liminality refers to a space/time in ordinary social practices that generally goes unnamed. Yet it is not difficult, as Turner demonstrated, to find postindustrial correlatives to the liminality of tribal rituals, and no extraordinary effort is required to locate liminals in science, as many graduate students would concur. However, Turner's examination of liminality sharpens our attention to the "not here-not there," the in between, and hence paradoxical nature of liminality. It also alerts us to its subversive potential, not just its transitory inversion of normative and mundane understanding. What Turner did not elaborate on are the conditions under which liminals transform their roles from marginals to subversives—the refusal to assume the roles of status quo practitioners. He did begin to examine these conditions, however, in his distinction between tribal liminals, who are involved in collective communals shared throughout the community, and what he has termed "industrial-liminoids," who are involved in smaller groups seeking communitas, groups organized through a social category or similar social characteristics, i.e., sex, age, ethnicity, trade, religion, or the like (Turner 1977, 47). The latter groups, according to Turner, experience not only the paradox of being both within and without, members and nonmembers, of the social state, but also the paradox of striving toward a sense of community while creating an insular, elite social group.

Given these anthropological concepts, contemporary feminist psychology can be configured as an event and a social movement within psychological science. The implications of such a configuration are multiple, for they entail refashioning the game board of this realm of psychology. If feminist psychology is a liminal science and if its marginality is conjectured as betwixt and between—as occupying a space/time of potential transformation—then the typical conversations about impasse, conflicting models, and contestation are at least partially in error. To occupy a liminal social zone is not necessarily to be *stuck in* or *stuck by* something, but rather to be *not* so encumbered or detained. Likewise, the paradoxes of that position need not be read as debilitating contradictions. Most importantly, liminality—as a suspended moment of transition when the ordinary and mundane are viewed in their strangeness and otherness—is not inextricably fated to one's reinstitution or reaffirmation of the ordinary social world; rather, the liminal (or industrial-liminoid) condition holds the potential to subvert, transmute, or transform. Liminality, then, lends an alternative understanding of some of the anxieties currently circulating in feminist psychology, and restores a vision of the transformational nature of that project.

It would be naive to think that feminist psychologists are unaware of their in-between status, for substantial thought has been given to the binds and well as freedoms of being not quite there. Numerous initiatives have been launched from this awareness; perhaps the most notable among these is the Association of Women in Psychology (AWP) whose structure and process were designed as "a model of feminist practice and a site for practicing feminism . . ." (Tiefer quoted in Parlee 1991, 42). The construct of liminality clarifies such understandings, but taken alone is an insufficient one for reconfiguring feminist psychology because it tends to flatten comprehension of social practices and fails to articulate the specific characteristics of liminal experiences. Liminality points to the paradoxical and potentially transformative valences of being in a marginal time/space, but it does not reveal the specific kinds of work activities that transpire within; nor does it tell how liminal agents are transformed and thus move out of liminality and into newer social relations and practices.

Resources beyond Metaphor

In the first chapter, the state of feminist psychology was portrayed through the narratives that are used by practitioners and critics alike to make sense of that enterprise. The narratives convey more than the tacit values of feminist psychology for they also contain plots that assign responsibility to various agents, identify what counts as progress, and convey the norms and aesthetics of appropriate scientific conduct. Like all stories, these narratives are *partial* and, hence, chronicle only some of the action, and concern themselves only with certain actors. They likewise are bound by particular premises of what is a *valid scientific action* and what is not. For instance, the empiricist narrative of restoration does not merely tell of imminent progress but, more importantly, sets certain conditions about *what counts as reality,* and *what attributes agents have* (animation, inanimation, physicality, sociality, consciousness, lack of consciousness, etc.). As noted in the previous chapter, the individual agent posited in classic empiricism accords with a liberal politics and its premises of an autonomous being who has, among other attributes, the capacities to engage in detached rational analysis. Yet underlying the empiricist narrative are axiomatic beliefs that scientists are passive—their beliefs and interests play no crucial part in the task of compiling veridical representations of objects in the world (Woolgar 1988). In contrast, the restoration part of the story imposes a somewhat contradictory view of scientists as responsible agents whose commitments are central to making an accurate science.

The notion of liminality counters this narrative of restoration by making a way for us to see science as a *human activity,* sustained by a set of *social relations.* The anthropological metaphor reminds us that science is a *collective* enterprise with organized *norms of conduct.* The more important insight offered by engaging this metaphor, however, is that whereas collective undertakings are routinized—or ritualized, as an anthropologist might have it—they are uncertain projects with untold possibilities for mutation or reformulation. Both the ideas of narrative and liminality, then, begin to move us away from conventional conceptions of science. Conceptions of science as a potentially identifiable set of rules, as a particular mindset about the world (paradigms), or as a special class of knowledge concerned with only certain characteristics of the world cannot readily be accommodated to science as it is practiced: these conceptions offer neither adequate descriptions of nor explicit prescriptions for scientific activities. There are now well-developed options to the conventional view of science in particular, and human knowledge in general. These emerging alternatives have influenced my work over the last fifteen years, and have served as resources for reimaging feminist psychology. The resources include work in several distant fields of inquiry as well as new theories in the human sciences. What follows is first, a compendium of these influences, a sort of resource index, and second, a brief introduction to a social epistemology of science that these sources have helped shape. A comprehensive exposition of a social epistemology of science is beyond the ambitions of this interchapter; the citations given throughout offer guides for further reading.

The first resource has evolved from new approaches to the *social studies of science*. Foremost among the achievements of these researches is the demonstration that science proceeds in distinctly different ways than is presumed in conventional philosophies of science. On one hand, science-as-practiced is notably different from science-as-recorded; that is, what scientists do in their daily activities is not what is inscribed in scientific texts, classic histories, or philosophical models. According to Latour (1991), these social studies of science show that "the whole edifice of epistemology, all the cliches about scientific method, about what it is to be a scientist, the paraphernalia of Science, was constructed out of science-made, out of science-past, never out of science in the making, science now" (7). On the other hand, these investigations of scientific activities have indicated that there is no distinctive or crucial difference between what scientists do and what everybody else does when they produce knowledge: Science is executed using reason, collaboration and talk—ordinary skills used in rearranging the world (Latour 1983, 1987; Woolgar 1988b). Like other forms of knowledge production, science is constructed in local contexts with local peculiarities.

Such findings support a substantially different conception of science and call for new epistemologies (Fleck 1979; Fuller 1988; Longino 1990; Rouse 1987). Among the implications of this recent work is the realization that not only disciplinary boundaries (Gieryn 1983) but also the most basic epistemic boundaries are the products of scientific work and not its pregiven conditions. The divides between nature and culture, physical and nonphysical, animate and inanimate, conscious and nonconscious, and representation and reality, along with the classic partition between science and society, are the *result* of scientific activities, and sometimes require effort to sustain. Steve Woolgar (1988b) has suggested, for example, that maintaining the boundaries between representation and the object of representation (reality) constitutes an ongoing problem for scientists. Scientists continually seek to manage this problem, and in analyzing these management strategies, science-studies researchers must undo the constructed divide between what counts as scientific activity and other knowledge-seeking activities. Likewise, Latour (1991) has described a historically constituted divide between what we take to be human and nonhuman, which has driven a differentiation in how truth is defined and sought in the human and natural sciences. As formulated in the seventeenth century, the dichotomy between human (provided with political representation) and nonhuman (provided with scientific representation) has underwritten a larger "political constitution of truth" that is more inclusive than a political constitution as it is conventionally understood, for it encompasses and directs both human and nonhuman representation. A political constitution of truth not only determines how certain objects in the world are to be represented in knowledge systems, it "also distributes powers, will, rights to speak, and checks and balances. It decides on the crucial distribution of competence: for instance, matter has or does not have will; God speaks only to the heart and not of politics . . ." (13). Divisions between human/nonhuman, political/scientific and social/natural are established in this constitution and create "two separate parliaments, one hidden for things, the other open for citizens" (15).

Another distinction enacted in this larger political world also concerns agency: the specifications of agents of representation "which mediate the world and its representations" (Woolgar 1988b, 101). In the drama of scientific investigation of the world, Woolgar has located a "moral order" that sustains scientific representation by assuming that the agents who are the observers are passive in terms of being thought to be incapable of "affecting the character of the world," yet they are taken to be responsible for the representations they furnish (101). This moral order of representation not only sustains a split between objects in the world and observers (analysts) of those objects but also poses inconsistencies regarding the nature of the analysts:

> The alleged passivity of the agent vis-à-vis the facts of the world is captured in the idea that facts are neutral, that they are there to be discovered by anybody. But the alleged irrelevance of the agent provides an interesting awkwardness when it comes to acknowledging and rewarding individual scientists for their contributions to science. . . . The dilemma is that the honoured individual is held to be especially capable of obtaining representations of the world, but that such representations do not arise solely in virtue of an individual agent. (101)

Further, this moral order sustains an intricate society whereby agents differ in their rights and responsibilities:

> Some are reckoned more capable than others, some particularly good at certain kinds of interpretive work, others as having outlived their usefulness, and so on. At any time, the culture of the laboratory comprises an ordered moral universe of rights and entitlements, obligations and capabilities differentially assigned to the various agents. This moral order can change with the introduction of a new agent into the community. (102)

Until recently, scientific knowledge itself has been more available for unpacking through science studies than has been the agent (self, analyst). This relative unevenness in treatment is understandable given the fact that scrutiny of the moral order of agents requires that critical analysts themselves must work within a moral order of representation; as we shall see, special reflexive senses must be engaged in these analyses (Rouse 1992; Woolgar 1988b). For Woolgar, "the task is not just to understand the moral order which sustains the ideology of science, but to seek ways of changing it" (105). Here we can begin to see how this rendering of science differs in another significant way from canonical philosophies of science in offering neither a bare descriptive account of scientific practice nor a normative one that ties prescriptions to those descriptions, but one that candidly stipulates expectations and aspirations for science—that acknowledges the simultaneity of political and epistemic engagements. Such science studies do not hold a preexisting or overarching distinction between the descriptive and normative features of science or a preconceived notion of its agents, but instead, set as one of the tasks a politically attuned analysis and reconstruction of these boundaries and entities.

Not all social studies of science are committed to changing the moral order or the constitution of truth that organizes scientific practice, yet they do illuminate opportunities for such changes. One of these opportunities for a change ensues from the recognition that science—and social science—has required the sort of divides named above: Science investigations proceed only by securing distinctions between representation, object, and observer (analyst). Once these separations are seen as fabrications serving particular interests, then not only the normative content but also the self-referential or reflexive properties of scientific statements about the world become evident. Reflexivity concerns the very relation between object (reality) and representation (accounts of reality). It refers to that back-and-forth process whereby making sense of an account of reality depends on pre-existing knowledge (on the part of the observer) of what that account refers to, and vice versa (Ashmore 1989; Woolgar 1988b). Once reflexivity is acknowledged and the awareness of the analyst and the awareness of object are seen to be bound up together, it then becomes possible to explore alternative relations between object, representation, and analyst that would be constitutive of radically different forms of knowledge and perhaps different political and cultural aims.

The second domain that serves as a resource in assessing feminist psychology is *feminist studies of science*. Whereas they share with the social studies of science an understanding of science as a historically constituted set of human practices, most feminist analyses of science examine how relations, particularly gender relations, have constituted and sustained scientific activity. Scientific agents do not participate in neutral or equal ways; rather, their involvements are typically arranged according to dominant social relations. Feminist studies of science name the ways in which science is gendered, and thus, point to the ways in which the gendered relations of production connect with gendered products, notably with sexist "knowledge" (Bleier 1984; Fausto-Sterling 1985; Fee 1983; Haaken 1988; Rose 1983, 1986). Some investigators thus have turned from studying gendered social relations of scientific work to examining how the underlying scientific epistemology is itself gendered (Bordo 1986, 1987; Fee 1981, 1983; Harding and Hintikka 1983; Harding 1986b; Keller 1985a, 1985b). For instance, the ideas of an objective knower and of objective observation appear to be grounded in a history of thinking of the knower as being separate from the object, passive in the observation, located in distant relation to the object, and, hence, a wholly cognitive and unextended creature. This knower, however, is vested with cognitive authority not only by virtue of having these qualities, but also because of his or her membership in ongoing social arrangements and hierarchies within scientific practice. These concepts of knower and objectivity have been found to parallel cultural concepts of masculinity and stand in opposition to feminine (and some feminist) styles (Addelson 1983; Bordo 1986, 1987; Merchant 1980). They also have been linked to psychological processes that may determine gender-specific ways of characterizing the world (Flax 1983; Keller 1985a, 1985b).

Feminist studies of science have engaged such historical understandings to ground new scientific epistemologies that avoid androcentric criteria for what counts as adequate knowledge, theory, and methods (Fee 1986; Harding 1986a, 1986b, 1987a, 1991; Longino 1990). They have moved beyond analysis of masculine bias to imagine alternative ways of doing science where, for instance, objectivity is defined in terms of the knower and his or her position (Haraway 1988) or where adversarial and hierarchical modes of making science are replaced by cooperative and non-dualist practices (Moulton 1983; Rose 1986). Such a successor science would mean that scientists "actively seek ways of negotiating the distances now established between knowledge and its uses, between thought and feeling, between objectivity and subjectivity, between expert and nonexpert, and would seek to use knowledge as a tool of liberation rather than of domination" (Fee 1986, 47).

The final resource informing this project consists of a constellation of projects that share an *interest in analyzing the dominant categories in society*. Familiar to most readers as race, class, and gender research, these studies have proceeded with neither common method nor singular subject matter. Rather, they converge on nothing more or less than a commitment to, first, "stories of the oppressed and an analysis of the meaning and nature of their oppression and, second, scholarly understanding that inequalities of power are organized along at least three axes" (Scott 1986, 1054). Gender, race, and class constitute at once *social categories* by which dominance and subordination are maintained, *and ongoing social relations*, which direct individual experiences and give them meaning. These categories and social relations are the social asymmetries of everyday life, and studies of race, gender, and class have delineated how they are constructed and change over time, despite some persistent intellectual efforts to define them as innate or immutable (Kelly-Gadol 1987; Hartsock 1984). For instance, recent studies have indicated how the history of American blacks, as a social group, is only understandable in terms of shifting economic conditions and specific gender arrangements (Mann 1989; Zinn 1989). Other research has shown how science and social science participate in these constructions. Psychology, for one, has moved from studying racial types or groups to investigating inner mental states of prejudice, discrimination, attitudes, cognitive schemata and the like, all of which are concepts that relocate issues of race within individual minds rather than taking them as concrete conditions of social reality (Henriques 1984; McLoyd and Randolph 1986; Samelson 1978). The sciences are one macrostructure of power that serves the organization of microstructural affairs; the human sciences in particular set parameters and give meaning to individual experiences, identity, and the choices available to individuals for acting in the world and interacting with each other (Gerson and Peiss 1985; Smith 1987a; West and Zimmerman 1987). The distribution of power according to race, gender, and class thus operates across all social relations, from academe (Christian 1989a, 1989b; Collins 1989; Zinn, Cannon, Higginbotham and Dill 1986), to shopping (Ayres 1991), wage earning (Reskin 1988), and housework (Hartmann 1981). Despite the fact that these studies of dominant social categories are informed by diverse and sometimes contesting theories and methods (Fraser and Nicholson 1990; Johnson 1986; Pfister 1991; Scott, 1986), they nonetheless have shown race, gender, and class to be far more dynamic and pervasive, far less stable and bounded, and certainly less responsive to conventional policy remedies, than has been assumed in the social sciences, including psychology (Morawski and Bayer 1991). Ongoing dominant social relations enter "into the research process itself—into the selection of a problem, into the methodology . . . and [into] the relationship with those we are researching" (Edwards 1990, 482).

Work on these dominant structures of social life has spurred recognition of other salient categories requiring analysis. For instance, although it is now generally known that psychology's constructs of gender cannot be transported to or considered to be connected in any simple way with sexuality and sexual preference, the project of conceptualizing sexual orientation or identity and of locating its importance in deciphering social experience lies ahead. Likewise, to begin investigating the dynamics of race introduces consideration of the varieties of ethnicity. Thus, just as we need to understand the racial categories of Hispanic to be a recent cultural invention, so we must interrogate the varied ethnic experiences and conditions associated with diverse social groups (Mexican, Puerto Rican,

Spanish, etc.) that have been labeled Hispanic. Such known and yet to be discerned classification and hierarchical arrangements in culture affect individuals' range of social action, structure social experiences, and as noted, enter into the very practices of doing science.

For feminist psychology, these new studies render problematic any notion of singular or stable identity or attempts to examine social relations solely in decontextualized environs. Most importantly, they make imperative the need to think deeply about how psychological categories are *produced* by, and are *productive of*, these social arrangements, rather than simply being objective *representations* of them.

Theoretical Choices?

Woven together, the resources of science studies, feminist studies, and cultural analysis direct rethinking about the processes of science along with its missions. They challenge older preconceptions about how to go about the work of science and, as will be considered shortly, they impart not just new descriptions of science but a politics of science as well. What the present index omits is an account of the varieties of theoretical options that have emerged over the last several decades, sometimes in alliance with the aforementioned resources. Notably relevant are the psychological approaches contained in social constructionism, postmodernism, and feminist psychoanalysis. There now exists detailed reviews of how feminist psychology might work with and through advances being made in social constructionism (Tiefer 1987; Unger 1989b, 1990), postmodernism (Flax 1990; Hare-Mustin and Maracek 1988) and feminist psychoanalysis (Flax 1990, Sayers 1986; Squire 1989; Walkerdine 1990). Yet, alongside these supportive analyses have appeared critical ones, which note the inability of these approaches to serve feminist inquiry (Bart 1977; Bleier 1984; Bordo 1990a, 1990b; Fee 1986; Hartsock 1990; Kitzinger 1991b; Nicholson 1990).

That such theoretical alternatives receive discrepant assessments is not a novel feature of either psychological work or these particular theories. For feminist psychologists, theory choices have always been enveloped in a field of antagonist tensions. While the previous chapter recounts a legacy of feminists' confrontations with established psychology, it does not give a full sense of the multivalent relations between feminist aims and psychological expertise that have ensued over the last century (and that have heightened in the last two decades with feminism's more visible presence). In her exploratory history of this most recent phase of feminism, Ellen Herman (1993) found that while feminists in general and feminist psychologists in particular compiled a large-scale critique of psychological expertise, they also appropriated "those aspects of psychological theory and practice perceived as potentially liberating for women or strategically useful to the women's movement" (620). More specifically, feminists utilized resources within psychology that aided in making connections between the psychic and the social as well as the personal and the political, and in forging investigations of the nuances of subjectivity and identity. Thus, feminist work on actualization, socialization, and identity formation, along with developments in feminist psychotherapy, have to various degrees depended on established psychological concepts. Feminist psychology was similarly informed by the politics of protest that had been enacted by other groups, notably the antipsychiatry movement. In acknowledging these paradoxical events, Herman suggested our need to appreciate that "while psychology helped construct the female, it also helped construct the feminist" (584).

Feminist psychology, then, even while distancing itself in important ways from the ethos of established psychology, has drawn from that intellectual corpus in its construction of theoretical alternatives. In retrospect, this pattern of events is not surprising for a complete break from all existing cultural understandings of psychic life is an unimaginable move. Further, both dominant cultural models and feminist alternative visions have contained only the simplest understanding of the relations between psychological and political phenomena: nowhere could be found a ready theoretical account of those relations. Feminist psychologists' simultaneous resistance to and accommodation of psychological knowledge has produced a paradox or, as Herman suggested, perhaps "it was merely wisdom in paradoxical form" (620). However the paradox is viewed, it needs to be understood not as an anomaly but as a fairly typical case of the oscillating operations of psychological expertise in the twentieth century.

> Capable of soothing and exacerbating social and political ruptures, psychological experts were technologists of pacification

> one moment and prophets of renewal the next. For feminists, who understood keenly the danger of reducing women's social status to the psyche, the challenge was to link the dots between self and society, between the personal and the political, without making either to be the byproduct of the other." (621)

When construed in this broader historical context, the theory options available to feminist psychologists at once become more plentiful and more risky. In the case of theoretical choices, our critical and creative interventions always carry the possibility of being refit into status quo representations. The question then becomes not one of finding *the* theory or theories that are once and for all rid of unwanted political context or consequences, but rather, finding the means to avoid or preempt the recuperation of new theoretical ventures into sexist and nonliberatory programs. In order to locate these means, we need to understand better the cultural workings of science—the practices and processes whereby our professional and scientific actions alter (or do not alter) the world. In turn, this task of situating our work depends on a broadened comprehension of scientific processes and practices; it essentially requires a different epistemic framework than the ones usually presented in our discipline.

Toward Social Epistemology

What is science once we take its embellished rules and textual products to be just one component of an extended social practice? What do we want from science once we detect and dissect its gendered heritage? How should we think about scientific work and, more importantly, how should we go about doing it? The resources noted above, especially the social and feminist studies of science, can frame an operative rapprochement to the dual necessities of thinking and doing science while continuing to labor within a professional/scientific community that still represents itself in mythic or otherwise inadequate ways (although the eventual objective of social epistemologies requires more thorough reformulations). A concept of science as a cultural activity opens to view the full range of practices that constitute that knowledge making enterprise; such a conception permits us to draw the contours of how science should proceed—the mapping of a social epistemology (Fuller 1987). To do so requires two crucial reconceptualizations: expansion of the definition of science to include those actions that are typically relegated to incidentals or epiphenomena (the so-called social aspects of science), and the reconsideration of power to incorporate (typically unacknowledged) productive forces as well as constraining rules or juridical systems of regulation (Fuller 1987; Rouse 1987). Expanding the definition of science requires attention to (1) the relation between the products or textual artifacts of science and the processes of science not represented in those artifacts; (2) the unacknowledged, indeed usually denied, interdependence of cognitive activities and social relations; and (3) the complex practices behind the formal organization of science, i.e., those behind the presumed prevalence of consensus among investigators, and the presumed distinctions between what is taken as theoretical and empirical, factual and political. To understand science as constituted through productive powers is to see how its organization, technologies, languages, and societal position at once produce the intelligibility of its claims and enable science to provide "us with a transformed hold on the world" (Rouse 1987, 211).

Adopting a social epistemology is *not* equivalent to rejecting or baldly relativizing knowledge claims. Rather, such a perspective treats the validity of scientific claims as social achievements (Janich 1988; Krohn 1988; Pinch 1988). Even epistemic beliefs are socially produced. Once this perspective is embraced, along with the idea that routine practices in their complexity and multiplicity make up the power of science, then it is but a step to begin contemplating the normative ambitions of epistemology.

In feminism (as in other liberation movements) these normative components of scientific epistemologies have received considerable attention, enabling us to locate inadequate or unacceptable grounds and to introduce viable alternatives. It is now apparent that the attempt to "arrive at the perspective from which nature and social life can be seen as they really are" is a derivative ambition of traditional epistemology, including the patriarchal association of knowledge and power (Harding 1986a, 647). Once it is known that such an Archimedean point necessitates erasure of the identity of the observer, or at least a safe distancing of subject from object, then that standpoint becomes undesirable. Likewise, once certain dualisms that sustain western intellectual thought are found to be intimately connected with the reproduction of oppressive gender systems, then it can be seen how our feminist analyses must continually encounter divides, oscillations, and conceptual instabilities (Harding 1986a; Snitow 1990). Finally, once we see how feminism requires both a negative project to dismantle sexist discourses and practices and a positive project to construct viable alternative ones, then feminist inquiry must be seen as requiring varied local strategies and arguments that, taken together, may not, and usually do not, look anything like an old-fashioned coherent theory (Gross 1986; Jaggar 1990). Intellectual projects in feminism then, cannot be patterned in any close way after the classic procedures for theoretical or empirical work. In epistemic terms, our projects cannot presume to manifest a stable, univocal, monolithic, or coherent form. In historical terms, our projects of the past must also be seen in their complexity, complete with tensions, contradictions, and multiple possibilities (Cott 1986, 1987; Snitow 1990). In all of these terms, it has become apparent that our epistemic foundations must inevitably be normative, linked more explicitly (although not more deeply) to politics than are traditional epistemologies.

In summary, social epistemology is all about seeing the constellation of interactions that constitute science. Efforts toward conceptualizations of feminist science have been particularly successful in locating both the sexist social organization and practices girding the positive production of knowledge. Feminist analysts have been motivated to engage science through its social workings and not its canonical guises. Growing from a suspicion that feminists, particularly feminist psychologists, have long operated with at least a tacit understanding of the sociality of scientific inquiry, our present tasks include explication of that insight, mainly by finding and assessing the ingredients of a maturing social epistemology.

Local Strategies (What We Do)

How, then, should feminist psychologists proceed with their science, especially when they seem to hold to problematic theories and tarnished epistemic images even as they see newer ones ahead? Put differently, where do feminist psychologists begin when they decide to move from liminality toward transformative science? The proposals from feminist theorists are diverse. Some theorists argue for an immediate and definitive resolution of ambiguous positions: They recommend various successor science projects, including those built from the standpoints of materialism, psychoanalysis, phenomenology, constructionism, and postmodernism (Alcoff 1988; Fee 1986; Harding 1986b; Hartsock 1987, 1990; Rose 1986). Still others find that ambiguity and plurality are essential to ensure both survival and the development of inclusive theory (Gross 1986; Jaggar 1990; Snitow 1990). This latter group of theorists posits the political necessity of taking *strategical* and *local* outlooks; of remembering the doubleness of the observer, her relatedness to her inquiry; and of forging an episteme that attends to the unstable complexities of the world. In advocating local and diverse tactics, Ann Snitow has noted that "each issue calls forth a new configuration, a new version of the spectrum of feminist opinion, and most require an internal as well as external struggle about goals and tactics" (29).

For feminist psychologists it is now apparent that the latter proposals have proved to be more common and more successful. Like feminists in related disciplines, many of us have spoken and written about how our inquiry pushes against the dominant narrative of scientific change, a story whose plot is overdetermined by the myths of positivism, progress, and democracy and by a politics of memory that over and over again forget the gender arrangements of science. Feminist psychologists at once stand within and outside that story, repeating what Naomi Weisstein observed twenty years ago: Psychologists "refuse to accept evidence if they are clinical psychologists, or, if they are rigorous, they assume that people move in a context-free ether, with only their innate dispositions and their individual traits determining what they will do" (Weisstein 1971, 222). Feminist psychologists, situated in a space in between, have seen the binds as well as the possibilities for strategic action: Since Weisstein's percipient observations, we have painstakingly colored the contours of our liminal space. The constraints of a narrowly defined methodology have been indexed (Lykes and Stewart 1986; Fine and Gordon 1989; Parlee 1979, 1991; Sherif 1982). The insularity of our discipline has been documented, and we have cautiously stepped out to explore other options such as those available in social constructivism and postmodernism. We have commented on the double consciousness of our liminality, and have broken the silence concerning the relationship of the analyst and the subject of inquiry (Fine 1989; Lykes 1989; Unger 1983, 1989b). The many vicissitudes of being a feminist *and* a psychologist have been charted (Kimmel 1989). These reflections are based on social experiences, on experiences generated within a particular organization of work, scientific psychology, and by a specific group, namely professional women working at one historical moment of North American feminism.

These experiences of liminality, in themselves, already defy the authoritative account of science. In fact, to name such experiences is to transgress not just the records of scientific orthodoxy, but its actual practice. Feminist psychologists, including the many who would count themselves as empiricists, *are* entrenched in alternative forms of scientific practice. The boundaries between analyst and the world, particularly between analyst and subject, have been unsettled. Indeed, the very enactments of observer (experimenter, analyst, knower) have been altered. While there continues to be talk about some parcel of information being "theory" or "data" or "method," feminist inquirers have moved beyond any pretense that these categorical terms represent separate or separable domains of knowledge. And although seemingly unchanged, the criteria with which knowledge is warranted are somehow different; certainly the lines between what is taken as pure and practical research, or as universal and specific, have been blurred beyond easy recognition.

Feminist psychologists have already reorganized scientific work, and already invented new practices. These practices, however, mostly occur in a space of betwixt and between, and for that reason are not always discernible. They are location-specific gestures, sometimes muted and sometimes bold. They are not always direct and overt but oftentimes oblique, vicarious, and coded. They are almost always contingent on varied settings and audiences. The practitioners in some way or another almost certainly hold uncertain status, and as liminoids our activities are sometimes tentative, partial, and of ambiguous meaning. Our identities as psychological scientists and as women are rarely if ever fixed: Our individual voices are often multiple, with the consequence that sometimes we face the unfortunate situation of being at odds with one or another feature of our own selves. And yet, we are almost always excited about what we are becoming. The remaining chapters of this book chronicle these increasing instances of transgressive or transformative activities; they make note of what we have accomplished and what we yet need to do. Only by, first, naming the new practices and, then, by elucidating their generative potential, can the social organization of feminist psychology continue on its transformative way.

Chapter 2

Objectivity

So foundational has been the idea of objectivity to psychology that titles of early books and articles often touted their "objective" contents. Over time, objectivity has become a taken-for-granted goal of all psychological investigations, a ubiquitous attribute requiring no special labeling. Objectivity now constitutes such a pervasive feature of modern psychology that it is difficult to locate a simple, inclusive definition of the word, or even to specify a fixed set of procedures that ensure its happening. It remains a primary aspiration for our investigations, all the while carrying multiple definitions: a specific criterion for what counts as adequate knowledge, a characteristic of the investigator, and a quality of methods.

This signature quality of objectivity is an unreflected reality of psychological research; only through analysis of its philosophical heritage and rhetorical forms do the complications of this ubiquitous concept become evident. If objectivity is analyzed in terms of its everyday usage in psychology, then we are forced to ask how it can be simultaneously referred to as an act, a goal, and a personal attribute? If objectivity in psychology is examined in terms of its common meaning of "not biased by someone's point of view" (Judd, Smith, and Kidder 1991, 5), then we must ask who can occupy the objective perspective, that Archimedian point? What perspective is the appropriate or desired one? Is this ambition realizable or even reasonable? Or is it, as Richard Bernstein has suggested, the enactment of a Cartesian anxiety about uncertainty, chaos, and irrationality? The search for an objective foundation or Archimedean point

> is more than a device to solve metaphysical and epistemological problems. It is the quest for some fixed point, some stable rock upon which we can secure our lives against the vicissitudes that

> constantly threaten us. The spector that hovers in the background of this journey is not just radical epistemological skepticism but the dread of madness and chaos where nothing is fixed, where we can neither touch bottom nor support ourselves on the surface. (Bernstein 1983, 18)

These sorts of queries pose a dual challenge to proponents of dominant renditions of objectivity: They question both the *possibility* of objectivity as an epistemic aspiration and the *desirability* of objectivity as an aim for generating knowledge.

Such questions also reveal a generally unrecognized multiplicity in psychology's definition of objectivity: its varied references to persons, procedures, and sometimes the object world itself. For this reason, the discipline's problems regarding objectivity are great, needing extensive analysis. They invite intrusive questions, insisting that what is at stake is analyzing not a singular referent to persons, procedures, or objects but also a host of terms like bias, value, control, and even the real. Questions regarding objectivity are only occasionally entertained in conventional psychology, but they have emerged as a problem area for feminist scholars and, hence, for psychologists engaged in feminist psychology. Feminist challenges to objectivity in science have taken many forms, but within psychology the challenge has been aimed primarily at research *methods*, specifically at the sexism embedded in them. As described in the first chapter, this line of criticism has fostered a demand for replacing sexist methods with unbiased or nonsexist ones. However, other solutions to the problems are possible. Some of these solutions derive from different interpretations of objectivity—renderings that expand the compass of what counts as scientific practice and that attend to the ways objectivity figures as an attribute of the knower, of knowledge, and even of the world to be known.

The study of objectivity is generally considered part of an academic niche within philosophy known as epistemology. As Naomi Schemen (1991) recently noted, "Feminist epistemology has an audience problem" (19): Whereas feminists find little value in the genderless abstraction and generality of conventional epistemology, philosophers often find feminist contributions to be irrelevant or unintelligible. When objectivity is the topic of discussion in psychology, a somewhat different audience problem arises. Psychologists have set most of their deliberations over objectivity in institutionalized terms such as *methodological procedures,* or to a lesser extent, the *qualities of investigators.* Many feminist psychologists become deeply engaged in these deliberations, unearthing less-evident ways in which issues of gender hinder the operation of objectivity in methodologies and investigators alike. Other feminist psychologists, however, often guided by personal experiences and critical analyses of foundational philosophy, reject these institutionalized frameworks for discussing objectivity, and instead, see it as an issue of power, language, and social regulation. In doing so, these researchers sometimes juggle between adopting empiricist criteria and poststructuralist critique; or, as Donna Haraway (1988) so aptly described it, they find themselves trying to "climb the greased pole leading to a usable doctrine of objectivity" (580).

The audience for feminist analyses of objectivity in psychology is, at best, diversified, but more often is simply distracted and disparate. This situation might pose less of a problem to the study of objectivity *if* we could find a way to mesh the varied languages and frameworks without naively reifying or rejecting any of them. With this collaborative aim in mind, the present chapter attempts to marshal some common understandings of objectivity that are present in the discipline. By singling out some of the taken-for-granted qualities of objectivity in psychology—those features pertaining to its existence as a scientific practice, an epistemic aspiration, and an attribute of investigators—we can begin to see the moral, political, and social choices that direct our practices of objectivity. The obvious risk in this venture is still the "audience problem," the possibility of having no audience since the review requires moving freely, perhaps too casually, through notoriously distinct paradigms and languages. In order to locate the routine ways in which objectivity is attained in research, the chapter begins with an unexceptional and concrete example of objective practice. That exemplar enables identification of some of the less obvious implications of defining objectivity through any narrowly constructed methods or through a de facto binary system that demands the opposition of objectivity and subjectivity and takes objectivity to be an attribute of observers. More importantly, elucidation of routine procedures and their limitations shows how objectivity in psychology is primarily a practical accomplishment, not an abstract ideal or personal attribute and, then, enables us to consider how a revised concept of objectivity as labored achievement connects with a view of epistemology as a moral and political project. Those large steps taken, it is necessary to deliberate the place and play of gender in the making of objectivity, from which point we can better appraise enactments of objectivity currently being made within feminist psychology.

Objectivity: Discovered or Invented?

Psychologists who identify their work as empiricist frequently pose objectivity as a research ideal that guarantees the separation of fact from value. Upon closer inspection, this ideal requires a distinction between subjectivity, which represents personal, valuational, and hence, idiographic takes on the world, and objectivity, which represents impersonal, value free and hence, universal takes on that world. In this form, objectivity is then connected with a set of research procedures, yet it simultaneously refers to a morality whereby science serves the rational pursuit of a valid understanding of nature and, therefore, demands an ethics of distanced and disinterested inquiry (Leary 1980; Pratt 1939; Toulmin 1975).

Feminist psychologists working with this binary definition (and ethics) of objectivity have found that, especially in research concerning gender, investigative practices have fallen short of the ideals. Cultural and personal values about gender have contaminated all stages of research (Hyde 1991). A task force on nonsexist research, created by Division 35 (Psychology of Women) of the American Psychological Association (APA), corroborated the claims of this contamination, enumerating a host of systematic gender biases in psychological knowledge. Research guidelines developed from the findings of that task force propose that such biases can be eliminated through the escalation or refinement of objective practices. The guidelines recommend "that we continue to subscribe to the claims that traditional methods can produce more valid, value-free knowledge" (McHugh, Koeske, and Frieze 1986, 880). The authors defined the "tradition" in terms of objectivity, and in turn, defined objectivity by contrasting it with subjectivity. The distinction between objectivity and subjectivity "rests on the equation of objectivity with value-free, repeatable methods of data collection and on the belief in the generalizability of objective data. In contrast, subjectivity is viewed as being value laden and unrepeatable, based on private events, and focused on unique experiences that cannot be generalized" (880).

The published guidelines reaffirm the prevailing position of feminist empiricism by demanding the continuation of usual means for attaining objectivity. These means include, first, the containment of values that may seep into the research at various stages and, second, the reduction if not removal of subjective biases of the investigator. Subjectivity, in this view, is a stable and distinct—if usually regrettable—attribute of the researcher as well as a set of alterable beliefs, values, or interests that leak into technical procedures. The authors of the guidelines acknowledged the manifested forces of subjectivity in noting that "perhaps one of the most difficult tasks of a scientist is to become disengaged from 'everyday' assumptions about the nature of reality and to generate alternative, testable conceptualizations of reality" (McHugh, Koeske, and Frieze 1986, 879). However, they also claimed that one such subjective condition, an investigator's social marginality, "can contribute to the individual's ability to view reality from an alternative perspective" (879). Here a feature of subjectivity seems to somehow flip over to the objective plane for it is being claimed that, at times, female psychologists have the attributes of marginals or outsiders and, therefore, are more able to disengage from dominant cultural values and beliefs. Male investigators have no such advantage and, therefore, are constrained from realizing objectivity, especially in studies with female participants where "the research setting most clearly reflects and reinforces the imposition of male definitions of reality on females" (880).

This portrayal of objectivity and its opposite, subjectivity, poses several problems. On the one hand, it argues for the bracketing of biases and values, and on the other hand, it suggests that such containment is less possible for certain investigators than for others (in this case, it is less possible for males). If the analyst's gender imposes limitations on the attainment of objectivity, then what about the influence of other personal attributes—what about age, ethnicity, race, religion, class, or physical appearance? What about feminism as a value or belief? In recommending containment of biases, what specific aspects of subjectivity are being successfully guarded against, and what aspects are not? Any answer to these questions would necessitate taking an exhaustive inventory not only of subjective states but also objective practices in order to ascertain what values are being eliminated and what values are not. In the end, it would require the ominous exercise of fully unpacking the meanings of objectivity and subjectivity for each-and-every step of an investigation. And if this inventory were to include analyses of investigators' personal attributes—their age, social status, ethnicity, political inclinations, or idiosyncratic preferences—then ensuring objectivity would be a formidable (if not impossible) goal.

To register these problems is not necessarily a claim that bracketing certain features of the subjective is undesirable or impossible; nor does it imply that we cannot pursue features that enhance objectivity. Rather, these problems simply signal the limitations of the dominant applications of empiricist thought in the discipline. It also must be understood that some of these problems are not unique to feminist empiricism, but have coincided with the maturation of empiricist psychology over the last century. They are embedded in the very project of developing an objective study of subjective experience, an aspiration that completely overwhelmed other ways to study subjective experience and that eventually yielded a narrow concept of what is objective. Some of these problems are also implicated in the self-appointed ambition of developing a socially relevant science while simultaneously aspiring to obtain objective knowledge of subjective experience. From this double-sided aim—a socially relevant but objective science—there have emerged numerous debates over the possibility of producing knowledge that is simultaneously disinterested and committed to social welfare. In feminist-empiricist research, motivated by a political commitment to women's rights and well being, the complications encountered in separating objective and subjective, and in balancing politics with a disinterested ethos have been magnified and compounded.

These various problems attending the construction of workable formulations of objectivity were joined by others arising from the admittance of women into the science, especially women who brought along feminist beliefs. The defining boundaries of objectivity have become blurred whenever researchers, mostly women, have detected some of the ways in which orthodox objective practices are, in fact, reflective of particular (in this case masculine) beliefs. The configuration of objectivity has been further complicated whenever researchers have indicated that the gender of an investigator determines his or her ability to act objectively. And these complications have become even more acute whenever researchers, again usually women, have acknowledged that they share certain subjective experiences with their research participants, and hence are better able to observe these experiences or their psychological consequences. Added to an already difficult project of identifying and securing objective practices, such feminist concerns offer undeniable evidence of the multidimensional qualities of objectivity as it is enacted in psychological research. Above all, these concerns demonstrate that one's questioning objectivity ultimately leads to interrogation of the way we construe the methods of inquiry, the investigator, and the investigative problem whenever we go about regular research practices.

An Objective Study of Subjectivity: Measuring Feminism

The compelling questions to be asked about objectivity, then, necessitate difficult answers. And the answers must (at some point) rest with reexamination of the *practices* of objectivity, including those practices through which attributes of investigators are identified and associated with the acts of being objective—or subjective. Before addressing these sorts of questions, more needs to be known simply about the normative practices that function to name the subjective and objective—practices equating objectivity with particular gestures of research and reserving subjectivity largely for certain actions and voices of participants. A case study is useful in tracing the routine conceptualization of objectivity in research as well as the assignment of surplus subjectivity (notably to the subjects). The case presented here is particularly illustrative for it concerns studies of a purported psychological phenomenon, feminism, that hypothetically could be associated with observers or persons being observed, or with both.

Several years ago Ruth Striegel-Moore and I began a study of the psychological investigations of feminism. We each became intrigued with the subject, albeit for different reasons. Striegel-Moore's research on eating disorders in women focuses on the relations between cultural values and psychopathology, and it appeared to her that feminism might be a salient construct in explaining the cultural axes of eating disorders. My historical work on gender and psychology led me to ask how feminist politics intersects with theoretical developments in gender research. We naively presumed that the project would be short lived, and that after collecting the handful of existing measures of feminism, we would be able to undertake a theoretical and historical analysis. We soon discovered that our data base was far larger than expected and that the aspirations motivating the psychological research on feminism were many. To date, nearly thirty measures of feminism or prowomen attitudes have been located. These measures have not been produced solely by feminist investigators, nor have they served the testing of any single hypothesis or subject population. They were conducted in a period spanning over half a century, and within diverse social climates. Our small, neat project almost spontaneously grew into a thick, ongoing inquiry (Striegel-Moore and Morawski 1993).

Given our own theoretical orientations, the examination of feminist measures also entailed a reflexive component, or rather, a doubly reflexive one. That is, our self-awareness as feminist scholars provided the impetus for the project: We began with a self-conscious concern about our own personal and professional meanings as well as the cultural meanings of feminism. We also were curious about the reflexivity actually exhibited in the research on feminist measures, and wondered, on the one hand, about the extent to which the researchers self-consciously positioned themselves in some relation to feminism, and on the other hand, about the extent to which they may have less self-consciously drawn on dominant cultural understandings of feminism. The discovery of so many different scales, produced by researchers working with diverse aims and in varied contexts, unsteadied our aspirations.

Historical complexities aside, the recursiveness of our inquiry still remains dizzying: We created a project in which feminist psychologists investigate psychologists' (some self-avowed feminists and some not) investigations of the feminism of other individuals (some self-avowed feminists and some not). Despite the recursive convolutions of our approach, the research literature acknowledged no such complications: The uncomplicated clarity apparent in these feminism studies was posed as the end result of objective practices. Without entering into the details of our findings to date, these objective practices can be delimited and shown to exemplify how hard cases of psychology research can be made easy—how objective practices ultimately engender clean and disengaged research. The fact that they may not tell us much about feminism, in either investigators or subjects, is another matter.

Beginning as early as 1936, psychological researchers studied the psychological correlates or consequences of feminism. They succeeded in doing so by deploying three common methodological practices. While ostensibly devised to maximize objectivity in controlled *observations*, these methodological practices also functioned to bestow objectivity on the *investigators* as well.

First, with few exceptions, the studies proceeded with a definition of feminism that was *referential*, that defined feminism by referring to some observed entity; in no study analyzed thus far was a self-referential definition proposed. Such referential definitions are constituted by making reference to some phenomena in the social world of which readers of the studies have some knowledge, and identifying the psychological construct, in this case feminism, with that reference. The definitions found across the studies refer to a wide range of phenomena, including social groups, clusters of political beliefs, or specific behaviors of individuals. In the earliest known measures of feminism, Clifford Kirkpatrick (1936) anchored his definition of feminism by reference to the propositions made by "feminist organizations" (422). In a study conducted nearly forty years later, J. A. Dempewolf (1974) mirrored Kirkpatrick's approach, defining feminism by reference to "the aims of the women's movement" (651). Other studies defined feminism in terms of specific beliefs or attitudes. Through this procedure, feminism is defined in reference to the perception of unjust treatment of women in one study (Smith, Feree, and Miller 1975), and the belief that men and women can take roles that traditionally have been associated with the opposite sex in another (Robinson and Follingstad 1985). By contrast, some research defined feminism by reference to sets of beliefs about personal choice and growth, or about social change (Arnott 1972; Dreyer, Woods, and James 1981; Goldschmidt, Gergen, Quigley, and Gergen 1974). Finally, several studies employed a more complicated strategy of defining feminism by reference to the specific findings from the measures being taken. That is, the definition of feminism was deferred until reference could be made to the actual scores on a scale, thus defining a feminist as someone scoring within a certain range on that scale (Renzetti 1987).

In conventional methods, referential definitions enable objective ones, for they point to a characteristic of the world that can be observed by others. The fact that different investigators select different references by which to define feminism remains a problem, but psychologists long ago devised means to adjudicate among such definitions, thus, ultimately resolving the problem (Hornstein 1988). What is more difficult to justify, however, is what is left out of the referential practices: the not readily visible, the symbolic, the as-of-yet unnoticed aspects of the world, *and* the investigator. For, if the investigators include themselves in their reference to what is out there in the social or psychological world, then they disrupt objectivity; they violate the taken-for-granted distinctions between object and subject. Yet these observers do in actuality stand in some relation to the psychological and social references to which they point.

A second and related methodological practice common to the psychological assessments of feminism is the construal of feminism as an *attribute of individuals,* a quality that is often described as bipolar—someone is or is not feminist. This research shifts the definition of feminism from activities (or behaviors) to individuals, usually to some internal character of individuals (a shift from behavior to mind that psychologists know is not always easy to demarcate). Research then proceeds by directly testing the amount or degree of feminism that those individuals do or do not possess. Sometimes this procedural move is made by testing the concordance between the referential definition and individual participants' responses, and sometimes by a further referential process whereby feminist and nonfeminist participants are identified prior to any testing. In either case, the practice entails the construction of an instrument or *inscription device* (Rose 1989) with which investigators can locate the phenomenon within individuals, thereby identifying both the presence and relative amount of the phenomena in those individuals.

Inscription devices further ensure objectivity because they provide a collectively shared means (an instrument) through which to observe the phenomenon, hence reducing the possibility of idiosyncratic or biased perceptions of the phenomena. At the same time, inscription devices also serve to give both form and content to subjectivity, to subjective realizations of the object under scrutiny. They locate and name subjective phenomena and, in doing so, they establish a firmer boundary between objectivity and subjectivity. So secure here is the difference between objectivity and subjectivity that *no* investigators applied inscription devices designed for assessing feminism to themselves. In fact, the very idea of such an application undoubtedly would have seemed outrageous.

The final methodological practice found in the research on feminism is the use of *quantification.* In all the studies located to date, the assumed subjective responses from participants are translated into quantitative units. This practice further serves the goal of objectivity in that quantification is held to escape the ambiguity and biases of language. By reducing variation and surplus meanings, the translation produced through quantitative inscription devices also provides means for investigators to reach consensus more readily. Translations of events in the world to quantitative units, an integral part of the inscription process, finally contribute to differentiating objectivity and subjectivity: Given their function in reducing personal and linguistic differences and in enhancing consensus, they facilitate erasure of the investigators' subjectivity just as they further distance the observer from the object of inquiry.

Most of the studies we located and analyzed share a set of investigative procedures—referential definitions, concrete tests of personal attributes, and quantification—that enable the production of what has come to be accepted as objective knowledge about feminism. The case of feminism measures is, on one level, an unexceptional example of how routine scientific practices do not just deploy some abstract notion of objectivity but function to manufacture and operationalize it. Trevor Pinch (1988) referred to this routinized process as the "externalization of observation" whereby observation is highly mediated by technical manipulations and whereby ordinary observations, the observer's sense perceptions, "get projected or externalized via the process of scientific observation." Observation, and hence, objectivity, *"reside in the apparatus* rather than in the immediate visual or audible fields" (229).

Using only this level of analysis, it could be argued that investigators have few choices to forgo the externalization of observation, especially given the strong regulatory forces operating on psychological research. However, if the analysis is taken to another level we can see a wider range of implications attending the externalization of observation through technical manipulations. First, in the process of observing something called "feminism," the studies under examination mark and double mark the difference(s) between observer and object: The most prominent difference being reproduced is the association of observer with method, and hence, with objectivity, and the association of the object with no such rational system, and hence, with subjectivity. Feminism is taken, through a system of referential definitions, to be *a subject*—an object of inquiry—and to be *subjective*—a value. Second, through the technical operations of the studies, the feminism of the investigators is securely bracketed from the feminism of others (notably the participants in the study). The research practices that were employed thus obscure or deny any existence of the investigators' feminism. Among the range of possible phenomena eliminated through such practices is double vision in the observers, despite many feminist psychologists' reported experiences of such double vision (of seeing both as feminists and as psychologists). In the end, these practices also discernably limit the relevance of personal experience in prototypical psychological research (Wallston 1981). In constricting what in the world is to be taken as feminism, these practices deny or overlook the possibility that individuals, notably women, act both in traditionally acknowledged ways—state opinions about sexism, join organizations—and also in subversive ways—imagine other possible ways of behaving, unobtrusively disrupt sexist affairs (Fine and Gordon 1989). When all is said and done, the conventional techniques of assessing feminism actually make a restricted place for feminism in psychology. We need to understand better precisely how these restrictions are made, and perhaps, how they can be unmade.

Ways to Make Objectivity

The case study of research on feminism highlights some of the ways in which objectivity is not simply invoked or used but is produced in relation to the object of study. Through conventional scientific procedures, feminism is located within individuals as a personal attribute, attitude, or belief—a subjective entity—thus making way for a regulated appraisal of that object. In turn, those controlled appraisal procedures at once signal that objectivity is being realized and that the observer is distanced from or devoid of subjectivity through engagement with these procedures. The object in the world is pointed to, measured, and analyzed; by performing certain technical operations the observer at once is behaving objectively and remains separate from the subjective material under scrutiny. Studies of feminism using different (qualitative) methods do exist, even studies assessing feminism in researchers (Kimmel 1989), but they usually make no claims of objectivity. Ironically, these other studies may inadvertently reinforce the desirability and superiority of objectivity by producing a contrast that reaffirms the common distinction between subjective and objective research, and the less common, although similarly polarizing distinction between nonsexist, or sex-fair and feminist research. These binary designations for research co-exist with a hierarchical logic: "Alternative (subjective) methods are often evaluated by comparison to traditional (objective) methods. That logic recommends that we continue to subscribe to the claims that traditional methods can produce more valid, value-free knowledge" (McHugh, et al. 1986, 880). Hierarchical arranging thus enters, almost undetected, into the evaluation of feminist studies: "Sex-fair research as encouraged here does not discriminate against women; feminist research works actively for the benefit or advancement of women" (886). The truly objective investigator is once again clearly identified and validated.

Through investigative procedures, then, objectivity is both produced and productive of a certain form of knowledge, knowledge that locates a decisive and decisively constrained set of characteristics in the object of inquiry. The analyzed studies of feminism hint at some of these characteristics of the objects. The studies ultimately juxtapose feminism and objectivity by divorcing the investigator from the object of study as well as by frequently identifying feminism as a committed point of view, a passioned belief, or a peculiar social attitude. Thus feminism is taken as a subjective, individual attribute. Many of the investigations implicitly make further claims about this feminism subjectivity by performing technical procedures that intimate its limits: By employing standardized scales and questionnaires instead of self-reports or interviews, using referential definitions that completely avoid reasoned or verbal responses on the part of participants, or shielding the purpose of the investigation from participants. In serving as means of assuring methodological control, or objectivity, these assessment techniques simultaneously convey substantial assertions about the participants (the world), specifically about the rational limits of their subjectivity. They reassert and therefore reassure us of the traditional view of feminism, ignoring its less visible or more subversive manifestations. The psychological studies of feminism exemplify (particularly poignantly, given their subject matter) the routine practices of making objectivity and deferring subjectivity, which are utilized in contemporary psychology.

Objectivity, as we have just seen it, is neither applied as a fait accompli, nor is it made simply in these individual studies; rather it is an accomplishment of years of routine investigative practices. Observers, or experimenters, were not always taken to be psychologically different from subjects, or participants. On the contrary, in early twentieth-century psychology, a plethora of investigative practices were deployed in experimentation that did not make such sharp distinctions, including the researcher's frequent exchanging roles of experimenter and subject. In a historical study of investigative practices, Kurt Dangizer (1990) has charted the shift, at first gradual and then careening, from diverse research practices to the monolithic one of designated, trained observers of individuals whose identities are selectively revealed or furnished by investigators. The development of a hegenomic technique whereby experimental roles of experimenter and subject (E and S) are distinguished has fostered the construction of particular subjects, and subjectivities: "For a discipline that took 'scientific' to imply reference to some universal truth beyond individuality, history, and local meanings, the establishment of claims to being scientific frequently depended on appropriate manipulation of the identity of the sources to which data were attributed" (Danziger 1990, 100). Danziger's study documents how experimenters' and subjects' roles were arranged so as to produce what could be taken as universal knowledge, to ensure the investigator's control of the investigative context, and to generate knowledge that was applicable to real-world contexts requiring the sorting and regulation of individuals. In doing so, these investigative arrangements furnished grounds for differentiating objective from subjective knowledge. Through these investigative procedures, what experimenters did became synonymous with objectivity, and what subjects did became synonymous with subjectivity.

The generation of objectivity through investigative practices has been an ongoing collective enterprise, one that has transpired in events ranging from everyday and oftentimes seemingly mundane laboratory negotiations to the establishment of a formal canon of scientific writing. What is to be counted as an objective statement about the psychological world has to be publicly agreed upon among investigators. Gail Hornstein (1988) has uncovered some of the ways in which practices of quantification enabled such collective agreement. Quantification offered more than a technique for transforming complex subjective phenomena into a uniform language: It offered a means "to objectify aspects of decision making that would otherwise be seen as clearly subjective" (23). Psychological research entails the making of nearly unending decisions about techniques, observation, and interpretation. Hornstein has shown that "by providing ways to 'package' these choices, quantification transformed the experience of the researcher into one of merely applying various standardized techniques, rather than having to make a series of complex choices" (23). The adoption of quantification techniques then, transformed the subjectivity of researchers into objectivity just as it made psychological research more efficient and less prone to social conflicts.

The making of objectivity extends from the preliminary organization and techniques of investigations to the ultimate stage of research: the written scientific account. Numerous studies indicate the ways in which scientific writing itself confers a sense of objectivity on scientific activities and, consequently, constructs its binary opposite, subjectivity. The history of writing styles in experimental psychology tells of a progression from writings in which subjects are portrayed as important actors in the story, and authors, using the first-person voice, appear as reasoners or persuaders who offer a narrative telling of experimental work, to writings that present subjects who emit highly specific actions or signals and authors, without a first-person voice, who are merely technical manipulators, rule-following calculators, and presenters of facts (Bazerman 1988). The rhetorical style that evolved through this progression has become a prescribed one—finely delineated and mandated in the APA Publication Manual and the editorial guidelines of journals—that effectively stabilizes the roles, relationships, goals, and activities of individuals within the research community in ways that are consistent with the community's beliefs about human behavior (275).

Rhetorical imperatives, however, exceed the mandates of official manuals: Objectivity is produced even in the fine-grained textual strategies executed in experimental write-ups. Using the case of experimental reports of "bias and heuristics" research, Lola Lopes (1991) has identified several textual maneuvers that cleverly position the authors, and even professional readers, as uncontaminated by irrational processing, while at the same time enabling them to posit (often unwarranted conclusions) that subjects are irrational or at least poor at judgments and decisionmaking. In the case of reports on unconscious cognitive processes, rhetorical strategies are deployed to secure some point of view that is undistorted by these unconscious processes, usually that point is the objective gaze of the investigator-author (Morawski and Steele 1991).

The notion that objectivity is an artifice of the social practices of investigation is hardly unique to psychology. This point is demonstrated in science studies' investigations spanning from studies of laboratory negotiations over the use of specific instruments to analyses of the structure of scientists' informal talk and textbook accountings (Gieryn and Figert 1986; Gilbert and Mulkay 1984; Latour 1987; Latour and Woolgar 1979). To acknowledge objectivity as a labored accomplishment, however, is not necessarily to imply that its constitutive practices are misguided. Rather, the acknowledgement opens the way for one's comprehending objectivity as an accomplishment that ensues from crucial decisions about the nature of the world, the possibilities of knowing that world, and the agents who desire that knowledge. In the end, decisions guiding our attempts to study the world objectively are actually questions about *who* we are and *what* we want; the decisions are, therefore, social and political ones (Rouse 1987). These decisions, although generally invisible in the day-to-day activities of science, are available for our measured and reflexive scrutiny. It is through such scrutiny that we can then begin to evaluate the adequacy of the political groundings of our science and move on to imagine alternatives to those grounds.

Gender and the Politics of Objectivity

To propose that objectivity is an accomplishment realized through specialized scientific practices is at once jumping ahead of ourselves in this evaluation and failing to go far enough in an assessment of the full play of objectivity. The proposal has not yet been related to contemporary renderings of epistemology, and given the sustained changes in this field, it needs to be set in that context. Nor does this proposal elaborate on its feminist premises or even speculate on how gender does or does not figure into accomplishing objectivity. The first of these skips in the evaluation of objectivity can be filled by reviewing the critical expositions of objectivity that have been made over the last three decades. The second skip, concerning the relevance of gender, has not usually been addressed in those critical expositions but is a central interest of feminist philosophers of science and will be reviewed in turn.

Assessments of objectivity have ensued from many disciplinary corners, and have often been tied to idiosyncratic problems of those disciplines. Ignited by the apparent relativist implications of the writings of Thomas Kuhn and W. V. O. Quine, philosophers of science have reconsidered the epistemological and historical groundings of objectivity. Among other issues, they have debated the very existence of the epistemological foundations of objectivity, and in so doing, the spector of relativism spawned duals between so-called objectivists and relativists (Bernstein 1983; Hollis and Lukes 1984; Rorty 1979, 1989). For social scientists, assurance about attaining objectivity had never been firmly cemented, and the age-old question of whether social science could be truly scientific, hence objective, was revived (Bernstein 1983; Rabinow and Sullivan 1979). In the humanities, poststructuralists challenged the authority of authors, readers, and critics alike, raising the ante on any claims of valid, enduring, or objective knowledge.

Given the multiple sites of these conversations, it would require a lengthy digression to enumerate the range of issues being contended. What has emerged from these conversations, albeit in very different forms, is an awareness of what is at stake in either defending some notion of objectivity or demonstrating its viability. In retrospect, this critical scholarship roused a sense that objectivity was a vulnerable target, one easy to hit. By bringing to the foreground the "Cartesian anxiety," as Richard Bernstein (1983) has described that peculiar dread of uncertainty and unfixedness that accompanies the desire for objectivism, the plausibility of abolishing such a foundation of knowledge seemed to diminish immediately. Eventually, questions of objectivity (for the most part) fell to the sidelines, and what ensued was a posing of relativism as the alternative to objectivism and, consequently, the formation of an oppositional playoff between relativism and objectivity. This binary game board has a long history:

"Each time that an objectivist has come up with what he or she takes to be a firm foundation, an ontological grounding, a fixed categorical scheme, someone has challenged such claims and has argued that what is supposed to be fixed, eternal, ultimate, necessary, or indubitable is open to doubt or question" (Bernstein 1983, 9). In psychology, as in many disciplines, the dual has entailed pitting objectivism or objectivity—understood as the belief in a distinction between subject and object, and an accompanying belief in the independence of what is out there (even when "out there" is inside people's heads)—and relativism—understood as the belief that there is no such fundamental distinction between subject and object and, hence, no definitive way to generate knowledge about what is out there except that which is relative to some cultural scheme, paradigm, or system.

In order to move beyond this stalemate, it is necessary to make not only what has been called a "linguistic" or "interpretive" turn but also a "practical" one: to assess epistemic or knowledge claims in the full context of their making—in their economics, material conditions, social arrangements, moral orderings, and symbolic and discursive practices. Advocates of these newer procedures for assessing knowledge claims agree that we must move beyond the deep Cartesian traditions that persistently recuperate and reinforce classic beliefs such as the independence of object and subject, and that continually impose transhistorical matrices of rationality or logical rules for decision making. There is an emerging sense that searches for knowledge, such as science and social science, are practical activities sustained by rules about the search and searchers as well as about the nature of the reality being investigated. These rules, in turn, are routinely altered through practices of research, and in the end, produce transformations of the world that are at once moral, social, material, and epistemic (Bernstein 1983; Fuller 1988; Latour 1987; Rouse 1987; Woolgar 1988b). Objectivity, therefore, can be seen as an accomplishment of multiple practices, one that has *moral* and *material* as well as *methodological* substance.

The morphogenesis from traditional epistemology to studies that construe objectivity in moral, social, and practical terms, is now well underway. This is a fundamental change and demands rethinking some central epistemological questions. If objectivity is a practical accomplishment, and not merely identifiable in terms of the knower (observer) or procedures (methods), then in what terms can we talk about objectivity? If objectivity is the product of social practices, then how can we call some practices objective and others not? Are there multiple objectivities? And can we continue to deem some observers, by virtue of their skills, actions, or personal attributes, more objective than others?

It is no coincidence that feminists, mostly though not always feminist philosophers, have engaged these questions. The epistemological anxiety that undergirds and sustains the Cartesian dualism (of objectivity and subjectivity) can be shown to have much to do with gender, particularly with masculinist thinking. Any plausible successor to classic epistemology must examine the place of gender in objectivity. (The marginal status of women in current science itself attests to the need to figure gender into any revision of scientific practice). This feminist inquiry has been (necessarily) both *backward* and *forward* looking: Historical and analytic studies have delineated just how objectivity is gendered, while more speculative and experimental studies have probed its possible alternatives. The inquiry also is one of *immediacy* and *specificity;* that is, if feminist revisions of objectivity depart from the nonfeminist reevaluations just reviewed on no other grounds, then they differ in the extent to which feminist work pushes forward to locate the specific dynamics of objectivity, to critically appraise them, and to experiment with them in the making of contemporary science and social science.

Primed with evidence of systematic bias in scientific representations of reality, and with women's experiences as marginal participants in science, feminist scholars have undertaken excavations of sexism in science. This work, informed by diverse methodologies and theories, has been categorized by Sandra Harding (1986b) as comprised by five distinguishable programs: (1) studies of the inequities surrounding women's participation in science; (2) studies of the sexist misuse of scientific knowledge; (3) analyses of androcentric or sexist bias in scientific research; (4), criticisms of the linguistic and textual biases in science; and (5) studies of alternative, sex-fair or feminist, epistemologies. It is this fifth research program that incorporates inquiries into the nature of objectivity, both as currently practiced in modern science and as it might be practiced. Harding elaborated on her taxonomy of science studies by delineating three paths toward feminist epistemology, or three feminist epistemological solutions: Feminist empiricism, feminist standpoint, and feminist postmodernism. This grouping of epistemological positions has proved useful in distinguishing general orientations toward science, as we saw in the case of contemporary psychological research in chapter 1, but is less helpful in appraising specific programs. A tripartite model of feminist epistemology obscures the extent to which new models are not always grounded in a single theoretical school, such as historical materialism or social constructionism, but in fact, traverse across conventional theory boundaries and borrow liberally from varied resources. Given such transgressions and blendings, adherents of quite different epistemic traditions are now appearing to propose some strikingly similar solutions.

However different these new visions may be, they all derive from Virginia Woolf's (1938) observation that "science, it would seem, is not sexless; she is a man, a father, and infected too" (139). Feminist epistemologies usually start by examining how science is a "man" and move toward thinking just how an alternative scientific enterprise might look. Carolyn Merchant's (1980) provocative history of the gendered dichotomies informing the epistemological and ideological writings of the scientific revolution has furnished a framework for connecting the shifting relations of the sexes to the maturation of modern science. Proposing a similar framework, Susan Bordo's (1986, 1987) analyses of both Descartes and Cartesian epistemology illumine the connections between masculine thought, including fatherhood, and the modern idea of objectivity. Descartes's project of separating knower from known, a move dependent on his differentiating the spiritual and corporal substances—mind and body—was at once "a defiant gesture of independence from the female cosmos" (1986, 451) and a rendering of that nature, marked female, as inert and mechanical. Bordo revealed how the separation, detachment, and purging of all things passionate and feminine actually constitute Cartesian objectivity, and how "the new epistemological anxiety is not over loss but is evoked by the memory or suggestion of union: empathic, associational, or emotional response obscures objectivity, feeling for nature muddies the clear lake of the mind" (452-53).

Evelyn Fox Keller's (1985a) historical studies also document the connections between the emergence of modern science and gender, namely the ideal of masculinity as it is signified by detachment, control, and domination of others, including women. Like Bordo (1986) and Jane Flax (1983), Keller analyzed these connections in psychological terms. She then extended her analysis to propose an alternative epistemology based on quite different psychological processes. What is conventionally taken as objectivity is carefully shown to be simply the cognitive counterpart, the mirror image, of the Western masculine ideal of autonomy: "Just as objectivity is to be understood as an interpersonal acquisition, here it is argued that domination, even of nonhuman others, is an interpersonal project" (71). Drawing on object-relations theory Keller suggested that males develop toward autonomy, seeking confirmation in domination and mastery, whereas females develop toward dependency, toward submission and seduction.

With this deeper understanding of the masculine essence of science, particularly as it shapes what we take to be objectivity, Keller submitted an alternative base for science, one that replaces the psychological stance of separation and control with that of "dynamic autonomy," and exchanges the cognitive ideal of detached, disinterested objectivity for that of "dynamic objectivity." These alternatives, however, depend on changes in the social relations of gender, specifically the termination of male domination and female submission. Dynamic objectivity comprises fundamental alterations not only in the social relations between knowers but also in the relations between knowers and the world to be known. A different (truer) world would be knowable once scientific inquiry is transformed "from the pursuit of unified laws of nature to an interest in the multiple and varied kinds of order actually expressed in nature" (124).

Other feminist theorists of science define objectivity in intrapersonal and interpersonal terms but either eschew the use of psychological mechanisms or utilize social rather than psychic ones. In conclusion to a comprehensive review of sexism in biological research, Ann Fausto-Sterling (1985) foresaw better science as partially dependent on the work of feminist scientists: "To hold out for a good versus bad science analysis is to ignore the important role feminism has played in *forcing* the re-evaluation of inadequate and often oppressive models of women's health and behavior" (213). But such a refashioned science also awaits social and political reforms because "neither the challenges to scientists to construct a more scientific and—yes—a more feminist research program, nor the challenge to all of us as world citizens to build a society that respects and recognizes differences while understanding and emphasizing human similarities, can be met separately" (222). Helen Longino (1990) continued this demand for changes in "the social relations of the context of science" (214) in order to eliminate the biased and oppressive assumptions that are masked by conventional claims to objectivity. Whereas Fausto-Sterling named these as necessary determinants of better, more objective science, Longino contemplated specifically how that objectivity would look. Sharing Fausto-Sterling's commitment to empiricism, especially beliefs in the possibility of accurate representations of reality and of a nominal separation of knower and known, Longino has advocated a "contextual empiricism" that insists on analyses of the social and political conditions surrounding scientific inquiry, encompassing "both the context of assumptions that supports reasoning and the social and cultural context that supports scientific inquiry" (219). Contextual analyses demand critical scrutiny of values encoded in the social relations of the scientific community, values that persist in both reasoning and observations. Guided by these revised rules of objectivity, feminist or other oppositional sciences proceed by unearthing dominant values or background assumptions in mainstream science and then by substituting those values with background assumptions that are at variance with mainstream ones. By using these objective procedures, oppositional science ultimately can become new science only when theories are the products of the most inclusive scientific community—a "genuinely democratic community." This caveat implies "that the problem of developing a new science is the problem of creating a new social and political reality" (214).

In these two proposals, objectivity awaits transformations in social relations; it necessitates nothing less than a democratization of political life both inside and outside scientific institutions. Whereas both proposals posit that the objectivity of the knower as well as the knowledge-seeking process depends on such desired social relations, Longino's model also intimates that some knowers at some historical moments, such as contemporary feminists, may have advantages in attaining objectivity. Overall, objectivity is a political project requiring new social arrangements and practices of accountability in science.

Other theorists, equally interested in the connections between social relations and objectivity in science, have grappled more directly with the question of which knowers, working in what concrete social and political circumstances, are most capable of objective practices. Whereas their theories bracket other questions about the social world, they hold that the social conditions of a knower strongly influence one's relation to the world, including those aspects of the world under scientific observation—the object of inquiry. Most of these theoretical propositions fit under Harding's rubric of "standpoint feminism," but the specific orientations of these propositions range from fairly orthodox materialism to what can be termed constructionism or postempiricism. Despite metatheoric diversity, these proposals center on one or both of two interrelated questions: (1) what social arrangements are required to create objective science? and (2) what characteristics of the knower are necessary for objectivity or engagement in objective work?

One set of answers to these questions has evolved from the historical-materialist perspective that credits the alienation and abstraction of scientific knowledge, including the idea of objectivity, to the sharp division of intellectual and manual labor characteristic of a capitalistic social system. Fashioned to serve that system, scientific knowledge harbors the ideologies that sustain its hierarchies and inequalities. Those individuals who benefit least from the system are best able to see the world without such ideological distortions. This perspective, however, fails to incorporate matters of reproduction and sexual division of labor. Feminist reworkings of materialism, Hilary Rose (1983) has argued, mean that we must analyze science in terms of the alienated categories of hand, brain, *and* heart. Women's experiences in reproduction, in caring relationships, place them in a better position as observers, and the fact that women are "by and large, shut out of the production system of scientific knowledge, paradoxically has offered feminists a fresh page on which to write" (88).

The fresh page refers at once to the identity of the objective observer and to the social arrangements through which that observer sets out to record the world. Suspecting that "there is good reason to believe vision is better from below the brilliant space platforms of the powerful" (Haraway 1988, 583), a number of theorists have begun finding out just what qualities and conditions enhance that vision. Here these inquiries take off where the claims of some feminist empiricists abruptly end: If it is to be claimed that women, or feminists, at times have a superior purchase on the world, then what enables this vantage point? In other words, these theorists earnestly engage the same claim made in the empiricist-minded APA guide to nonsexist research that an investigator's social marginality "can contribute to the individual's ability to view reality from an alternative perspective" (McHugh, Koeske, and Frieze 1986, 879).

Just as these programs delineate how social arrangements of excluded or oppressed persons situate them in a less-biased observational position, they have also begun to consider *how* the conventional social relations of scientific work might be altered by feminist science. Elizabeth Fee (1983), for instance, has asked how this affirmative feminist position, one knowledgeable of systems of denial and suppression and receptive to critical interrogations, enables a critique of male-created illusions about science including mythic concepts of the antimonies of objectivity and subjectivity, thinking and feeling, and science and society. In comprehending science as constituted through particular social relations and hierarchies, Fee (1986) has suggested that it is possible, and indeed necessary, to understand how critiques of science result from different social relations (of race, class, and gender) and how an alternative science ultimately depends on a variety of critiques of domination.

Close analyses of the social relations in conventional science have guided proposals for alternative practices. Janice Moulton (1983) has uncovered the adversarial attitude that shapes the structure as well as communication of intellectual work: Conventional writings are offense manuevers that aggressively pit a selected idea against other persons' work. Through socially isolated and intellectually piecemeal attacks, the adversarial method allows no means to question larger axioms, introduce novel systems, or engage in cooperative enterprises. Competition, a correlate of adversarial methods, has also received attention (Keller and Moglen 1987). Moulton speculated about how different relations of science might work: The adversary paradigm, at least in philosophical pursuits, might be replaced by reasoning processes that assume experience to be a necessary element. Concurring with the need to bring experience (reasoning or observation) into our scientific jobs, theorists have named some of those experiences. These include the insights gained from women's marginal or outsider status, the critical edge sharpened by experiences of exclusion, and the caring attitudes that have been built by undertaking nurturing roles.

More inclusive alternatives must attend to the multiple dynamics of marginalization and, as Fee suggested, to a variety of critiques of domination. For instance, by studying the marginal and oppressed social positions and experiences of black women, Patricia Collins (1989, 1990) located a "self-defined standpoint" that can serve as the foundation for black feminist thought. Collins began with black women's unique experiences, their political and economic status, and their distinctive consciousness of that reality as a "taken-for-granted knowledge" that can be transformed into a specialized knowledge. Until this point in time, such knowledge is suppressed whenever black women are permitted to enter the dominant institutions of knowledge production. This alternative epistemology, she argued, is composed of core values of an Afrocentric perspective; common experiences of oppression; awareness of the contradictions, multiplicities and "both/or" orientations of being black and a woman; and considerations of social class. In turn, this relational and experiential composite calls forth radically new criteria for knowledge generation, including valuing wisdom and concrete experience in the ascertainment of meaning, using dialogue in assessing knowledge claims, and incorporating ethics of caring and personal accountability in the pursuit and evaluation of knowledge. Although Collins' model has been criticized as positing but not demonstrating a singular black women's standpoint, and as giving little attention to wide-ranging class differences among black women (Higginbotham 1992), it successfully articulates how varying social and personal positions afford opportunities to consistently observe and describe the world on different terms.

The focus on social relations of science is connected to the questions of the observer's attributes: power relations are reproduced in science and "the scientist, the creator of knowledge, cannot step outside his or her social persona, and cannot evade the fact that he or she occupies a particular historical moment" (Fee 1986, 53). Thus, *how* and *what* we come to know are increasingly being understood as dependent on *who* and *where* we are. The conception of an adequate knower, bequeathed from Enlightenment philosophies, presupposes a rational, reasonable, generic person who is removed from the physicalities of time, body, and place; but in fact, that knower is gendered male. In place of this abstracted yet gendered knower, the feminist work informed by a materialist framework recognizes the knower as *situated*, located within dynamic social structures, knowing as *relational*, dependent on the person's position and participation within a community of would-be knowers. Knowing also is *historical*, a transitory process in specific locales and moments.

In linking the sociopolitical context of knowledge production with the identity of knowers, feminist theorists have followed two paths. Those who, like Rose, are committed to a materialist perspective work to name those historically unique features of the knower that engender objectivity. Other theorists, intrigued by the specificity and mutability of the identity of knowers, are working to elucidate the fragmentary, shifting, and sometimes conflicting features of the knower's identity. These latter theorists eschew the project of locating basic or stable qualities of knowing; instead, following postmodern inclinations, they focus on process, plurality, and instability. Feminist theorist Jane Flax (1990) advised that such knowing "should encourage us to tolerate, invite, and interpret ambivalence, ambiguity, and multiplicity, as well as to expose the roots of our needs for imposing order and structure no matter how arbitrary and oppressive these may be" (183). Not only is the knowledge process, including objectivity and the identity of knowers, recognized as multiple and mutable, but "if we do our work well, 'reality' will appear even more unstable, complex, and disorderly than it does now" (183). In these terms, alternative science in both its form and ambitions would be tentative, deconstructive, and interpretive, and would seek the shifting meanings in everchanging representations of a changing world.

Postmodern thinking has alerted theorists to the dangers of preconceived notions of identity and reality and, perhaps most importantly, has posed serious questions about our linguistic and symbolic systems of representing that reality. However, these claims in themselves offer no concrete guide to the project of reconfiguring objectivity. The relativism apparent at the heart of postmodern propositions risks operating much like traditional, totalizing notions of scientific authority: "both deny the stakes in location, embodiment, and partial perspective; both make it impossible to see well" (Haraway 1988, 584). Without casting off the lessons of postmodern thought, Donna Haraway (1988) and Sandra Harding (1991) have proposed models of objectivity that avoid such relativizing but nonetheless retain tools of deconstruction and, at the same time, insist on seeing knowers as situated in social relations. Both Harding and Haraway's projects offer more precise visions of objectivity, and hence, afford concrete resources that researchers can apply to everyday scientific activities.

Harding's (1991) project takes up the difficult question of what makes a standpoint objective or, of the many possible positions of observing the world, which are most objective? Rejecting the relativism of post-structuralism, with its refusal to grant special status to any particular position over others, Harding has proposed a "strong objectivity" that evaluates its own epistemic legitimacy. Strong objectivity demands that scientific research include systematic and critical appraisal of the deeply embedded background beliefs that inform scientific practices. Drawing on the contributions of standpoint feminists, strong objectivity can be understood to begin research "in the perspective from the lives of the systematically oppressed, exploited, and dominated, those who have fewer interests in ignorance about how the social order actually works . . ." (150). Added to this starting point is the recognition of how observers, and their ostensible attributes like gender, are produced through historically specific social relations, particularly through struggles over dominance and control, coupled with an awareness about how members of dominant groups have constructed others in science and in social life more broadly. From these acknowledgements, the step to strong objectivity can be taken: "To enact or operationalize the directive of strong objectivity is to value the other's perspective and to pass over in thought to the social condition that creates it—not in order to stay there, to 'go native' or merge the self with the other, but in order to look back at the self in all its cultural particularity from a more distant, critical, objectifying location" (151). The others in this instance must include not only the subculture of women but also all movements of subjugated, disenfranchised, or marginalized peoples. Strong objectivity includes too what Harding called "strong reflexivity" or the requirement that the researcher gaze back at his or her cultural situation, recognizing all the while how the object of inquiry gazes back; strong reflexivity thus enables "the development of oppositional theory from the perspective of the lives of those others" (163).

For Harding, strong objectivity is a political program starting from the oppositional and reflexive positioning of the knower, a being who places him or herself on the same causal plane as the object of observation. Strong objectivity is neither simply a vision nor an exclusive practice: It already exists in some feminist science and it can be adopted by anyone who is willing and able to adopt "traitorous" identities, selves built in solidarity with oppressed others. In this latter claim, Harding departs from those feminist theorists who believe that solidarity and identification with other disadvantaged peoples depends on common experiences of oppression.

Whereas Harding's project loosely relies on metaphors of role, or perspective-taking, which is common and comfortable contrivance of modern social science, Haraway's (1988) undertaking assumes a metaphoric play with vision. Discarding the Cartesian separation of subject and object—vision as distanced and disembodied—Haraway began with the premise that "there is no unmediated photograph or passive camera obscura in scientific accounts of bodies and machines; there are only highly specific visual possibilities, each with a wonderfully detailed, active, partial way of organizing worlds" (583). The viewing, or standpoints, of the disadvantaged are taken to be better, but not "innocent" positions and, therefore, are not exonerated from critical scrutiny.

The viewpoints of those whose worlds are "less organized by axes of domination" (585) should be privileged, but Haraway has taken this as just one move in the making of objectivity that also must be situated, multiple, and mobile. Haraway has insisted that concerns with identities of investigators, and with what has become known as "identity politics" is misplaced, and that seeing from critical positions can not happen through an isomorphic identity or being. Rather, such seeing involves mobility and partiality of self; the kind of splitting that is known to feminists admits this partiality, and the knits connections between both the rational and the fantastic as well as the various positions of subjugation. Thus, as Haraway argued, "Identity, including self-identity, does not produce science; critical positioning does, that is, objectivity" (286). Just as objectivity requires such multidimensional, mobile, and critical positioning, so it also needs to be grounded in responsibility for such scientific practices. In other words, "moral and political discourse should be the paradigm for rational discourse about the imagery and technology of vision" (587). Like Harding, Haraway has conceived of the rationality of scientific processes, objectivity, to be inclusive of moral and political examinations; these concerns are constitutive of scientific rationality. While sharing Harding's refusal to employ simple identity claims and her emphasis on observer positions, Haraway also has reconfigured the observer's stance as mutable and partial. Feminist embodiment is not about a new identity, "is not about fixed location in a refined body, female or otherwise, but about nodes in fields, inflections in orientations, and responsibility for difference in material-semiotic fields of meaning" (588). This idea of the situated knower makes it possible to discard the assumed dichotomy between observers and the technologies of observation, those continually refined apparatuses of vision, and in turn, invites exploration of how these technologies are complexly implicated in our visualization.

Haraway's project includes another substantial departure from the scientific canon in its consideration of objects, or reality, as central to rethinking objectivity. Just as the attributes of the observer need to be radically reconsidered, so do the characteristics conventionally granted to objects. Instead of being taken as a passive or inert thing, the world is perceived as an active agency; it must be granted agency. In some areas of social science where the object of inquiry is persons or personhood, such agency has already been acknowledged; Haraway proposes that *all* objects be so recognized. The purpose of taking objects of the world as agentic or active is not to anthropomorphize them but to become aware of their generative capacities in scientific production and to realize that their boundaries materialize in those social interactions (595). Haraway's conception of objectivity as situated knowledge, then, encompasses a radical reformulation of the knowing subject and the world to be known (Birke 1991).

Feminist epistemologies, starting from the desire to understand science, particularly in its masculine or patriarchal forms, are now immersed in the task of reimagining and even refashioning scientific practice. With diverse epistemic groundings, these feminist theories refuse Cartesian bifurcations of mind and body, fact and values, and the Enlightenment ideal of generic knowers laboring in relative freedom from historical circumstances. As noted earlier, knowing is *situated* and *historical:* It is located in intricate webs of social interactions and transpires in particular temporal planes. Knowing is *relational* in multiple senses: the knower's position in a social order, interactions within a community of knowers, and connections of knowers to the world to be known. In this last sense, knowing is also *reflexive:* It can be comprehended only in terms of various gazes, back and forth, in the processes commonly known as observing.

Even with these skeletal similarities, recent feminist epistemologies are not united; they contain some basic, provocative differences. Their unique and sometimes controversial claims will not be settled in further epistemic writings alone, but through practical experimentation. Feminist theorists have from the start taken actual practiced science far more seriously than most philosophers of science. With a keen regard for their precarious footing at the uneasy divide between science as talked about and science as made, feminist epistemologists have pledged themselves to a scientific vision grounded in the concrete—of the observer's identity/identities, social relations, technologies, and the world. Nevertheless, stepping from the zone of philosophical writings to laboratory floors is tenuous, requiring stretching and sometimes balancing.

Objectivity in Feminist Practices

The interest in reaching from theory to the lived science of psychology is motivated by an additional desire. Research psychologists have a peculiar reputation regarding their conceptualizations of objectivity: They are often accused of epistemological simplicity because of their beliefs in the feasibility of separating objectivity and subjectivity, fact and value. However, what is usually not acknowledged is that psychologists frequently engage in critical evaluations of objectivity. Feminist-empiricist research, when perceived as a partner of malestream empiricist psychology, is likewise ascribed this reputation of epistemic naiveté. One consequence of this perception is that many feminist scholars, a few psychologists included, spare little time or patience with psychological research. Once marked as blandly empiricist and naive (at best), even truly "experimental" feminist research programs get bypassed. This gesture imposes a compound neglect for and prompts a general disregard of feminist psychology research. It also dismisses the work of those psychologists (especially feminist) who are diligently critical of objectivity and its vicissitudes. By ignoring these unnamed activities and the accompanying acts of diligence, we know little about their forms and functions. Therefore, we must abstain from such stereotyping of research and ask what is happening in these critical appraisals, including the possible reformulation of epistemic terms and rules.

Aside from the fact that the negligence of certain research causes self-embarassment, I became captivated by the question of what is accomplished in feminist psychologists' ongoing revaluations of and experiments with objectivity. In turning to these studies, what becomes apparent is the double-sidedness of their mission. Many of the researchers are not behind the epistemic or feminist theoretic times. On the contrary, they occupy that very political and historical moment. Yet their accounts generally are produced and evaluated in another institutional space that is governed by staid rules of scientific authority, largely by psychology's latest version of positivism. In order to accomplish this double mission, not a few feminist psychologists employ strategic practices, meshing and mobilizing in such a way as to produce a certain subtleness in the final scientific account—a subtleness that unfortunately masks their subversions and innovations. (It should be added that a very different condition holds for those feminist researchers who manufacture psychological studies outside the disciplinary boundaries: Although they may have less need of complex strategizing, they have an even smaller audience, and when their investigations are appraised by psychologists, they fall prey to criticisms of methodological infirmities.)

Feminist psychologists who choose to alter normative practices of objectivity in accordance with visions of feminist science are using diverse strategies to do so. Their tactics range from the crafting of barely detectable changes in conventional measuring instruments to the selection and even creation of "friendly" publication outlets. Somewhat protected through these strategies, feminist psychologists have begun experimenting with objectivity, remodelling (however slightly) its definitions, languages, rules, and enactments. Paralleling some of the advances in feminist epistemology, these experiments with refashioning objectivity have proceeded on three fronts. The first involves identifying the situated knower, as objective observer, and appraising the relation between that knower and the knowledge produced. The second concerns generating new appreciations of objective knowledge both in terms of how it is canonically understood and how it might be reconceived. This is sometimes cojoined with a recasting of the world and its objects. The third front consists of reflexive interrogation where the knower and the world are redefined and repositioned. Selective exemplars of the first two of these revisionings, of knowers and knowledge, illustrate how they are strategic, experimental, and transformative.

Knowers

In psychology as in other mature human sciences, altering what is taken to be the knower is a necessarily radical move, for it involves unveiling the abstract generic scientist. To many feminists working outside the sciences this disclosure hardly seems drastic, but when we examine the feminist psychology that attempts such an alteration, we are reminded afresh of the analyses of science discussed earlier in this chapter, particularly of the political stakes grounding the idea of the objective observer in modern science. As Elizabeth Minnich (1990) has reminded us, "It is certainly not crystalline clarity, nor consistency, nor avoidance of contradictions that has held the dominant system in place for so long; power, exercised and suffered directly through acts of exclusion, internalized in a sense of entitlement in some, in a sense of vulnerability or inadequacy in many others, is at play here" (180). To locate or mark yourself as observer—whether by gender or gender preference, ethnicity, personal experience, psychological state, age, or other social status—is to disrupt a mythic but powerful concept of the scientist as an observer without agency or identity, and along with that, a plethora of methodological rules. To furnish different identities and pose them as integral to scientific objectivity is also to remind readers of themselves as situated knowers. And if these two disruptions are not disturbing enough, then it must be seen that an even greater challenge in this situating of observations lies with its essentially experimental nature: The knower confronts unexpected responses and consequences *everywhere* in the course of investigation, from observing and validating to compiling a written account. Control and mastery—and the order they ensure—are no longer feasible.

Some practicing social scientists have made calls for a situated knower, and many of their appeals parallel the proposals of feminist epistemologists (Mies 1983; Oakley 1981; Westkott 1979). With increasing frequency, these guidelines have been applied to actual social science. The work of sociologists Joan Acker, Kate Barry, and Johanna Esseveld (1983) illustrates one means whereby the metatheory of situated knowers is translated into concrete research practices. Their problem entailed studying how changes in a particular structural situation of women, the movement from domestic, unpaid work (as mothers and wives) to paid employment, were related to changes in consciousness. The study was guided by several principles of feminist research that included commitments to using methods that are not oppressive and to developing a "feminist critical perspective that questions both the dominant intellectual traditions and reflects on its own development" (137). The knowers in this study were situated in at least two ways: By replacing the subject-object dualism with a more publicly stated and reciprocal relation between researchers and participants, and by positioning the investigators according to their own social structural locations (as professionals), personal experiences (as women who may be mothers and wives), and political orientation (as feminists).

The study exemplifies how such modifications of knowers mean that minute methodological details and conceptual terms must be renegotiated: What, for instance, is a process of change and how can feminist consciousness be categorized? It candidly discloses the actions involved in positioning investigators, or rather, in *re*positioning them someplace other than at an abstract vantage point. Finally, the study necessitates confessions and resists closure. In confiding in the reader, for instance, the investigators acknowledged a contradiction in their newly formed positioning: The closeness to participants was seen to create "certain kinds of blindness in the researcher" (147), and the analytic measures developed to reduce such putative blindness consequently distanced the researcher from participants. This contradiction is sensed more acutely in psychology where most research is performed in specially designed spaces, usually laboratories, and participants' responses are rarely examined in other than quantitative form—even in feminist studies (Lykes and Stewart 1986). Any attempt to build more honest relations between experimenter and subjects automatically jeopardizes validity by implicating the experimenter and her passions. Yet some investigators are abandoning these practices and experimenting with ways to eliminate the subject-object problem without circling back to such contradictory stances. These projects begin, like that of Acker, Barry, and Esseveld (1983), by naming some of the axes of domination determining the investigator's gaze, by connecting the experiences of investigators with subjects, and by undertaking self-critical analysis. They push toward close interrogation of the persistent tensions in situated and relational observations.

One direction taken in these experiments with positioning

entails simultaneously fixing and transforming the investigators' objective stance. From a paradoxical aim of at once *locating* and *moving* objectivity, investigators have learned more about participants and themselves. In her studies of Guatemalan women Brinton Lykes (1989) has examined the consequences of the observer's relational self. Lykes credited the actual experience of working with these women as the resource for moving beyond conventional methods; as she recalled, that work "enabled me to depart . . . from the *quantitative* methods of my training toward a more qualitative participating model of research" (172). Just as experimenting with participatory social relations inspired Lykes to develop cooperative methods, so it led her into sometimes uneasy conversations that revealed more about her own positioning, her participants' expectations, and the unexamined space between them. When Lykes introduced the standard informed-consent form used in psychological research, she discovered something about that uncharted space. To her participants, the form was a declaration of mistrust between the researcher and themselves. Originally formulated in a liberal democracy with its customary atmosphere of legal rights and consumer awareness, informed-consent agreements are taken to ensure protection of subjects and investigators alike. However, Lykes discovered that for the Guatemalan women invested in the study, "the introduction of the form threatened to undermine our previously renegotiated contractual arrangements of trust" (178). From their refusal to consent, she learned how resistance served both as power and as affirmation of cooperative involvement; she learned too of vestigial maneuvers of control still operating behind her participatory stance.

Lykes situated her objectivity in and through social relations, particularly through arrangements that decreased the distance between how and what she and the participants saw, and that admitted their mutually peripheral situations. Michelle Fine (1989) established a similar stance in her study of North American minority women who were rape victims. Fine began her investigation with a critical perspective on the normative model of victimization that assumes that victims cope most effectively if they take control over some facet of their lives. This model ignores or obscures the stratification of power according to race, class, and gender that limits many individuals' access to control. Fine's report does not simply assert this criticism but rather shows how it can alter the investigator's objective viewing.

In listening to her participant, given the name Altamese Thomas, Fine realized the multiplicity of her objectivity: Her roles as psychologist, volunteer rape-crisis counselor, author, and Michele Fine, are all present in her written account (Morawski and Steele 1981). From each viewpoint, or with each voice, Fine was able to differentially understand Altamese's responses and then, to critically evaluate her observational purchases. It is as a volunteer counselor, the least powerful of her textual roles, that Fine most directly challenged—and was challenged by—inequities of social power. This was the "self" with whom Altamese was most able to talk, question, and share her suspicions. This was the self, then, who could apprehend the sense of Altamese's refusal to participate in social and legal systems where justice is unlikely, and who could understand her sustained priority to family and community concerns. This was also the self who could best comprehend the limits of psychological theory that is built on the lives and opportunities of a white middle class.

In Fine's study, situating knowing was neither stable nor singular; nor were the knower's voices harmonious. Fine confronted the subject-object problem, the problem of objectivity, through a conversation in and between the researcher's positioned selves that was sometimes congenial and other times conflictual. Fine preempted the possible contradiction in a purportedly democratic relationship between researcher and subject by loathing the contradictions within the observer, and then resolving them through her own transformation. Objectivity is her gift: Her participants taught her "a lot about being a psychologist and being a woman" (198).

Both of these studies situate objectivity in social relations and through changes in those relations. A different experiment in positioning the knower, by Wendy Hollway (1989), likewise attends to the relational dynamics of investigator and participants, but names limits to the shared experiences and then executes analyses both inside and outside those experiential boundaries. In other words, Hollway admitted her position in relation to the participants and used methods to enhance interaction—to situate the researcher in relation to participants. However, her analysis also "depends on rejecting the assumption that I necessarily use the same discourses as my participants" (36). Although this decision resembles the normative objective premise of distinguishing the experiences and meanings of subjects from those of researchers (object from subject), it nevertheless differs markedly from that tenet. Hollway decided to abandon any attempt to create interpretations that correspond to the "theory of the participant." Her decision was based on the realization that she proceeds with questions that are very different from the participant's, which, in turn, leads her to find different meanings in the taped transcripts than they might find. Her ultimate research interpretations are the product of her interests, not a reflection of the world of the participants; her distancing is thus contrary to conventional tenets of subject-object separation that impose distance to ensure accurate representation of the world. Objective observation for Hollway is not a claim to veridical representations of reality, but is a constructive act where "text is produced—in this case for research. It is not the expression of immanent ideas awaiting expression" (36).

In differentiating the experiences and positions of researchers and subjects as a means to establish an objective stance, Hollway has rejected not only a correspondence theory of truth but also what might be called a transparency view of actors. Subjects' accounts do not directly reflect their consciousness or experience; their "subjectivities are produced within discourses, history and relations, and the meanings that they produce in accounts of their experience and themselves both reproduce these subjectivities and can modify them" (41). Hollway took seriously her awareness, from science and personal life, that people can generate a plethora of accounts of experience and can similarly attach a host of meanings to those accounts. Subjects, therefore, can give a great variety of descriptions of these experiences and "if, as social scientists, we elicit such accounts and reproduce them as fact legitimated by our 'scientific practices,' we are reproducing sexist regimes of truth" (45). From this perspective on how people generate accounts and meanings, Hollway grounded her claim that researchers must give *different* accounts: Not only are they participants in different social relations and discourses, but they need to ask different questions in order to end the perpetuation of certain "regimes of truth." In order for feminists to claim that their position as women is a more objective one, it is necessary to break out of that reputedly neutral accounting.

Hollway's research parallels other feminist theorists' calls for a political epistemology and for traitorous identities, just as it points toward the need for substantially revising notions of subjectivity. Here the political grounding of objectivity implicates the observer's stance, in particular the ongoing decisions between echoing or rejecting the ideological meanings that are cloaked in the (presumedly transparent) apparel of neutrality. Discarding the garb of neutrality occasions the opportunity to take traitous or at least uncommon observer positions, yet it leaves open the matter of what positions or identities can and should be selected.

A final instance of bringing situated knowers into psychological investigations extends several of the methods found in the first three cases. Nancy Datan (1989) found multiple points of vision through autobiography, and deployed these points to engage critical and political dimensions of objectivity—to explore "feminist cognition." Datan analyzed the latent contradictions of prowomen or feminist self-help literature for women recovering from mastectomies. Her analysis proceeded through observations of a multiple situated-self—woman, feminist psychologist, and breast cancer patient—and through mobilization of these privileged stances to see problems in this specific literature on women's bodies. Autobiography does not necessarily resolve the subject-object problem faced by feminist researchers, and Datan made no pretense that it could. Rather, the play of identities enabled her to locate troubles in one particular feminist program wherein its language of individualism, victimization, and female passivity worked not against but along with a message that the removal of breasts leaves a woman's body defective and in need of disguise. What had been taken as a liberatory program for breast-cancer patients to rise above cultural stereotypes actually harbors a rhetoric of damaging assumptions about women's bodies and desires. It is through making public the private world of the investigator, and the political lessons she learned from feminism, that Datan could bring new meaning to a self-help literature that is ordinarily taken as politically acceptable.

It is through the "I" that is multiple that Datan could find that "if socialization is viewed as the transmission of values from one generation to the next, it may be argued that feminists are failures in socialization" (186). Rendering alternative meanings to the texts, through textual and self analysis, yielded a repudiation of this socialization and an objective stance from which to construct new visions of illness, women's bodies, and feminist cognition. Risking a stance that was traitorous even to herself, as someone who had experienced breast cancer, Datan revealed hidden gender ideologies, and in doing so, prompted a reevaluation of subjects as more complex agents than was assumed in the programs she assessed.

These four studies represent true experimentation for they bring new visions to the doing of science. More importantly, each of these experiments moves into the unknown, both in terms of novel methods and of observers' identities. Whereas each study at least implicitly assumes the privileged stance of observers who are marginal to the dominant social orders, and each engages the ongoing relations between observer and subjects, they nevertheless experiment in very different ways with the knower's objectivity. Lykes (1989) has been committed to exploring the social-relational dynamics that inspire the investigator; for her, critical positioning is a participatory accomplishment. Fine (1989) has sought critical positioning in ways consistent with Haraway's (1988) conjecture that objective viewing involves mobility and partiality of self rather than simple "identity politics." Hollway (1989) has examined not just the relational dynamics between object and subject but uses reflexive analysis to probe the limits of those relations. She sought objectivity at the boundaries of these relations, particularly by bringing political analysis into the rational discourse of science. Finally, Datan (1989) has drawn on political and personal experiences (reflexively) to achieve objective analysis that has the potential to be critical not just of dominant ideologies but of feminist ones as well.

The different practices represented in these four cases attest to the opportunities awaiting scientific studies that abandon the generic, yet gendered, observer whose gaze has predominated in modern social science.

Knowing

In feminist as well as traditional epistemology, objectivity concerns more than the attributes or positioning of the observer because objective viewing operates through an array of practices in and with the world. Just as feminist epistemologies differ on matters of the observer's characteristics, differences ranging from calls for simply "unbiased" observers to more elaborate considerations of privileged stances, so too they diverge in describing the sorts of practices constituting objective science. No feminist theory eschews the desire to eliminate androcentric conventions or premises. From that shared starting point, some models, like those of Fausto-Sterling and Longino, call for replacing sexist social relations in the larger context of science; they seek nothing less than to change the societal order. Other proposals call for the inclusion of feminine as well as feminist practices in scientific work, for a science structured through caring and empathy as well as through advocacy of women's rights and inclusion. Still other theories call for a more radical alteration of scientific practices by insisting that the subject, the world itself, as well as observers are active agents in objective science. In distinct ways both Harding and Haraway advance such propositions.

It is with this last epistemic move that the most challenging experimentation begins. Including reality, or objects of the world, as a participating presence in scientific practice means that we reformulate not only the knower but also the world to be known. It also requires, as we shall consider in the proceeding interchapter, serious self-interrogation or -reflexivity. For now it is sufficient to consider how investigators might go about the task of creating and naming scientific practices that reconceive the larger world and its generative capacities.

One approach to rethinking scientific practices is necessarily critical, and proceeds by scrutinizing what is conventionally taken as objective practice. Feminist scientists in biology and psychology have been enormously successful in this undertaking: they have deconstructed the language, models, instruments, and social systems that constitute standard objective scientific practices to show just how such scientific practices conceal undisclosed beliefs and assumptions. Taken further, this approach allows investigators to connect these practices to the world—to show how reality is shaped by, or resists the view of, the world embedded in scientific practices. Employing this approach, Emily Martin's (1987) study of the "woman in the body" begins by analyzing the scientific and medical practices that produce contemporary understandings, or reality, of the female body. Dominant scientific knowledge describes a body that functions like a hierarchically organized factory, a mechanical system requiring technical management. Metaphors of production and waste, of machines and engineering, do more than undergird scientific practices, they actually change the reality of women's bodies. Martin's interviews, with women of varied race and class memberships, indicate how women's bodies, and experiences of their bodies, get structured through such scientific representations. However, her conversations also show that alongside the denigration and shame that women experience as a consequence of scientific renditions of their bodies "are a multitude of ways women assert an alternative view of their bodies, reach against their accustomed social roles, reject denigrating scientific models, and in general struggle to achieve dignity and autonomy" (200). Martin's study, then, demonstrates how the objective world is given form through scientific and medical practices, yet it also discloses another viable (if contradictory) world that, in paralleling the contradictions of women's lives in our culture, enables them to sometimes resist hazardous representations of their bodies.

Critical analyses of the objective world as it is shaped and represented through the practices of knowledge acquisition are not simply projects of deconstruction. Quite the contrary, these analyses challenge researchers to see the world afresh and to reformulate knowing to encompass a much larger parcel of activities. Martin's study not only yielded evidence that scientific practices give form and meaning to the world as it is experienced, but also located another world, or dimension of the world, in women's resistances. These discoveries suggest how we might restructure research practices to accommodate that world.

Mary Parlee's (1991) sociohistorical examination of the premenstrual syndrome (PMS), also displays the vast range of activities that constitute scientific practice. Most importantly, her work establishes that our "knowing" about PMS has involved a great variety of actors working in diverse cultural locales, and that the reality of PMS is a *cumulative product* of these activities. In order to understand how the world is constructed through practices, Parlee did not unpack or deconstruct biased scientific beliefs or procedures. Instead, she began by retracing the scientific practices that gave rise to the phenomenon of PMS, and in doing so, included actors and events that are normally left out of histories of science. Among the actors, feminist psychologists were instrumental in initiating research on the psychological correlates of the menstrual cycle, and they viewed that research as a means to correct the biased scientific accounts of women's nature. But they were not the only participants in the project to learn the reality of premenstrual experiences. Other interested agents included activists in the women's health movement who were challenging medical treatments of women's bodies, physicians and researchers in the biomedical fields who were developing careers by producing authoritative scientific accounts and regulation of women's reproductive systems, pharmaceutical companies who were seeking markets for their products, psychiatrists and therapists who were attempting to secure paying patient populations, and ordinary men and women who were trying hard to comprehend the conflicts and contradictions of gender relations in contemporary culture.

Enumeration of the many interested parties in the search to know PMS illustrates how practices of knowing extend far beyond laboratory walls and transpire through complex social engagements. Parlee found through this complex sociogram that scientific practices are "an arena of cultural contestation " (12) in which groups with diverse interests forge reality.

> "PMS" is a gendered concept of illness which came into being in our culture in the early '70s when social relations of gender and the ideologies supporting them were under challenge by feminists. It furthers interests reflected in the routine activities of specific and powerful social institutions. In both the interpersonal and more broadly social domains, "PMS" serves to contain potential social protest by women by channeling interpretations of their suffering and actions into medical rather than political forms. (11)

The world and the "truth" about the world are recast through sustained cultural practices that include but encompass more activities than those that are normally called "scientific." Parlee also found that the complexity and multiplicity of this cultural arena is such that some invested participants may discover retrospectively that their scientific involvements have inadvertent or opposite results. For instance, feminist social scientists who in the 1970s demanded thorough and precise scientific research in order to eliminate sexist scientific truths, in the end, yielded control of that research to biomedical scientists who had the institutional and financial resources to produce that work. In so doing, they ultimately collaborated in a process of making PMS a biologically based disorder. From this series of events, Parlee concluded that "one lesson feminists might draw from this case study of the cultural imbeddedness of a gendered illness is that contestation within the domain of science is not likely to be effective" (11). As a corollary, her analysis indicates that reality can only be understood through relations of power both *within* and *outside* the hallways of scientific institutions, and that this expanded understanding can be a resource in generating alternative objective practices.

The studies of Martin and Parlee expand as they critically interrogate knowledge-making processes, and they signal how the knower is implicated in those processes. Additional and somewhat different analyses are needed to explicate the relations between knowing and the knowers. Just as technologies of social control can be seen to impact on the controllers of those technologies (Kipnis 1987), so procedures and technologies of scientific knowing can be found to influence their scientific observers. Some studies indicate that technical procedures for inquiry shape investigators' thinking about the world. For instance, Gerd Gigerenzer (1991) found that psychologists' use of statistical inference altered their theory of the mind. The transference of concepts from the methodological realm to theory illustrates how knowing, knower, and knowledge are connected. While psychologists joke about a two-by-two mentality arising from researchers who appear overly fascinated by that routine experimental design, and feminist psychologists jest about the manipulation and control fetish exhibited outside the laboratory by some male experimenters, further attention must be given to the dynamic interplay of knowing and knowers. The features of this interdependence that have been explored are but a few of the myriad systems of interaction between experimenter and technologies of experimentation. Betty Bayer's study of the use of automation in group research indicates that these technologies are purportedly implemented to augment and substitute for the experimental observer but they also virtually transform the observer. As the varied functions of the experimenter (such as those of instructor, coordinator, observer, and analyst) are replaced by technologies ranging from audio tapes and electronic switchboards to completely computer-automated experiments, the observer becomes cyborgian, and human interactions are radically altered. Such technologies do not merely entail an "externalization of objectivity" by substituting instruments for the observer's sense (Pinch 1988), they also alter the distinctions, sometimes blurring them, between the natural and artificial of human functioning. Contrary to the typical concern that such technological interventions raise questions of the "external validity" of experiments, Bayer's analysis of small-group research suggests that what really is at stake is the "nature" of the experimenter and his or her social relations. The study introduces new questions about what is the "social" of social psychology, reaffirming the need to reevaluate the identity of experimenters (Bayer 1993; Bayer and Morawski 1992).

The investigations reviewed above turn on critical analyses of science, rotating them in their multidimensionality to find new objective means of knowing. The rudiments of routine objective practices are overturned, but in doing so, what is uncovered allows us to comprehend knowing as being far more dynamic and extended than previously thought to be the case. Objective practices occur every day, in politics and personal life, just as they convene in systems of expertise and in technologies. As recast in these studies, the world, too, is dynamic: Both Martin and Parlee exposed a reality uncharted by conventional science, a reality of vigor and generativity that at times disobeys or pushes back. Studies such as those by Kipnis, Gigerenzer, and Bayer intimate how observers inhabit that same world and are produced or transformed within it, sometimes by their own engineering. Objective knowing always takes place in a specific cultural context, and is produced in and through that context. Objective knowing depends on seeing the world itself—and the observers situated within—as the agents in this production.

Conclusion

The modern configuration of objectivity, in both its theoretic form and technical functioning, has been radically refashioned by both critical philosophers and feminist theorists alike. These transfigurations, begun by plying the historical, political, and social substance of modern objectivity, involve not just a revolution in epistemic discourse but also experimentation with techniques of knowing and identities of knowers—ways of seeing, hearing and touching—and with rituals of telling, accounting, and defending. Psychology has not failed to participate in these changes, despite its longstanding reputation as an archaically positivist enterprise, as a vestigial science of "physics envy" and "method fetishism." Rather, within psychology some feminist investigators are experimenting with a transformed objectivity guided by reconfigurations of theory and practice.

This reconfiguring, according to Elizabeth Gross (1986) is central to feminist theory in the sense that it is

> both a "theoretical practice"—a practice at the level of theory itself, a practice bound up with yet critical of the institutional frameworks within which the production of theoretical discourses usually occurs, a practice involving writing, reading, teaching, learning, assessment, and numerous other rituals and procedures; as well, it is a "practical theory"—a theory openly seen as part of practice, a tool or tactic playing a major part in the subversive, often dangerous assault on one particular site of the functioning of patriarchal power relations—the sphere of knowledge . . . (202)

The experiments visited in the final part of this chapter elucidate the concurrence of theoretical practice and practical theory; they unsteady the boundaries that have separated what we have taken as distinct actions and actors of research. The strategies invented and deployed in these experiments are at once critical—of dominant regimes of truth—and productive—of new scientific practices. The experiments exemplify the possibilities for, and the actualities of, transforming objectivity in psychological science.

Interchapter

Reflexivity: Observer Positions

To whom are we accountable? And what social relations are in/scribing us?
—Barbara Christian, "But What Do We Think We're Doing Anyway? The State of Black Feminist Criticism(s) or My Version of a Little Bit of History"

The adoption of the "professional" standards of academia is no more an activity devoid of gender politics than the current fashion in women's tailored suits and large-shouldered jackets is devoid of gender meaning.
—Susan Bordo, "Feminism, Postmodernism, and Gender-Scepticism"

To inquire into what social relations are inscribing us or to name what gender politics sustain our professional standards is to engage in self-conscious reflexive thought. Feminist revisionings of objectivity insist on the reflexive work of self-consciously gazing back on one's situation, one's special place in social relations, one's embeddedness in a concrete location. Once it is claimed that objectivity must be construed in terms of the identities, positions, and relations of the observer and that it is a partial, located, and multiply formed process, then objective practices must circle back and incorporate the observer in objective research. Figuring out the social relations of research and then refiguring them through the perspectives of the "others," those agents who are silenced or devalued, changes and multiplies the scientific gaze. Self-reflexive research "starts thought in the perspective from the life of the other, allowing the other to gaze back 'shamelessly' at the self who had reserved for himself the right to gaze 'anonymously' at whomsoever he chooses" (Harding 1991, 150).

Tracing the circle of objective practices, however, merely outlines the process of reflexivity. What are we to gaze back on? That is, who are we as subjects, and what about that subject status is relevant to our objective undertakings? In other words, how do features of our subject-being, (self as subject) and subject-acting (self as actor) influence or fashion our visions? And on a more practical level, when and where should reflexive work be done? Such unresolved questions regarding reflexivity form the mission of this interchapter. Going beyond the raw assertions that reflexivity exists, or the bold demands that reflexive analysis be undertaken, quickly brings us to the realization that reflexivity has several meanings, each with very different implications for investigative practices. It also brings us, as intimated in the questions above, to the necessary, if ultimately unresolvable, task of deciding what self or selves, and what features of self or selves, should be reflected upon.

Of course, all these journeys into new social relations of science depend on permission, or at least the absence of resistance, to make such passages. Current investigative practices forbid such passage, given the entrenched understanding of observer as outside the scientific action, as a passive bystander whose observations are dictated by techniques and technologies of control. Thus, most of this interchapter works with speculations and proposals whose realizations will be in the future. The few reported reflexive practices appear outside the mainstream publication system in psychology. The interchapter proceeds, therefore, from a cursory review of the leading (and sometimes incompatible) interpretations of reflexivity to more complicated ruminations on the subject matter of reflexive analyses. It concludes by screening several experiments with reflexivity.

A caution: Simply concentrating on the backward gaze or self-awareness of the researcher does not complete the circle of objectivity, nor does it embrace the totality of reflexivity, because the object of that gaze, as an *agent* as well as a *subject* of our scrutiny, is also a part of that circle. The need to radically reformulate the positions and attributes of our objects of inquiry (subjects), as well as the relations between them and investigators, is considered in a later interchapter. The organizational decision to treat the two subjects separately risks reinstating the classic separation of observer and subject that has long been mandated in psychology's methods and metaphysics. Nevertheless, this separate treatment facilitates detailed exploration of each issue and, in the end, aims to underscore their interdependence.

Definitions

Although a relative stranger to the vocabulary of psychology, the term *reflexivity* has become a familiar one in varied intellectual pursuits, and over the last two decades the word has been used variously—to describe phenomena ranging from a general property of social action to an inescapable condition of science and social science. In its most prevalent use, reflexivity is defined as "a turning back on oneself, a form of self-awareness" or self-regard (Lawson 1985, 9). Reflexivity, in this case, is a potential property of all human action, from the esoteric practices of critical reading to the routine actions of getting in a car. When applied specifically to intellectual practices, reflexivity is usually defined as the self-referential quality of theory. Thus, in intellectual activities where the objects of inquiry are humans or human action, reflexivity is seen "as an aspect of all social science, since any statement which holds that humans act or believe in particular ways, under particular circumstances, refers as much to the social scientist as anyone else" (Gruenberg 1978, 322).

If extended even further to refer not just to *self* or to *theory*, reflexivity can be taken to the epistemic realm, and then, can be seen to enter into the *relation between reality and accounts of reality*. Reflexivity is a back-and-forth process whereby an account of reality depends on preexisting knowledge of what the account refers to and vice versa (Ashmore 1989; Woolgar 1988b). This form of reflexivity concerns not only scientists whose observations of cell walls depend on their prior understandings of cell walls, and whose understandings depend on prior observations, but also the explanatory processes involved in everyday living. For example, we connect the reality of genitals and accounts of gender though a reflexive process: "The reality of gender is 'proved' by the genital which is attributed, and, at the same time, the attributed genital only has meaning through the socially shared construction of the gender attribution process" (Kessler and McKenna 1978, 155).

Reflexivity is alternatively defined as self-awareness, the self-referential property of theory, a central feature of furnishing representations of reality, or some combination of these. These definitions share an understanding of reflexivity as a fundamentally social phenomenon, despite their divergent understandings of where reflexivity occurs in scientific practices. They all take reflexivity as a process of turning or reflecting back, despite the varied explanations of what is reflected back. Yet, in order for reflexivity to be a functioning tool in scientific or social scientific work, these definitions need greater specification, and at least four open-ended issues must be addressed.

First, *where does reflexivity operate*—at the levels of the individual agent, methods, or theoretical activities, or all of these? Viewing reflexivity strictly as a self-awareness or self-consciousness implies that we interrogate the identity of the perceiver or knower, whereas positing it as a feature of organized work activities suggests scrutiny of collectivities. Second, the various definitions differ in their rendering of reflexivity as *either intended or unintended*—and consequently as either desired or scorned, celebrated or denied. Although the turning back or self-awareness of the contemporary literary critic is readily apprehended as an intended act, the same cannot be said for all reflexive activities. In fact, most of the studies of reflexivity in science and social science concentrate on unintended manifestations of reflexivity. Working within this framework, historians of psychology have identified how theories reflect the cultural knowledge and anxieties of the period in which they were produced, how for instance, Solomon Asch's conformity research mirrors the concurrent cultural obsession with compliance and obedience (Richards 1987; Buss 1978; Flanagan, Jr. 1981). Or they have shown how individual psychologist's work refers back to their personal lives, as in the case of Sigmund Freud's psychology of women or William James's ambivalence about the scientific status of psychology.

The third issue follows from the second by asking to what extent reflexivity is *acknowledged or unacknowledged* regardless of whether it is desired or not, intended or not. The matter of admission presents some sticky problems, most importantly in terms of deciding what it means to acknowledge reflexivity. For instance, does it mean merely being aware or does it mean acting in some particular manner because of that awareness? In psychology reflexivity is rarely given explicit consideration, yet it can be argued that psychologists have routinely and recurrently developed ways to avoid, manage, cover, and deny it. And if psychologists dismiss the self-referential properties of their theories, if they deny that their self-regard is of significance to their science, and if they assume an independence of representation and the represented object, then these dismissals themselves are (ironically) reflexive acts (Morawski 1992). One solution to this problem entails incorporating acknowledgment of reflexivity into its very definition. Seeking this solution, Kay Oehler and Nicholas Mullins (1986) proposed that reflexivity consists of two processes: "(1) an awareness on the part of research communities of the social bases of their theories and (2) some kind of institutional arrangement to encourage the development of that awareness and its public display" (2). As defined by Oehler and Mullins, reflexivity is a self-critical operation aimed at improving research through critical analyses and corrective measures. This definition affords one possible resolution to the fourth issue regarding reflexivity: whether it is to be taken as a *positive or negative feature* of investigative activities. Paralleling Oehler and Mullins' proposal, other theorists have similarly construed reflexivity as a *possibility* rather than a problem, and have advocated a "reflexive" science that derives from the self-awareness of the researchers and sometimes the recursive awareness of the object of theory, the ordinary actor (Giddens 1979; Gouldner 1970; Wolf 1986). To these ends, numerous feminist social scientists have made similar recommendations (Fonow and Cook 1991a; Mies 1983; Stanley and Wise 1983).

However, there exists a pervasive countertendency in scientific life, a deeply structured resistance to both acknowledging and actively using reflexivity. This reluctance is especially strong when reflexivity challenges the idea of representation, a foundational tenet of modern science. That is, the very possibility of representation is at stake when reflexivity demands rejection of the idea of the independence of the act of representation and the object being represented, and instead, indicates how the representation is changed to accommodate prior perceptions of the nature of reality and vice versa. Challenging representation in this way is so dangerous that reflexivity can be counted among the "methodological horrors" that science practitioners continually struggle to manage (Woolgar 1988b).

For psychology, issues of reflexivity are multiple and complexly so: Reflection or self-referential actions can be located in the knower or the investigation, the object or the participant, and in the subject matter itself since psychology includes in its purview those social and cognitive processes that constitute reflexivity (i.e., perception, memory, attribution). Although canonical investigative techniques have functioned to circumvent or deny reflexivity, and although no substantial program for its acknowledgment or utility has been advanced in psychology, its unintended and sometimes intended appearances warrant attention. And even if psychologists were to eschew the more radical implications that reflexivity raises for representation, they must repeatedly face the realization that their subjects ultimately have resorted to the same cognitive resources that they do, that their objects of study may not be the same in 1992 as they were in 1942 and that this may be true partly *because* of psychology, and that their subject matter (humans) can potentially be changed through its own self-evaluation. The variety of implications that reflexivity brings to psychology might, indeed, be genuinely horrifying.

Reflexivity in Feminist Psychology

That a fair number of feminist investigators can be counted among the few psychologists who have entertained the vicissitudes of reflexivity is not surprising. The disciplined *denial of self-reflection* has had adverse consequences for feminist thinking in particular, and women's participation in psychology generally. The empiricist tradition of psychology assumes that the observer is a sensing conduit of observations and that the particular identity of the observer as a historical subject or rational agent is irrelevant. Self-reflection is deemed inappropriate, unnecessary, and even antithetical to that cognitive program. Hence, reflexivity is a nonissue. When women psychologists have turned to investigate gender, and they have done so at least partly in order to understand their own place in modern society (a reflexive turn), their explorations often have been restricted by the cognitive system in which they worked. The philosophical worldview in which they have participated has denied the very act that motivated their inquiries. Its epistemological rules have further restricted inquiry into their very gender bases: The rules are gendered through rudimentary categories of subjectivity and objectivity, rationality and irrationality, reality and illusion, and of gender itself. In turn, the system and its rules have been tied to the governing arrangements of the social world; they are inextricably part of a larger system of patriarchal values that feminist psychologists were attempting to question. Paradoxically, these women confronted limits to their reflexive inquiries precisely because psychology *is* reflexive, but what has been reflected in that social structure of science are social relations fitted most comfortably to the experiences of Western males in a hierarchical social world.

There are at least two distinct ways in which the denial of reflexivity has restricted women psychologists' work, especially feminist research. First, the prohibitions against self-reflective thinking as a legitimate tool has limited the inclusion of experiences and cognitive structurings that may be particular to women. By not admitting certain experiences and ideas into scientific work innovative questions and investigative procedures are arrested. Second, the inability to incorporate these experiences and cognitive structurings has preempted any comprehensive critical analyses of psychological theories and their social conditions. With such restrictions, early twentieth-century feminist psychologists were frustrated by the conceptual and methodological constraints placed on their studies of sex differences. One psychologist gave up the effort to comply with the canonical system for assessing sex differences, claiming that "the real tendencies of women cannot be known until they are free to choose, any more than those of a tied up dog can be," and that sex differences "cannot be demonstrated until men and women are not only nominally free but actually free to enter any profession." (Tanner 1896, 9-10). Contemporary examples of such cognitive restrictions are not scarce and are particularly evident whenever feminist psychologists delineate power structures, alter the application of psychological findings, or even write experientially.

Materializing against or outside the dominant system of knowing are feminist propositions for developing an explicitly reflexive science, suggestions whose implications would infuse every pore of disciplinary practice. Rhoda Unger (1983) has posited that reflexivity is the key feature of any social science that admits values, as a feminist social science does. Such a science requires *emphasizing* and not just *recognizing* the reflexive nature of the relations between subject and object, person and reality, and psychologist and the subject matter. Unger stressed the need to radically rethink the relations between experimenter and subject and, therefore, to consider entering "into different research arrangements with them" (27). Further, a reflexive psychology would press toward a realization of its political mission, which, among other aims, includes the objective of making "our subjects more self-aware than they were before they involved themselves in our procedures" (28). Articulating and accommodating such moral or evaluative objectives of research and designing reflexive methodologies are essential to realizing reflexivity, and they certainly interrupt the normative patterns of keeping reflexivity conscientiously unacknowledged, denigrated, and/or purportedly unintended. To broaden this positive project, Sue Wilkinson (1988) has called for reflexivity in feminist psychology that is not only personal and functional, that not only assures self-consciousness and methodological revisions, but that also demands "a discipline or subdiscipline to explain its own form and influence" (495). Therefore, in addition to ongoing scrutiny of methods and personal predispositions and replacement of faulty methods with participatory and self-monitoring ones, feminists need to ask how the discipline currently functions to bracket or marginalize feminist work. From that understanding, Wilkinson proposed that feminists can work against these forces to make feminist science more visible and legitimate. Only through awareness of the institutions of science and the covert as well as the accepted means of altering them can feminist psychology advance.

To these requirements for reflexive science must be added the need to understand how the discipline is implicated in the governing of social life generally. Taking Unger's and Wilkinson's proposals seriously means reflecting on the macrostructure of our work as well as its microstructure, and thus, interrogating the "implicit ideological freight our theories carry" (Kitzinger 1991b). It means analyzing how feminist psychology, as well as the dominant paradigms, may be useful in sustaining status quo relations of power in society; for instance, how women-centered theories may reinforce discriminatory practices, or how studies of gender similarities may be useful in masking social inequities. To varying degrees, the case studies discussed in the previous chapter undertake such macrostructural analyses of how dominant social relations of power direct and circulate through psychological research. Each of them exposes social relations embedded in investigative practices that limit the realization of emancipatory knowledge. As such, these studies represent one crucial move toward reflexive acts: They constitute a precursory exercise for an eventual wholesale reanalysis of selves and experiences in investigative practices. Most of the proposals for reflexive work cannot be implemented by proclamation or fiat. Nor can they be engaged at a single moment or without enormous and sustained efforts. Feminist psychologists have been successful in naming the moral and political features of conventional research and in introducing a disciplinary reflexivity that attends to and restructures the science's institutional constraints. What lies ahead as relatively uncharted work is the reformulation of self, agency, and the personal as they constitute the science we produce. In this challenge even the most modest explication or elaboration of researcher self-awareness will probably seem heretical, a breach beyond the merely subversive. The remainder of the interchapter entertains some of the speculative and sometimes spectacular thinking that may emerge in this realm of reflexive practice.

Selves and Their Knowing

As mentioned earlier, reflexivity can be seen as going beyond disrupting normative investigative techniques in that it is also related to the taken-for-granted process of representation. At this point reflexivity finally concerns the very relation between object (reality) and representation (accounts of reality) by undermining the purported *independence* of the two. Steve Woolgar (1988b, 1989) has described how reflexivity is actually instrumental to the art of representing reality yet is routinely denied by scientists. In normative practices, representation is sustained as a feasible action only by burying the methodological horrors of reflexivity and by instating what Woolgar has called a "moral order" of representation. This order presumes an interesting, asymmetrical role for the agent or self (analyst): Whereas agents are taken as incapable of changing the character of reality, as passive spectators, they are held responsible for the character of the accounts of reality. Given this curious role that, in the end, is absolutely crucial to representation, Woolgar has advocated critical analysis of the "self"—that "disregarded agent of representation" (1988b, 109).

Woolgar's exposé of the privileged self, situated in the moral order of representation, comprises but one additional reason why feminist psychologists must further refine their reflexive procedures in order to further transform their comprehension of self as knower. The selves behind or within scientific representations are neither abstract, neutral, nor unmarked: All selves of knowing are not equal, and their identities are relevant, but not fixed, matters of fact. Considered in the previous chapter were feminist projects that insist on reflexive analysis of these selves or agents of representation; however, while those projects start with the assumption of selves as embedded in complex social arrangements, they entail no specific scrutiny of those selves or agents. Hence, they bracket some significant questions.

What features of the self constitute the material for examination? Is "feminism" a pertinent feature of self? Indeed, what is the self (or, what are the selves) to be analyzed?

In raising these questions, it becomes immediately apparent that they are not new ones: Feminists have long been engaged in the reflexive task of examining self, particularly in the social relations committed to generating knowledge (and power). Feminists have been especially intrigued by two dimensions of these questions: the *connections between identity and social relations,* and the *extent to which the personal is political.* The first dimension turns the critical analyses of men's gendered participation in knowledge production onto women's gendered participation. This turning involves reasoning that "if both men and women are formed in and through gender systems, then the thinking of women (or feminists) as well as that of men (or nonfeminists) must be shaped in complex and sometimes unconscious ways by gender relations" (Flax 1990, 139). Jane Flax has urged that feminists explore how the psychological consequences of the gendered social relations in our culture affect the very shape of feminist theorizing. Susan Bordo (1990a), pointing to the analogy of women's almost manlike dressing, has insisted that we consider how our "professional" conduct is not gender neutral but rather is coded male or female in systematic ways. More specifically, Bordo has suspected that what currently passes as professional may be nothing more than a refurbishing of the long-reigning epistemology of value neutrality, one that thoroughly effaces the gender structuring of knowledge as well as any distinctly female ways of knowing. In her probing of professional activities, Bordo is asking us to move a step beyond what feminist scholars have long recognized as their double visioning or double consciousness (through which they can see simultaneously as intellectual workers and as women). Unpacking the connections between knowers' identities and social relations, both relations of professional practices and of the entire gendered life structure, introduces new opportunities for pursuing knowledge.

Such multifocal seeing, if used consciously, disrupts the clear narrative of science, casting it as neither cohesive nor comprehensive, and renders transparent some of its usually invisible tensions and contradictions. The multiple positioning of feminist observation—the dual consciousness—comprises one strategy for theoretical critique and reconstruction. However, the advantages of seeing our identities as enhanced by multifocal vision depend on continual self-critical scrutiny of what is hidden, contradicted, or even denied in those multiple sightings.

The desideratum of knowing our identities in their ongoing social relations is, of course, simpler said than done. First, locating and naming the connections between identity (or identities) and social relations immediately reveals a highly populated world of interacting beings. The analysis of androgyny research, described in the first chapter, only begins to decipher how investigators' experiences and circumstances as women proceeding in a man's world influence their scientific productions. In that case, reflexive inquiry brought to the fore a play of professional life on the identities and cognitions of investigators; such analysis serves as a starting point for "contextualizing in the investigator" (Wertsch and Youniss 1987). But the androgyny study is simply a beginning that needs to be supplemented by interrogations of other features of identity (including but not limited to the now commonly known ones of race, class, age, and social status) along with consideration of the multiple social relations through which these identities are produced or affirmed. Such an extended evaluation must go even further by examining the impact of the collective rewritings that are part of our institutional life, just as they have been found to be part of the narrative repertoire of our research participants (Helson 1992). As with any emerging practice, feminist investigators have few ready methods and rare opportunity to commit to these sorts of identity studies. The one notable exception appears with introspective examination of our activities in the classroom and our functions in educational and clinical settings. There is now considerable writing on these sets of social relations that tease out the politics and contradictions of identity, such as how women's studies is at once the aggressor and the victim in debates over political correctness or how as teachers we must deal with the confusions and complexities of our personal identities in relation to those imposed on us in the classroom (Crawford 1992).

If this were not enough, feminist scientists who desire reflexive awareness of the connections between identity and social relations must simultaneously confront the theories of identity and agency implicit in mainstream science. What Woolgar (1989) has referred to as the "ideology of representation" houses assumptions about the passivity (or irrelevance) of the agents of scientific representations that actually mask a complex hierarchy of rights and responsibilities distributed among those agents (who include humans and inanimate entities). If we agree with Woolgar's account of science and identity, then we can appreciate even more the difficulty of realizing reflexive practices in psychological research, since the ideology of representation routinely and repeatedly denies the significance and sometimes even the existence of agents and, hence, social relations in science. Reflexivity and science, it would seem, are incommensurable, and feminist psychologists are left without a theoretical vocabulary for speaking about the social relations of observers.

The questions of self in inquiry are further complicated once we take seriously the second dimension of feminists' reflexive thinking: reconfiguring the personal as political. This reconfiguration has been a prominent slogan of contemporary feminism, and analysts have been "fueled by taking the personal as a category of thought and gender as a category of analysis" (Miller 1991, 14). Despite this waving banner of personal and political, many academic feminists retreated in the 1980s and were more likely to engage in a "self-conscious depersonalization" of their work (Miller 1991, 14). That is not to say that they ceased to examine personal or personally relevant facets of gender but that those issues were removed from the personal of the investigators. Thus, although feminist psychologists have studied such life events as marital rape, self-esteem, menstruation, and even the connections between personal and political life, they typically distanced these phenomena from their own lives, a separation that is accentuated whenever these phenomena are described in the stylized, technical language of the discipline.

This central assertion of feminism—the personal is political—is relevant to reflexive practice and to redefining the self and identity in knowing. Yet to reassert the personal as political is not to collapse the two terms, to merely take the self as a particular political creature. Postmodernist thinking has signalled the insufficiency of traditional philosophic notions of autonomous selfhood and coherent identity, and has replaced them with concepts of multivocal, shifting, and plural selves that, in turn, suggest new mappings of the personal and political. However, studies engaged with the lives of subjugated, disenfranchised, and nondominant peoples have highlighted the conceits and limits of such postmodern concepts. These studies have yielded at least two necessary reconfigurations of personal and political. First, as Iris Young (1990) has noted, claiming that the "personal is political" does not mean rejecting any distinction between the public and the private, but it does mean denying "a social division between public and private spheres, with different kinds of institutions, activities, and human attributes" (108). These spheres are interdependent but are made and maintained in particular ways in particular social orders with the consequence of sustaining certain exclusionary practices:

> The modern conception of the public, I have argued, creates a conception of citizenship that excludes from public attention most particular aspects of a person. Public life is supposed to be "blind" to sex, race, age, and so on, and all are supposed to enter the public and its discussion on identical terms. Such a conception of a public has resulted in the exclusion of persons and aspects of persons from public life. (109)

Further, these divisions and the politics of personal life they maintain are different for different people, depending on their social status. As Aida Hurtado (1989) has shown, American women of different races and social classes experience differently the oppression of the culture's public-private distinction. While white middle- and upper-class women benefit even as they are oppressed by the distinction, women of color are aware that for them "the public is *personally* political" in that welfare programs have altered their family life, intervened in their reproductive rights, and otherwise affected the destinies of their people. Raising similar questions about cultural diversity in the realm of the personal, Hope Landrine, Elizabeth Klonoff and Alice Brown-Collins (1992) have questioned whether psychological experiments are the same for all women: "Do women of various ethnic cultural groups who complete the Bem Sex Role Inventory, or the PAQ, or the MMPI, or the Beck Depression Inventory complete 'the same' questionnaires?" (150). Their research indicates that the answer to this question is no, and that traditional interpretations of psychological data obscure variations in personal experience among women.

With the realization of the relational meaning of the personal as political, and its grounding in dominant political orders, has emerged a second reconfiguration of the personal as political: Identity and the personal are produced through the social relations of struggle. The simplest idea of identity politics—the view that I am something and therefore I can or do represent some claim or objective—must be refashioned with awareness of identity being made through social and political struggle (Mohanty 1991). This second reconception affords a better understanding of how location, relations, and practices make possible the formation of politically oppositional identities who can effect social change. Sometimes standing against a postmodernist idea of fractured identities is that of agency produced through specific histories, sites, and interactions such as

> in the minute, day-to-day practices and struggles of third world women. Coherence of politics and of action comes from a sociality which itself perhaps needs to be rethought. The very practice of remembering against the grain of "public" or hegemonic history, of locating the silences and the struggle to assert knowledge which is outside the parameters of the dominant, suggests a rethinking of sociality itself. (138–39)

Naming that sociality and locating its silences and struggles is crucial. For instance, Rebecca Shuster (1991) has described the oppositional identity of bisexuals as a positive possibility arising from their stance as both lesbian or gay *and* heterosexual, combined with acknowledgement that in that position "no activity or belief secures our standing; we can stop searching for hospitality" (269). Oppositional agency may depend, then, not on a frozen identity politics, however brave the particular assertion of difference. Rather, as Ed Cohen (1991) advocates for gay politics, it may depend on working with ongoing constructions of identity and "incorporating ('self'-) contradictions into the processes of political transformation as moments/sites of possibility" so that "movements may be able to consciously affirm the political significance of their own complex (e)motions rather than be driven, and riven, by the struggle to fix 'identity'" (88-89). Therefore, in these reformulations the personal is ongoing, emerging in day-to-day events that are themselves political.

These reconfigurations abandon the slogan "the personal is political" as it sometimes has been used to differentiate individual identities, and however inadvertently, double mark (further ensuring containment of) whatever it is that is taken to be personal. Instead, such reconfigurations ask how our personal histories and identities emerge or recede as we fashion representations of the world. Taking the personal as political need not imply identity politics that inscribe certain characteristics of one's identity (attributes such as gender, age, or color), and that firmly affix those salient markers to one theoretical achievement or another. Exploring the personal as political steps beyond any simple rendition of identity to traverse the broader cultural horizon along with the landscape of personal histories. It involves learning how "identity is not the goal but rather the point of departure of the process of self-consciousness . . . how the subject is specifically and materially engendered in its social conditions and possibilities of existence" (de Lauretis 1986, 9). Identity, then, becomes a shifting and sometimes self-contradictory process "that one decides to reclaim from a history of multiple assimilations, and that one insists on as a strategy" (9). Identity is not a marker of personal self; it is neither a fixed nor singular state but a process integral to critical ends of both *resistance* and *revisioning*.

If we take to heart these two dimensions of feminist reflexivity the connections between identity and social relations and the reconfigurations of personal as political—we need more than a formula that equates reflexivity with the identification or confession of some personal experience, characteristic, or trace. To divulge that I am a woman (or even a white middle-class woman participating in certain regimes of scientific authority) is an insufficient premise for examining how my intellectual accomplishments themselves might reflect my subjectivity, or even how I am not a woman all of the time (Riley 1988). Such admissions, however horrifying to other psychologists, do not adequately explain how my subjectivity itself might be reformed through scientific practices or against them—how my identity might be used strategically and altered in the course.

Thinking reflexively, then, not only pushes hard against the ways of orthodox psychological science, it also presses up against our common notions of self. Even in its moderate constructions, reflexivity challenges the idea of an agent who earnestly, yet passively, monitors representations of reality. In its stronger versions, reflexivity demands new constructions of self that take identity not as fixed or as asocial (autonomous, independent) but as the *effect* and *cause* of social relations. Feminist self-consciousness starts from a recognition of the historical social relations through which self and self-awareness are constituted, and continues by delineating how that self-consciousness can motivate politics whether that politics is rendered through changing theory, practice, or self.

Writing Selves

Toward these ends, some experiments with reflexivity will entail strange and chancy ventures, the use of novel forms of writing (and performances generally), and occasional moments of embarrassment or even failure. These experiments have taken place, and most likely will continue to take place, outside the formal settings where psychology happens, and they usually are reported in lesser-known journals and at special conferences. However or wherever they occur, these exploratory risk takings are crucial, at once reminding us of the limitations we live by when we participate in "acceptable" scholarly projects and showing us where we need to stretch or lunge to shift those limits. Two examples show how more radical reflexive work can underscore the regulative qualities of conventional research and signal possible alternatives to that research. Both examples draw on and from the autobiographical as personal, but they each use different theories of self and self-consciousness to accomplish their reflexive analysis.

The first experiment is an ethnographic study of holocaust survivors in which Ruth Linden (1990), the analyst, reflexively positioned herself both throughout the duration of the study and within the final written account. As such, Linden's experiment exemplifies the forefront in an emerging transformation of ethnographic methods whereby "instead of a choice between writing an ethnographic memoir centering on the Self or a standard monograph centering on the Other, both the Self and Other are presented together within a single narrative ethnography, focused on the character and process of the ethnographic dialogue" (Tedlock 1991, 69). Linden challenged the ethnographic dualisms of subject and object, self and other; she also transgressed both beliefs in historically specific events and transhistorical knowledge "by inscribing myself in the text, as a partner in dialogue or as an active commentator or 'native' discourses" (6). Linden wove her account of survivors' accounts of their lives with *her* changing accounts of those accounts over the years. The weaving is not of disparate strands, for Linden attended to the mutual interdependence of tellers and creators of accounts. In particular, Linden reflected upon her earlier bewilderment over one of her interviewee's decisions to join the resistance and, thus, further risk her life during the war years:

> The limitations of my lived experience—and hence, of my imagination—are reflected in the fact that I didn't understand the force of her words, and perhaps I still do not. Now as I reread my interpretation of her decision to join the underground, my own hypothesized meanings of resistance are reflected back to me. I feel as though I am staring into a mirror at my own image. (17)

From this revelation it became more obvious how ethnographic subjects are constructed through multiple forms of social relations, varied positionings of self and other, and inscription techniques that are bounded by culture and historical resources, including language and epistemic rules. The intersubjective writing also unveiled the indexicality of representation and the respective agents participating in it.

The use of reflexive ethnography refuses to abandon or cover over the self-conscious presence of self in method. By extending the boundaries of what self is acceptable in ethnography and in interview methods generally, researchers are able to uncover features of self-making that are routinely hidden or ignored in such methods. The second experiment with reflexivity also entails interventions in methodology but does so by showing the parallels (and nonparallels) between the lives of the objects of inquiry, the psychological "subjects" in the study, and the subject of knowing, the analyst or investigator. Drawing on extensive studies of the acquisition of feminine identity, Valerie Walkerdine (1990) has developed a theory that incorporates home life, formal education, social-class conditions, and unconscious processes. Critical analysis of the gender discrimination embedded in pedagogical practices and of the authority of education is juxtaposed with gender- and class-related accounts of her personal decision to become more than a primary-school teacher. At another moment, an exposition of the "fantasies" or unconscious dimensions of feminine identity is illuminated by a psychoanalytic account of her father's images and fantasies of her identity in childhood (as well as his own). Through a personally illustrated interpretation of the multiple gazes of self and other, Walkerdine reveals "the powerful fantasies and anxieties which keep those representations circulating and provide us with the basis of other narratives of our histories and the claiming of our power" (155). Using personal photographs, poems, and essays, Walkerdine inserted herself as the interpreter *and* the interpreted; her autobiographical inserts work recursively to dissolve boundaries between the object and subject, thus making even her powers as critical theorizer available to other selves. Likewise intentionally blurred are the lines between fiction and fact, fantasy and social science.

These two experiments encourage a moving beyond the modest reflections that can be taken as reflexivity. They remind us that our identity as investigators, even as self-consciously identified investigators, warrants further development both as a presence in our methods and as agents who act and are acted upon. Our self-consciousness begins with the recognition of identity but must continue toward an understanding of how identity is a position and/or a strategy whose features are not always acknowledged even by ourselves. Just as Linden's study inverts the relation of self and other, and illuminates the changing form of self-consciousness, so Walkerdine's text indicates the varied ways in which the self is implicated in theoretical practice, being both subject and object of theory and being politically situated in both positions. And although all experiments with reflexivity need not be and cannot be as bold as these, they are necessary if feminist psychology is to achieve a "strong objectivity" or "critical positioning" that transcends the current gender arrangements in scientific practice, transverses between the politics of practice and practice of politics, and transforms self-consciousness along the way.

Experimenting Selves

Left suspended through much of this interchapter is a tremendous problem for attaining reflexive practice by observers/scientists. The worldview of modern science has no place for the agency of its practitioners: Its language, notions of representation, and social arrangements all effectively conceal the workings of agency in the processes as well as the products of inquiry. The "ideology of representation" preserves the presumed absence of agency by insisting that agents are not responsible for or actively implicated in the "discovered" relations between objects in the world and their representation in scientific knowledge. However, once we uncover this concealment of agency, either by probing Woolgar's hidden "moral order of selves" or Harding's "critical positioning" or Haraway's "situated knowing," a plethora of reflexive activities is made accessible to us.

Removing the veil of neutrality that cloaks agency in scientific practice, however, is a massive project that obviously disrupts normal scientific routines and that, perhaps just as obviously, could not be attempted by any investigators desiring to retain their scientific status. Thus it appears that feminist psychologists, scientists who have ample reason to unearth reflexive practices from their sealed vault, have no available (read permissible) tools to do so. That being the case, it then would seem that feminist psychologists must choose to either artfully disguise their reflexive work in public forums (so much so that this work might go unrecognized) or else continue with the restrictive techniques of unreflexive science (and, hence, with the consequences of enacting little if any change). A study of interpersonal power or rape or equity or of any other social phenomena of feminist concern that its author would aspire to have appear on the pages of the *Journal of Personality and Social Psychology*, for instance, will at most have only the faintest traces of the selves of its manufacture. There would be few if any places for sharing details about the identities making that representation or about how they were altered in the process; very faint traces would be the best that could occur.

There are options to handling self-conscious reflexivity in the shadows of the prevailing investigative codes or to not handling it at all. At least three means toward reflexive work are intimated in the previous pages. First, as illustrated in the experiments on writing selves, researchers can use novel literary forms to expose hidden agency. Varied experiments with this technique now have been conducted in the social studies of science to correct the tendency for researchers in that area to exonerate themselves from the kinds of analysis that they impose on the science and scientists whom they study (Ashmore 1989; Woolgar 1988a, 1989). For example, by forgoing the standard textual form of a univocal author and disrupting the linear progression of textual argument by introducing a second authorial voice (produced by the same agent as the first), Woolgar challenges the reader's conceptions of "the author as a passive, neutral agent of representation" and reveals something about the hidden moral order of selves (1989, 141). This methodological intervention has the virtue of directly exposing agency and reflexive acts, but it carries the high cost of stigmatizing if not disenfranchising the author as a "good" scientific citizen.

A second course avoids such social/professional disadvantage by making an intervention into the scientific work of others. Through a range of analytic techniques it is possible to locate agency and reflexivity even in the standard genre of scientific writing. This approach too has been used in the social studies of science as a way of locating agency, its contradictions and variations, in science (Latour 1987; Woolgar 1989). Rhetorical signs and gestures of agency are not difficult to locate in psychological texts, and the example of psychological studies of feminism described in the last chapter intimates how agents are neither neutral nor passive in the production of representational knowledge. In another exploratory study of research writing, Robert Steele and I found that psychologists/authors display interpersonal power in specific and specifically gendered ways (Morawski and Steele 1991). Sometimes revelations of the selves of science are most apparent in quasi-scientific places, like prefaces to texts (Stringer 1990), but they occur throughout scientific writing. In science and quasi-science writing alike, psychologists have often bifurcated the observer's self, talking about a passive agent and a more passionate self (Morawski 1992). Such studies of writing expose the dynamics of scientific agency, but they also have educated me about the limits of such analyses: They depend on an "ontological gerrymandering" (Woolgar 1989) whereby I differentiate myself, as sort of a scientific observer, from the selves under study by claiming (or pretending) through traditional scientific rhetoric that my analysis is somehow a representation without agents. Despite such a paradox in the analysis of others' reflexive selves, this approach offers one preliminary direction for charting the selves of scientific inquiry.

The third approach to reflexive observation is perhaps the route most commonly followed by feminist psychologists. In what some researchers have called "weak" reflexivity there are no radical literary ventures, no dramatic multivocality, but instead there are the author's insertions (into texts) of their "critical, political, ethical, or moral passions" (Cozzens and Gieryn 1990, 10). Although such passions may not be readily detectible in feminist research appearing in the mainstream psychological journals, they are sometimes present;

and in other places, notably feminist or specialty journals, textbooks, and book chapters, their presence is increasingly undisguised.

Two themes are common in these reflexive insertions: *resistances* to conventional theories, interpretations, and social relations of science, and *narratives* of personal transformation (see for examples, Kimmel 1989; Richardson 1991, 1992; Unger and Crawford 1992, 23-24). Accounts of resistance and self-change echo the liminal status of feminist work, but more importantly, they represent new understandings of identity and social relations that (in their very articulation) alter ongoing scientific practices. In particular, narratives of transformation disclose the processes of identities and insist, however quietly, on the ubiquity of these emergent selves in science. It is but a step from these narratives to the institution of quite different practices. As noted earlier, these changes are occurring first in places other than the laboratory, often in classrooms and applied settings. For instance, Susan Hawes (1993) has introduced a reflexive model for supervision of clinical psychologists in training. By bracketing the taken-for-granted supervision procedure, Hawes located its implicit power relations and hierarchy of agents, and then designed an alternative procedure in which multiple discourses are brought to discussions; truth claims are submitted to contextual and critical analyses; supervisor and supervisee together engage in dialogues of self-critical reflection; and power relations are exposed and examined. This explicitly reflexive and collaborative arrangement modifies relations of supervisor and supervisee. It also effectively intervenes in what is taken to be personhood: "By its very instance on the role of implicit oppressive power relations hidden in dominant discourses and its assertion that the intentional engagement in deconstructing these discourses is empowering, a reflexive stance entertains a view of persons that is less patronizing, patriarchal and pathologizing" (15–16). Hawes's model indicates how even local alterations can have consequences that extend beyond the specific context.

The culture of science, from its epistemic beliefs to its social order, leaves no space for self-conscious reflexivity: Only through interventions and experiments, such as the three approaches just described, can a place for cognizant reflection or agencies and identities be imagined. Even this very writing, charged by resistance to gendered science and by sober skepticism about our ways of making representations of the world, still relies on the rhetorical conventions of representation without agents. As author, I have adopted those conventions to persuade, leaving aside my weighty doubts about classic causal explanations of the world, the power relations of textual persuasion, and not the least, about myself as positioned on all too precarious a precipice between belief and disillusionment, commitment and abandonment, reform and rejection, hope and anger. And while the interchapters provide a literary opportunity to balance these dimensions, they also call forth additional reflexive contemplation that, in turn, insists on going further.

Chapter 3

Subjectivity

When we move from considering objectivity to examining the very objects of objective observation, a move to what most psychologists routinely call "subjects," we immediately encounter problems of nomenclature. Why are the individuals who are studied in psychological research "subjects" and not "objects," "reactors," or "agents"? Why are they not "observers," "actors," or "variable movers"? What is the difference, if any, between the more recent motion to call these individuals "participants" and the previously predominant fashion to call them "subjects" (aside from the rhetorical politeness of the former term)? At the surface, such decisions of nomenclature concern methodological expectations about the representativeness of the individuals whom investigators have selectively sampled from some larger population, or assumptions about their behavior that are built into the methods of inquiry. The recurrent criticism of the "college sophomore" syndrome is but one challenge to these methodological norms: Psychologists' heavy reliance on white college students (to serve as subjects) may be providing a psychology of the human nature of late adolescence rather than of some universal human nature (Sears 1986).

But the complications of nomenclature are not just word deep: They call forth central questions about that which is being named. Questions of *representativeness* in a sample selection can be extended to more serious questions of *representations*, and here semantic variations can become substantive concerns. What is being represented through the routine use of subjects to produce psychological data or subject matter? Are the productions by research subjects truly representations of subjectivity, of some psychological essences? Do subjects' research enactments reveal the true nature of subjectivity? Yet again, semantic problems are re-encountered in these questions because psychologists frequently refer to subjectivity, sometimes in themselves as well as in their objects of inquiry, as a bias or state other than that of normal cognitive rationality, i.e., the subjectivity of experimenter biases and its effect on experimental outcomes. Is this subjectivity in any way related to the subjectivity of subjects? Or is it related to what, in other contexts, is called "consciousness"?

On yet another semantic plane subjectivity calls forth objectivity as its opposite. In fact, subjectivity is often defined in relation to its opposite: The guide to nonsexist research (McHugh, Koeske, and Frieze 1986) discussed in chapter 2 enacts such an operation by defining objectivity in contrast to subjectivity. In such binary semantics, the terms are not fixed, but rather, the definition of one term shifts its point of reference (along some continuum) in relation to the other term. This shifting or indexically defined polarity imposes not a balance but, in fact, differential effects on the meanings of each of the terms. The opposition encourages an escalating flight from subjectivity "under the pressure of an assumption that everything must be something not to any point of view, but in itself" (Nagel 1979, 208). That is, in the privileging of an objective point, subjectivity has become not just elusive but undesirable: We avoid identification with it.

The construct of *subjectivity,* along with the more classic epistemological construct of *subject,* then, must be considered within an elaborate play of language and within the particular histories of their imaginings (the history of theorizing the subject). The constructs also must be examined within their practical context-specific usages in both texts and laboratories. Deciphering the linguistic and historical conditions that attend constructs of the subject comprises a preliminary step toward thinking about—and rethinking—subjectivity in feminist research. That is, in order to reconceptualize the *subjects who are the objects* of our inquiries, it is first necessary to map the landscape upon which subjectivity is routinely defined and observed in research.

This chapter proceeds, then, by reviewing the larger history of subjectivity, including recent considerations of the postmodern subject. This history provides a guide for revisions in our thinking about subjectivity. The chapter moves on to revisit one "factor" of subjectivity that is central yet perpetually troublesome to feminist psychology: The category (attribute/quality/variable) of "gender." Cataloguing the prominent troubles with gender reveals the limitations of such categories, including the tendency to seek differences between and within categories and the problems posed by multiplying categories of analysis, notably by adding to gender the concepts of race, class, and sexual orientation. But perhaps more important, exposition of such categories raises crucial issues about subjectivity and identity, and about agency and resistance. Several proposed resolutions of the tensions between the need for subjectivity that is accessible to empirical analysis and a more accurate portrayal of its dynamics follow, and the chapter concludes by citing several feminist experiments with expanded conceptions of subjectivity.

Historical Subjects

Until this point, subjectivity has been examined in terms of the *forms of talking* about it. We find that our talk about these matters is riddled with apparent semantic complications, but that is just one of the complications. Our talk is not univocal but includes mixed traditions of describing the composition of psychological subjects. Yet, neither examining the language nor its variability fully exposes the theoretical conceptions of subjectivity that underlie modern psychology. And if we were to undertake a detailed investigation of those basic concepts we would find that they too are neither linguistically pure nor singular but are continually shifting and multiple (Chorover 1985; Flanagan 1981; Levine, Worboys, and Taylor 1973) To complicate matters further, our theory talk is filled with antimonies that recurrently trigger or guide debates; these oppositional points include nature-nurture, cognition-emotion, rationality-nonrationality, individual-society, mind-body, and volunteerism-mechanism, among others.

Despite such oppositions, oscillations, and flip-flops, practitioners regularly reach some agreement on the operative concepts of subjectivity, or what is usually referred to as "human nature." Beyond the idiosyncratic differences and nuances of particular psychological theories there persists shared knowledge about the characteristics of subjectivity—a metaphysics of the subject that resonates with the predominant features of Western philosophy. Among the core characteristics are the beliefs that subjects are autonomous or independent in their cognitions about the world; that they are whole, unified, or self-contained in their independence; that they are capable of or designed for enacting rationality (a preferred mode of thought or action); and they are a "natural" kind, ultimately unaltered by artifices of time and place. Whether one contemplates behavioral theories or parallel distributive-processing theories or some other more recent variant of theorizing, these characteristics of subjectivity are taken to hold.

However stable or coherent these core features of subjectivity appear at any particular moment of theorizing and practice, they are not seen by everyone as either representative or desirable. At least three lines of critique within psychology have challenged these reigning features, and they have proceeded initially by detecting fatal cracks in the metaphysics of subjectivity and then by proposing radically different conceptualizations. The first line is now well known: The *humanist critique* finds subjectivity, as modelled in much psychological work, to exclude or minimize creative and self-transforming impulses. Narrow understandings of rationality (read mechanism) and subject independence (read isolation) obscure the self-conscious, self-generative capacities of humans. The humanist perspective generally traces these omissions in the prevailing metaphysics to psychologists' overdependence on natural science methodologies, a reliance that neglects the "human" in human nature. Thus, for example, arguments for "a view of man [sic] as an active, self-directing, self-monitoring agent whose acts occur in a social framework constructed out of meanings" (Harré and Secord 1972, 297) typically have been accompanied by programs for reforming research methods to accommodate that view. Seen from a slightly different perspective, the humanist critique has not implied abandonment of classical notions of subjectivity. Rather it has reaffirmed the qualities of freedom and autonomy by showing how they are obscured or erased by psychology's use of narrowly construed scientific methods (Toulmin and Leary 1985). In the end, this critique ties the reformation of methodologies to the realization of an essential theory of subjectivity, one that brings to the fore certain neglected yet cherished characteristics.

A second form of critique, one descendant from the tradition of *critical theory*, identifies the operative parameters of subjectivity with ideology. The dominant concept of subjectivity in psychology is seen to be ideologically grounded both in the sense of representing "false consciousness" or distorted understandings of the world *and* as the actual consciousness of a particular historical situation (Sampson 1981). Subjectivity, as modelled in Western thought and distinctly elaborated on in human sciences like psychology, is suited to a social order that grants privileges to some and not others, justifies social and economic hierarchies, and regulates actions in particular ways. The self-contained individualism that is presumed, examined, and certified in modern psychology is found to be compatible with a larger system of competition, exchange, and inequality, and hence, with a historically specific ideology (Sampson 1977). A model of the mind that reduces experiences to the level of individual and subjective life—as does cognitive psychology—can be seen to complement the maintenance of a dominant social order by encouraging people to "accept a change in their subjective experience as a substitute for changes in their objective reality" (Sampson 1981, 735).

Ideological critique contests the idea that subjectivity is universal and stable. Analyzing the social politics of subjectivity as it is construed in different research programs at different times, whether in concepts of aggression (Lubek 1979), development (Bronfenbrenner, Kessel, Kessen, and White 1986; Kessen 1983), social psychology (Archibald 1978; Henriques 1984) or sex differeces (Lewin 1984; Shields 1975), challenges such universality and substantiates the context specificity of subjectivity. These analyses reveal the paradox of ideology as being both false and true consciousness: "It is true insofar as it accurately represents the reality of a given sociohistorical era or group. It is false insofar as that truth may itself be a systematic distortion which serves the interests of some groups over others" (Sampson 1981, 731). This paradox, as Edward Sampson has shown in the case of cognitive psychology, points to the *interdependence* rather than independence of subject and object.

> Consciousness and thinking reflect something about the subject's perception and experience; yet they also reflect something about the objective world within which that individual works and lives. To understand cognition therefore requires that we grasp both subject and object. If we stop our inquiry at the individual subject, we participate in the same kind of distortion that he or she reflects; yet if we ignore the subject in favor of the object, we miss the important constituent that the subject's active consciousness contributes. (731–32)

To grant the context-dependence of subjective experiences and of objective renderings of these experiences is to acknowledge the material and social groundings of our notions of subjectivity. It invites critical reanalysis of the assumptions underlying dominant psychological models, assumptions such as the autonomy of cognitions or even the priority of the cognitive over emotional and social experiences, since those very categorical assumptions of mental life are produced through certain material and social conditions.

Close analysis of ideology is the starting point for a third critical stance that views subjectivity as a *historically determined* (and a history determining) *phenomenon.* From this perspective, subjectivity is transient and mutable; there is no universal subjectivity, only historically specific forms. Scientific studies absorb and reflect these historically formed phenomena, and at the same time they also participate in the very generation of subjectivity or subjective experiences. Psychology, then, both *reproduces* cultural manifestations that are taken to be subjectivity *and* contributes to *producing* these forms. Studies of the ideological and cultural foundations of psychological knowledge supply evidence for the first of these functions of psychology by elucidating the correspondence between scientific concepts of personhood and dominant discourses of the prevailing social order. Studies of the prescriptive and inventive features of psychology illustrate the second. For instance, psychology has contributed to new expectations about the self and social interaction, and social psychology in particular has facilitated the making of an externally driven personhood or "at least the appearance of anomic, cross-pressured, easily swayed people who seem to warrant the gloomy verdict" (MacIntyre 1985, 902). What is taken to be the substance and potential of the self has changed dramatically over the last two centuries (Baumeister 1987; Cushman 1990; Sass 1988; Verhave and van Hoorn 1984), and in the last hundred years psychology has become one generative force in these transformations.

Far from being a monolithic system, what is called here the historical critique is actually a covering term for a variety of accounts of historical changes in subjectivity and psychology's participation in those alterations. There exists several postulated connections between the science of psychology and the formation of subjectivity. Although most accounts locate more than a single link and represent the connections as multidynamic, it is possible to enumerate some of the more common postulates. Of these, the most readily identifiable link between psychology and the formation of subjectivity is to be found in the science's relatively uncritical adoption of cultural norms and practices and its consequential assimilation of popular understandings of persons at a given moment in time. Graham Richards (1987) has revealed this cultural absorption and reflection in the case of Solomon Asch's research on conformity in the 1940s. Asch's findings of high levels of conformity (results that apparently cannot be replicated in contemporary research) are intelligible only when we consider "the entire historical setting of high-status European professors vis-à-vis earnest, respectful, young U.S. college students in a culture where conformity was a widespread pre-occupation of science-fiction writers, film-makers, folk-singers, and social commentators generally" (207). The relation between scientific productions and cultural formations, as illustrated in the Asch experiments, is not one where an external cultural pressure is exerted on scientific ideas but one where science *is* culture. Viewed in this manner, "Asch's experiments were not *separate* from the phenomenon they were studying—they were themselves part of it, one further level of expression of the general cultural pre-occupation with conformity, just as later U.S. psychological work on prejudice and the roots of racism was part and parcel of the wider civil rights movement" (207). Such studies exposing the correspondence of the historically specific and the scientifically specific make it apparent that contemporary social psychology, as Michael Billig (1990) has argued, has not fully reinvented the social but rather, in its conflicting principles and argumentative structure, actually "resembles the more ordinary common sense it seeks to replace" (59).

As a *cultural form*, a *mode of cultural production*, and an *institution that serves society*, it is not surprising that psychology has integrated dominant concepts of personhood. Nor is it astonishing that psychology has generated a subjectivity that *needs* the institution of psychology. Philip Cushman (1990) has investigated the creation of the "empty self" in psychology, a self that suited an industrial economy of overproduction in need of individuals to consume its products: "The Western world and America in particular constructed a new type of bounded self that was the perfect complement to the postwar economy built on a system of universal, worldwide credit. Credit is only necessary when the individual's wish to buy outstrips his or her capital . . . with an empty self people *always* need" (604). The making of a self ever in search of change, novelty, and growth, ever in some kind of need for fulfillment—an empty self—transpired hand in hand with the growth of a psychological industry to minister to that self. Thus, "the empty self has become such a prevalent aspect of our culture that much contemporary psychotherapeutic theory is devoted to its treatment" (604) and an extensive psychotherapeutic industry has accompanied its emergence.

These examples illustrate how psychology participates in the cultural formation of subjectivity. They also indicate yet another relation between psychology and subjectivity: Psychology is an instrument of macrosocial life. That is, psychology is a positive force "in constructing the subject both as the object of its study and as a site for social administration and regulation" (Henriques, Hollway, Urwin, Venn, and Walkerdine 1984, 203). Modern psychology of the individual emerged not just as a science, however culturally infused or defined, but also as an institution implicated in the regulation, government, classification, surveillance, and therapeutic modification of people. As a positive force, psychology has produced not only abstract constructs of mind and self, but also a technology that is crucial to these constructions. In addition to creating books and reports on subjectivity, psychology also has "consisted of a set of practical instruments and techniques which embodied the explanations proposed and deployed them in relation to the practical problems which had occasioned them" (Rose 1985, 8). The technology of psychology, its devices of *description* and *inscription* (Rose 1990a, 1990b), constitute a set of practices that impose new relations between people, e.g., notably but not only psychologists and their investigated subjects, and hence, further contribute to the making of subjectivities. The creation of a field of experimental social psychology, for instance, required a reconceptualization of what counted as "social" such that what experimenters did in the course of scientific investigation was not taken to be social and what subjects did in the new laboratories was taken to be such (Morawski 1985). The social came to be defined through specific and painstakingly managed relations in research settings and through the technical devices, assessment scales, forced-choice situations, etc., used in those settings. Even ostensibly minor research conventions like debriefing produced distinctive social relations, especially as the device was borrowed from specific military practices (Harris 1988).

In addition, the very practices of subject selection, the social identities (age, gender, education) written onto these subjects, and the nomothetic assumptions built into data analyses contribute to the formation of subjectivity. These technical conventions have endowed notions of the independent individual who could be understood, indeed, is best understood when abstracted from his or her social environment and involvements. Through these practices psychology "essentially adopted culturally established categories and treated them as psychological" (Danziger 1990, 92) and did so by deploying research techniques for exercising social power that were compatible with (if not identical to) techniques used in beauraucratic institutions including the school, industry, and hospital. As Kurt Danziger has illustrated in his history of the psychology subject, through these routinized and institutional practices "mid-twentieth century psychology had been transformed into an administrative science" (190).

Viewed from these multiple historical purchases, psychological science is not an innocent consumer of some pregiven model of subjectivity. Although informed by ideas going back to at least the Enlightenment—ideas about an independent, unified, and more-or-less rational subject—modern psychology has participated in its ongoing reformation. Psychology has been involved as *producer of cultural knowledge,* as a *system of social practices,* and as an *institution structured to serve* a certain social order. To acknowledge the historicity of subjectivity and the engagement of psychology in that historical process is not a condemnation of the scientific project. On the contrary, such awareness bequeaths new ways to imagine and study human action.

Postmodernism, More or Less

Taking subjectivity to be a historical construction is one theme of postmodernism. As an epistemology or, perhaps, an antiepistemology, postmodernism counters modernist convictions about progress, truth, and democracy, as well as the idea of a unified or stable subject (Flax 1990; Gergen 1991; Lyotard 1984). Under analytic and deconstructive scrutiny, the universal, free, stable, and coherent subject is seen as a mythic figure masking fragmented, shifting, and conflicting subjectivities. Through new studies of language, history, and power, the Enlightenment subject has been found to be a confected protagonist of a Western metanarrative. Alternatively, postmodern subjectivity is seen as a historical phenomenon continually being refashioned by the discourses and politics of postindustrial culture. Hence, "Subjectivity is now read as multiple, layered, and nonunitary. . . . No longer viewed as merely the repository of consciousness and creativity, the self is constructed as a terrain of conflict and struggle, and subjectivity is seen as a site of both liberation and subjugation" (Giroux 1992, 60–61). Despite the extravagances of this thinking about the subject, it should be noted that the idea of the self as multiple or mutable is hardly the invention of postmodernism. Classic psychoanalysis can be understood as positioning a multiplicity of self, although desiring a more or less integrated one, and more recently experimental psychologists from a variety of theoretical vantage points have contemplated plurality and even fragmentation in selfhood and identity. While postmodernism offers rich possibilities for reconceptualizing subjectivity and the self, conceptualizations that are more appropriate to the world in which we live (Flax 1990; Gergen 1991), it harbors unsettling problems. First, and most obviously, once the subject is understood as multiple and mutable, as contradictory and fragmented, it is necessary to consider how this assemblage is held together.

> What accounts for the continuity of the subject, and the subjective experiences of identity? What accounts for the predictability of people's actions, as they repeatedly position themselves within particular discourses? Can people's wishes and desires be encompassed in an account of discursive relations? (Henriques, Hollway, Urwin, Venn, and Walkerdine 1984, 204)

However fractured and mutable subjectivities may be, most individuals proceed with a seemingly integrated sense of self, monitor and recreate actions and interactions, and report coherently on a flow of experiences. Postmodernism leaves unsettled the problem of how individuals operate with coherent selves and with multiply structured subjectivities.

Whereas the question of a functioning and coherent sense of self is sometimes apprehended by social scientists, a second problem is more often heeded by critical and poststructuralist investigators. The problem consists of ascertaining what enables subjects to become aware of their subjugation, their own "inauthenticity," in order to overcome or transform oppressive conditions (Smith 1988, 60). How are destabilized, contradictory, and partial subjectivities capable of innovation and resistance? This problem intimates the political girders of theory building that are sometimes eschewed in the elitism of poststructuralist enterprises. Richard Johnson (1986) posed this problem for cultural studies, linking it with the prior problem of coherent subjects:

> Above all, *there is no account of what I would call the subjective aspects of struggle*, no account of how there is a moment in subjective flux when social subjects (individual or collective) produce accounts of how they are, and conscious political agents, that is, constitute themselves, politically. To ask for such a theory is not to deny the major structuralist or post-structuralist insights: subjects are contradictory, in process, fragmented, produced. But human beings and social movements also strive to produce some coherence and continuity, and through this, exercise some control over feelings, conditions and destinies. (69)

For theorists whose projects are grounded in politics, as are projects on race and gender, the postmodernist rendition of the subject is evidently problematic (Fraser and Nicholson 1990). As Judith Butler (1990b) argued, "If it is not a female subject who provides the normative model for a feminist politics, then what does? . . . What constitutes the 'who,' the subject, for whom feminism seeks emancipation? If there is no subject, who is left to emancipate?" (327). The lacuna fashioned in postmodern subjectivity might itself be a political move, not an oversight (Bordo 1990a,1990b; Hartsock 1990). As bell hooks (1990) warned, "Should we not be suspicious of postmodern critiques of the 'subject' when they surface at a historical moment when many subjugated people feel themselves coming to voice for the first time" (28)? The poststructuralist critique of essentialism "should not be made synonymous with a dismissal of the struggle of oppressed and exploited peoples to make ourselves subjects" and to "find ways to construct self and identity that are oppositional and liberatory" (28–29).

These problems, and the questions they engender, intimate an inadequacy of postmodern subjectivity. While deconstructive practices reveal delusions and fabrications behind normative concepts of the subject, and while historical and ideology studies document the microsocial constructions of subjectivity, including those produced in and through social science, an adequate theory of the subject is still wanting. And it is these very absences, these gaps in theorizing subjectivity, that feminist psychologists must begin refiguring, for without a subject who provides a normative model, without agents capable of struggle and change, the project of feminist psychology is bereft. However, to commence with this generative project of theorizing a (post-poststructuralist?) subject (or of reconstructing subjectivity) is not to refute or ignore the lessons of historical, deconstructive, and postmodern studies. On the contrary, our investigations can only proceed with and through these sorts of analyses. The practices of feminist psychology must incorporate—and are already doing so—the methods of critical studies.

Reworking Gender in Psychology

Even *with a theoretical project in sight,* however blurred its contours, and with *more than an armful of critical lessons and promising new investigative techniques,* feminist psychologists confront momentous decisions about where to begin. Historically we have started from (and with) analysis of gender, and did so for obvious and necessary reasons. Gender was not only a neglected category in psychological studies but also much more: It has been routinely misconceived, misperceived, and mismeasured. Primed with a feminist sense that gender is a dominant axis passing through and affecting most (if not all) the phenomena treated in psychology, feminist psychologists have had enough work to keep themselves occupied just by examining gender—its causes, correlates, and consequences. Yet in doing so, we have continued to participate in psychology's dominant paradigm of subjectivity, specifically its reductive individualism, that focuses on individual experiences, prizes cognition over other events, and parses the world into units of individual, society, nature, culture, and so on. In pursuing this line of work, we have circumscribed the questions that are asked and responses that are deemed appropriate (Kitzinger 1991b; Squire 1989), and have restrained new or more radical theoretical projects. In psychology as in other disciplines, it has now become evident that gender analyses alone are not enough, and that inclusion of race, class, and sexual preference (among the most obviously omitted axes) necessarily alters our theories and research practices. Thus, our analyses of gender must be further transformed: Inclusive theorizing forces visualization of a very different terrain of theory and configuration of subjectivity.

Gender as an object of psychological inquiry has a history as old as the discipline itself (Fausto-Sterling 1985; Shields 1975), but it was with the feminist wave beginning in the late 1960s that gender came to be viewed as *more* than a stable variable or personal attribute. In psychological investigations of the last twenty-five years, gender has been submitted to multiple reconceptualizations, including substantive proposals about its status as a social/biological/psychological category; as a continuum of difference (male vs. female); as a social process or relation; and as a form or consequence of power. Each of these propositions challenges, to varying degrees, some central tenets of psychology's metaphysics of subjectivity, and taken together, they destabilize the entire endeavor in ways resembling the effects of deconstructive critiques. For these reasons feminist psychology entails a *critical* and *self-critical* as well as *productive* field of research: "Feminist psychology is fundamentally a contest over meanings and definitions: it is a struggle about what is sayable within our discipline, and about what need not be said—about what can be assumed and what requires explanation, about what questions can be asked, and what constitute legitimate answers" (Kitzinger, 1991b, 49).

Immersed in such a widescale undoing and revisioning, in an emancipatory project, feminist psychology in some respects is far from being emancipated inquiry. Celia Kitzinger (1991b) described how we are repeatedly recalled to answer standard research questions like, "Is lesbianism a sickness?" and how, in debating these issues

> we tacitly agree that the answer "yes" would be reasonable and intelligible: ironically, we contribute by consensus to the underlying structure within which these questions are *possible* even in

> attempting to reform or deny the values they imply. . . . It is precisely these sorts of rival claims and counterclaims which sustain psychology as an institution, and that feminists who engage with psychology in this way, far from representing a subversive or radical threat, in fact support and extend the discipline. (51)

Kitzinger has highlighted how feminist psychology, as a project conducted within an already structured scientific institution of knowledge production, cannot extricate itself from the dominant norms of that institution without constant vigilance over the kinds of questions asked, constructs used, and methods deployed.

If these concerns are taken to the feminist psychologies of gender, then it becomes necessary to interrogate those studies, not in order to compromise or fractionalize the overall project, but to strengthen it. We need to revisit the propositions made about gender, taking with us those promising lessons and investigative techniques gleaned through critical analyses. The reassessments of basic propositions inventoried below simply offer initiatives for rethinking subjectivity and identity more generally. In the interrogations of theory categories, concerns with difference, and reimaginings of process and power, we then can establish practices and articulate theories that transcend conventional confines of the subject.

Sex/Gender Categories

The term *sex* has a long history in psychology while *gender* has only recently attained common usage. The ascendancy of gender as a central category of investigation corresponds with the rise of feminist research that, among other objectives, sought to separate scientific myths from empirical facts about the nature of women (and men). In 1979, Rhoda Unger argued that in order to distinguish between biological and social theories about male and female differences, and hence, to weed the empirical garden of unwarranted nativist assumptions, an appropriate terminology had to be devised. Her proposal that the term *gender* should refer to "those characteristics and traits socio-culturally considered appropriate to males and females" (1085) was intended to separate social from physiological arguments and reduce the common conflation of all psychological differences with biological origins. Many investigators have adopted this distinction, yet there exists no consensus in usage. Janet Hyde (1991), for instance, used only the terms *gender* or *gender differences* in her psychology of women textbook; the term *sex* was reserved for discussing sexual behaviors. Hyde found that a dual terminology (sex and gender) obscures the fact that many studies provide no causal evidence about origins, whether psychological, cultural, or biological, and that "the sharp distinction between biological causes and cultural causes fails to recognize that biology and culture may interact" (3).

Here is another instance where differences of opinion are not just word deep. Contention concerning the terms *sex* and *gender* is tightly tied to both *political* and *theoretical* goals. On a political level, using two distinct terms restrains (although does not eliminate) the tendency to equate male and female differences with some underlying natural order. The terminology simultaneously carries a certain political safety by implying an openness to theoretical possibilities; that is, someone using the term *gender* and assessing its sociocultural components cannot be so readily accused of close-mindedness about biological determinants of difference.

On a theoretical level, the contention over language involves numerous troubles, and the choice of a particular venue of terms sometimes (but not always) serves to contain these problems. For instance, despite their different word choices, both Hyde and Unger (in her 1979 article) tacitly accept the idea of an external world divisible into the biological and the social and cultural, the natural and artificial, and an accompanying idea that human bodies exist in a binary system—male and female. Yet, these ideas have been challenged by claims that sex and its binary configuration are themselves culturally constructed categories, not eternal ones. To take the existence and duality of sex as natural categories "obscures the social, political, and economic origins of the differences between the sexes and of women's subordination as a class" (Bleier 1984, 73). In other words, it ignores the social and political origins of these ostensibly natural categories. Like Ruth Bleier, Suzanne Kessler and Wendy McKenna (1978) have taken the categories of sex and gender to be socially constructed whereby "a world of two 'sexes' is a result of the socially shared, taken-for-granted methods which members use to construct reality" (vii). As members of this world, scientists' thought "is grounded in the everyday gender attribution process" (ix). Understanding the cultural invention of categories opens the way for seeing the circularity of the sex-gender distinction such that "If the immutable character of sex is contested, perhaps this construct called 'sex' is as culturally constructed as gender; indeed, perhaps it was always already gender, with the consequence that the distinction between sex and gender turns out to be no distinction at all" (Butler 1990a, 7). Even usages of the category of gender that are plural and multidynamic (Sherif 1982), participate in a culturally derived, regulated system and sustain its reproduction.

Regardless of how the categories are derived or divided, the sex-gender system poses yet another set of troubles in assuming that sex and/or gender are properties of individuals (Stacey and Thorne 1985). Taking sex and/or gender as a *variable* of individuals tends to push analyses back to the individual level—a reductionist move. It further essentializes the categories and precludes examination of how gender structures experience, how gender relates to other axes of social organization such as race and class, and how gender figures more generally in social relations of power (West and Zimmerman 1987). Just as fixed categories of sex and gender foreclose on interrogations of the possible gendered *forestructuring* of the world, so they also circumscribe our perception of where and how gender *operates beyond its immediate influences* on individual identity and behavior.

Once the tacit implications of these terms are examined, sex and/or gender categories become available to a range of theoretical possibilities and these, in turn, have varying consequences for what comes to be taken as subjectivity. Two theoretical approaches, broadly defined, illustrate both the available choices and the consequences. Social constructionist and poststructuralist theories alike often indicate that sex/gender are invented categories, representations produced through the dominant order and practices of social life (although they differ in postulating how these categories structure or intersect with individual experience). Essentialist and what are often called "cultural" feminist theories (predominant in the social sciences), while challenging male-centered theories of sex/gender, still claim that there are locatable genders. They assume, for instance, that the term *woman* has identifiable features and has some degree of stability or universality. Both sets of theories pose somewhat perilous consequences: The first abandons the idea of a coherent subject, one who *has, does,* and *is* along with the grounds for treating people as agents, whereas the second collapses gender identity into a single, stable form, ignoring how history, race, class, ethnicity, and sexuality are constitutive and differentiating features of gender. Abandonment of theoretical categories leaves no notions of the subject with which to work, yet retention of unanalyzed categories reinforces certain disturbing and sometimes essentialist notions of the subject.

Given this apparent impasse, we need to treat our theoretical categories as problematic, constantly experiment with their boundaries, and repeatedly ask what implications are attached to them. Specifically, we must examine whether *and* how these categories replicate psychology's dominant ideology of individualism, autonomy, and reductionism (Kitzinger 1991b). We also need to incorporate the advances we have made in understanding gender as constituted through social relations and structures, and take seriously the poststructuralist analyses of gender as a system of signifying power. Following Joan Scott's (1986) advice to historians, we might proceed with a multidimensional concept of the elements of gender: as culturally available symbols (containing multiple and sometimes contradictory representations); as normative concepts (delineating most aphonic possibilities); as a political construction; and as subjective identity (of persons). And to these dimensions must be added an escalated investigation of how gender is connected to other central, theoretical categories of identity, notably (but not only) race and economic status. Although feminist psychologists working with conventional theories and methods have heeded the last suggestion namely by investigating differences among women (of different classes, races, or other life experiences), they have largely done so without questioning the culturally symbolic and normative bases of their theoretical categories.

How feminist psychologists travel across this landscape of theory options continues to be a *political* as well as *theoretical* issue. As Teresa de Lauretis (1990) has suggested, the debates over various feminist theories can be "read not only as a crisis *over* identity, a metacritical doubt and a dispute among feminists as to the notion of identity, but also a crisis *of* identity, of self-definition, implying a theoretical impasse for feminism as a whole" (261). Identity then becomes a political goal in two senses: the subjectivity of feminists and the subjectivity of those whom they try to understand.

We need, then, to acknowledge the doubleness, oscillations, and paradoxes of our analytic categories as productive forces in our research practices, and use them in strategic ways. That is, our analytic categories must be fluid and continually scrutinized. In turn, this scrutiny may require syntheses of purportedly opposing theories, for instance, coupling the proposition that gendered subjectivity is a property arising from an individual's experience with "the notion that identity is an active construction and a discursively mediated political interpretation of one's history" (de Lauretis 1990, 263). It also necessitates realizing that synthesis is not always desirable or feasible (de Lauretis 1990; Gross 1986; Snitow 1990). These theoretical practices involve a political reflexivity, an awareness of the ways in which theoretical categories like gender and sex, and the forms of agency and identity they inscribe, are at once products of historically specific agents and also are productive of agency and identity. Such practices include strategic use of analytic categories, being ever mindful of their revisability, and a readiness to expose, contest, or replace the investigative techniques that frame gender and subjectivity in restrictive ways. Thus, pushed to its limits "the task is not whether to repeat, but how to repeat or, indeed, to repeat and, through a radical proliferation of gender, *to displace* the very gender norms that enable the repetition itself" (Butler 1990a, 148).

Difference

In psychology the idea of difference is immediately understood as a comparison of individuals on some psychological trait, characteristic, or state. Difference thus implies individualism; the equation of subjectivity with individual attributes; and the existence of distinct categories of being, acting, or having (such as masculinity and femininity). The idea of difference, however, also is *evaluative* and *prescriptive.* As Kurt Danziger (1990) found in his history of psychological methods, the categories of assessing individuals are not socially neutral categories but decisively evaluative ones that fit larger commitments: "It was not an academic interest in the psychology of human cognition that motivated the normative study of individual performance but an interest in establishing who would most effectively conform to certain socially established criteria" (108).

Over the last twenty years, many feminist psychologists have warned about the evaluative component in gender difference research, specifically how gender difference makes a difference in the ways that individuals act, in the ways that they perceive themselves and others, and in the ways that social institutions are organized (Hare-Mustin and Marecek 1990b, 4). In fact, feminist psychologists have become increasingly wary of difference research and their reservations are, indeed, manifold. The noted problems with difference research include the following:

1. The assumed binary nature of gender difference that posits two distinct sorts of genders—male and female.
2. The biologic or reductionist bias accompanying difference research that enables a slide from detected difference to biological causation.
3. The neglect of variations within gender (those variations within one gender related to age, circumstance, race, class, and sexual orientation) that influence manifestations of gender.
4. The biases of standard and research methods and reporting conventions that sometimes exaggerate differences and sometimes minimize them.
5. The neglect of gender similarities that skews the picture by emphasizing gender differences.
6. The false symmetry assumed in the binary model of gender difference that obscures the differential valuing of the two types.
7. The tendency to assume female differences as "otherness," as something varying from an implicit norm of being.

This list is actually shorthand for many worries, and as such, blurs their complexity and overlap. Consider, for instance, the dubious assumption about the symmetry of gender difference. Underlying much of the research that takes for granted the binary of male and female is the belief that the dichotomy balances two unlike but comparable phenomena. Through this tacitly held symmetry "classic gender-role theorists have portrayed male and female roles as opposite, complementary, reciprocal, and equal" (Hare-Mustin and Marecek 1990b, 185–86). Buried or forgotten in this assumption are the actual hierarchical relations between masculine and feminine roles and their interdependence in ongoing social relations. Also closeted are functionalist assumptions about the individual's relations to social institutions: the symmetrical polarity subsumes ideals of social stability and consensus in social organizations, such as the family, and neglects the basic gendering of these very functions and ideals (Stacey and Thorne 1985). The symmetry of the gender dichotomy presumes that gender is *two*-something, obscuring awareness of how gender experiences are multiple. Individuals may have multiple and incongruent experiences and understandings of their assigned gender, and the meanings attached to gender may vary across social groups, situations, and times.

The false symmetry of gender constructs flies in the face of generally recognized dyssymetries and a history of valuing one gender over the other. Deconstruction has provided one means of examining the preferential and hierarchical structure of binaries, showing how language veils both the interdependence of ostensibly oppositional terms and the absence of any essences underlying those terms (Poovey 1988; Rabine 1988). Without seeing how the assumed symmetry of gender difference hides an interdependence of the terms, masks unequal social practices and experiences, and sustains hierarchical relations, those researchers who seek to celebrate gender difference, often to extol feminine characteristics, fail to see the double edge of difference: the other side of celebrating difference and symmetry is the invocation of essentialist claims, the reinforcement of denigrating stereotypes, and the underestimation of gender inequities built into social structures (Jaggar 1990).

Whereas male and female operate as one binary pair in models of gender difference, the term *difference* has been identified as one pole in another commonly held dichotomy of difference-equality. The dualism is evident in psychological research, for instance, just as caring and responsibility are seen as complementing justice styles of moral decision making, so these supposed gender-related styles are taken to be unequal. Just as verbal ability is seen as a skill symmetrical to math ability, so these abilities are taken to be unequal. And just as the cycling brain, with its surges of hormone production is taken to complement the non-cycling brain, so these gendered organisms come to be seen as unequal.

Deploying deconstruction and critical or historical analysis, feminist scholars have challenged the truth and universality of this dichotomy. The binary of difference-equality actually is nonoppositional.

Joan Scott (1988) has traced the historical and political circumstances whereby "difference was substituted for inequality, the appropriate antithesis of equality, becoming inequality's explanation and legitimation" (43). The historically confected opposition forces an "impossible choice" (43): Choosing difference means surrendering equality and choosing equality means rejecting difference. Once the historical picture of equality is sketched, it becomes apparent that equality arguments have begun with, and have depended on, a prior recognition of differences, but the difference-equality dualism denies this past political theorizing. However, to substitute a difference-sameness binary for the faulty difference-equality one, invites other problems. Difference-sameness can only be understood in the specific context of *what* qualities are being compared. Even then, the difference-sameness polarity not only collapses women's experiences into the normative (male) template but also masks the diversity of women's experiences.

For feminist psychologists (many of whom are already wary of the very project of difference research), critiques of difference-equality and difference-sameness, along with those of the assumed symmetry of gender, might appear to erode all available theory avenues. However, the way out may not mean reinstating one option over the other, but rather, refusing to use these dichotomies. Scott (1988) has recommended that these dichotomies be replaced by investigations of *differences* that challenge the dualities while still enabling study of how differences operate through individual and group identities. Such investigations disrupt the assumed oppositions and help reveal the hierarchical arrangements perpetuated through them. Alison Jagger (1990) also has argued for ongoing critical analyses of the polar terms, not through a new category but through strategies based on a politics of location in which circumstances determine which terms should be used: "Sometimes equality in outcome may be served best by sex-blindness, sometimes by sex-responsiveness—and sometimes by attention to factors additional to or other than sex" (253). For Jagger, the opportunity to construct understandings that transcend gendered, Western oppositions must await a more hospitable social environment. Until then, it is necessary to use dynamic and context-specific strategies to investigate the historical nature of differences and perceptions of them. Taken together, these strategies begin with refusal to proceed further with normative terms and the questions they invite—a refusal to engage restricting and sometimes dangerous narratives—and instead move forward by studying the multiplicity of differences, within and between individuals—an exploration ever alert to record the social and political conditions attending these differences. Here again, as in the examination of analytic categories, conventional psychology procedures for studying a variety of differences fall short of what is needed. They fail to permit scrutiny of the politics underlying the assumption of existing differences, and they are too tightly bound by orthodox methods to allow for the necessary diverse investigative strategies; difference thus remains located within individuals and connected to larger normative models.

Situations, Processes, and Performances

Critical awareness of the problems associated with difference research and the core categories of sex and gender has led some feminist psychologists to wholesale reconceptualizations. Rather than assuming gender to be an attribute or something-ness of individuals, it also can be seen as an effect, a situational occurrence, a social process, or a performance. Both Bernice Lott (1985) and Barbara Wallston (1981) have suggested viewing gender-linked behaviors in their socially specific contexts. Lott has urged attention to the antecedents and correlates of these behaviors, arguing that "it is not sex that matters but those life conditions that are systematically related to it by cultural prescription, regulation, or arrangement" (162). Similarly, Kay Deaux and Brenda Major (1987) have proposed that gender is a "component of ongoing interactions" (369) and that multiple influences such as expectancies, self-schema, and situational forces "account for the variable appearance of sex differences" (370). These proposals afford several promising moves. They enable investigation of how "one is not a woman all of the time" (Riley 1988), or the "now you see them, now you don't" feature of gender effects (Unger 1989b). They allow more substantial analysis of social conditions and groupings other than gender, and although still informed by classic psychological tenets that warrant further scrutiny, they nevertheless resonate with other studies that abandon such premises.

These situational models signal a shift away from gender-as-fixed-attribute, but they do not abandon that notion entirely. The models still stipulate the subject as individual with all the conceptual baggage attached, and generally reduce gender phenomena to the individual level. Gender is yet a cognitive variable, whether it is located in the head of the perceiver or the object of perception (the target subject). As Rhoda Unger (1983) has warned, "A focus on events that take place 'inside one's head' may also make it easier to ignore external realities that are not under the person's control" (23). For these reasons, working with a situational or context-sensitive model can actually eclipse consideration of material conditions and social power. And as long as such models proceed with a reductionist individualism, the efforts to include other factors or to tap variations among women and their experiences will result in research where these factors, too, are psychologized and translated into conventional categories like race and class (Squire 1989).

Another but related reformulation of gender views cultural and situational conditions not as codeterminents of gender and gender-linked behaviors but as the very material of gender. That is, gender is a process of social relations, a complex and ongoing performance. From an ethnomethodological perspective, Suzanne Kessler and Wendy McKenna (1978) have argued that gender is constructed through social interaction and the routine use of socially shared everyday rules for naming and explaining experience. The existence of two genders (or sexes), then, is a social accomplishment. Candace West and Don Zimmerman (1987) have advanced a similar theory that views gender as a routine accomplishment, one constituted through ongoing interactions. Rather than holding to an assumption that gender is a property of individuals, it is seen as emerging from social relations. Gender is taken both "as an outcome of and a rationale for various social arrangements and as a means of legitimating one of the most fundamental divisions of society" (126). Drawing on a very different theoretical tradition, that of object relations, Jane Flax (1990) has offered a compatible theory of gender as social relations that, like the other theories, begins by granting that even "our concepts of biology and nature are rooted in social reality" (25). Where Flax's theory departs most notably from the others cited here is its psychoanalytic focus on the impact of early-life social relations.

Understanding gender as performative—as constituted through ongoing social relations—affords a way out of several impasses posed by more classically psychological, individualist, and reductionist frameworks. First, shifting from internal mechanisms and an "indoor psychology" to external mechanisms and an "outdoor psychology" (Genova 1988) ordains investigation not just of immediate, local, and idiosyncratic forces, but also, historical, pervasive, and repeating forces on the constitution of gender and the meanings rendered through it. Once these "institutional" processes are no longer psychologized or reified, we can better detect means for social change (West and Zimmerman 1987). Second, a performative model escapes the conventional assumptions about subjectivity and their consequential homogeneous concept of woman (or man). As Flax (1990) observed, gender "is a social relationship that is both independent and autonomous from and at the same time shaped by other social relations such as race and economic status" (25). Finally, this perspective permits us to continue studying gender as a category of thought, and to examine how it operates through language via metaphors and other symbols to structure cognition at every point of experience from epistemology to common-sense.

A performative or relational theory of gender is not without hazards. Most crucial of these are the connections made between the enactments of gender and subjectivity. Theories invoking the cultural foundations of gender tend toward a determined view, one where gender is not fixed by nature but by culture (Butler, 1990a). The active subject is lost, or at least subjectivity comes to be flattened and mechanical, leaving no simple way to explain resistance, rebellion, or subversion. A person's compliance with or participation in gender-forming processes thus can become indistinguishable from his or her self as an agent (Unger 1989b). Perhaps excepting psychoanalytic variations of this theory, like Flax's and the model recently proposed by Maureen Mahoney and Barbara Yngvesson (1992), these theories ultimately contain no explanation of how experiences in social relations affect the formation of subjective identity, of a person's sense of self.

The matters of agency and subject formation are not grounds for abandoning relational or performative approaches, but they do indicate the need for more detailed work. One solution entails positing "gender consciousness" as something that is "based on gender awareness but goes beyond the descriptive attributions to a recognition of the rights and obligations associated with being female or male" (Gerson and Peiss 1985, 325). This postulate (one open to further exploration) sees consciousness as produced through an individual's location in a historically specific gender system, and shaped by the kinds of negotiations and concerns available in that system. Judith Gerson and Kathy Peiss have distinguished several types of gender consciousness. Among them is "feminist consciousness," which is identifiable by an articulated challenge to dominant gender systems, adoption of a shared collective identity, and engagement in organized responses. Subjectivity or consciousness can be investigated by attending to how boundaries of gender relations are negotiated, defended, and altered. Another route toward resolving problems of subjectivity is one that regards the subject as plural and partial, as subjectivities (rather than a subjectivity) coalescing in specific locations with specific identities. As we have seen, this avenue still skirts the ultimate issues of agency and self-consciousness, for it also produces a political absence that further blocks "the quest to find ways to construct self and identity that are oppositional and liberatory" (hooks, 1990, 29).

The problems of connecting social relations with subjectivity, and with finding some explanation of agency and empowerment, are tremendous ones, yet they are precisely what feminist psychologists must confront. Needed is a notion of subject as both constituted and constituting, one where the internal world is not divided categorically from the external one, and where self-consciousness, however fragmented or revisable, can be located. One viable starting point might be to document those expressions of subjectivity that are not typically catalogued in conventional psychological research and that yield clues to the constructive yet more subversive dimensions of subjectivity. Following this strategy, Michele Fine and Linda Gordon (1989) have advocated a project of distinguishing between what women do *traditionally* (which is usually what psychologists investigate traditionally) and what women do *subversively* (which is usually not what psychologists study). Taking a somewhat different approach, Rhoda Unger (1989b) has proposed a project of interrogating social *paradoxes,* both the paradoxes that ensue from contradictory theories, like realist and constructionist ones, but also those of everyday life. Determining how these paradoxes form, and how individuals endure or transform them, provides further understanding of subjectivity, possibly including its own paradoxes. Thus, although the theoretical problem is substantial, there already exists a repertoire of strategies for working on it.

Power

Circulating around and sometimes through formulations of gender (as well as those of subjectivity) are matters of power. Carolyn Sherif (1982) called for gender as a social category including an understanding of how the gendered asymmetry of power relations is incorporated into identity. Mary Parlee (1979) concluded a synoptic review essay on psychology and women with a similar call for addressing the play of social power. Despite these and other comparable invitations, and despite substantial research using power as a variable, feminist psychology has not yet systematically addressed the matter of power.

The fact that power remains unfinished business is no surprise given that psychology itself has produced no concept of power comprehensive enough to be utilized or even refashioned. In a provocative review of feminist psychology and power, Celia Kitzinger (1991a) documented the poverty and naivete of the discipline's understandings of power. In feminist psychology, power is usually absent, or nominally present as bland rhetoric. When power is more actively studied, whether in feminist psychology in particular or feminist theory in general, it is depicted in simplistic typologies. At times power is taken to be "bad," or is divided into "bad" and "good" forms; at other times it is seen as neutral and accessible to everyone. Without clear definitions, Kitzinger found that feminist researchers tend to configure women either as "powerless" or "powerful." The first approach poses women as incapable agents and continually risks reinstating the victimization of women, whereas the second poses women as personally empowered and risks a psychologizing of power. The former approach, powerlessness, depends on a passive subject, yet hides a tacit assumption that if women could just understand their oppression, they would be empowered and free. The latter approach, powerfulness, depends on an agentic self, and conveys the idea that other (structural) sources of power are relatively insignificant. In either case power is fashioned only as an individualistic property, variable, or asset.

The virtue of Kitzinger's analysis (1991a) is twofold: It connects notions of subjectivity with theories of power and introduces an option. That alternative is informed by Foucault's theory of power as productive force, as unstable and changing, but is modified by a feminist reluctance to accept the arbitrariness of power purported in Foucault's model (Bleier 1984; Bordo 1990a; Hartsock 1990). With this in mind, power is not simply oppressive "but rather promotes, cultivates and nurtures (particular types of) identity. Power is not a force which acts on people from the outside, at a distance: it is intimately involved in the construction of the individual and her sense of selfhood" (Kitzinger 1991a, 124).

The idea that power is productive and facilitative raises exciting possibilities for theorizing gender and subjectivity, but it also prompts concerns about power as it applies to our own professional practices. As discussed earlier in the chapter, psychology has served human governing in the broadest sense: The objects, techniques and knowledge of psychology help sustain, regulate, and control society. Dorothy Smith's account of the practices of sociology holds at least equally for those of psychology: "They perform a work of ruling" (1987a, 152). Not only do our *theories* of gender possess a tacit politics of power and subjectivity, but the *discipline* "as a whole is deeply implicated in the maintenance and reproduction of power relationships" (Kitzinger 1991a, 111). Thus, figuring power more centrally into gender theories must have as its parallel a critical awareness of power in our science and how our investigative practices are themselves accomplishments of power.

In summary, this visitation of the lumpy ground of gender theory has been a necessarily extended one, for feminist psychology has as its primary focus the analysis of gender. Reviewing errors in previous work helps orient the task of reshaping our central constructs and theories, a revitalization assisted by the advances of feminist work outside the discipline. Several lessons for future practices emerge from the review. Our working constructs must be severed from those psychological paradigms and techniques that repeatedly push us back to an unexamined individualism with its attendant story of an independent, autonomous, and (nearly) rational subject. Our work needs to be similarly released from a language that establishes gender as a natural phenomenon, one that is bipolar, symmetrical, and stable in form. Instead, gender must be understood as historical, relational, and contextual in its manifestations. We must better articulate the relations between subjectivity (or identity) and gender, as well as those between subjectivity, gender, and power. Finally, we must be ever ready to look back on our practices as *political* and continually assess how theorizing, and research practices generally, are productive elements in gender and gender experiences.

Work Ahead: Consciousness and Social Structures

Rethinking the construct of gender has yielded a more sophisticated analytic framework, facets of which already can be seen in much feminist psychology. However, these reconstructive efforts have made even more apparent our lack of sophistication in analyzing two other domains: subject awareness (consciousness) and social structure. While the cautious modifications of gender constructs have intimated the importance of attending to subject awareness and social structure, our understanding of these notions remains vague and uneven, sometimes contradicting other core features of our investigative labors.

This chapter began by reviewing studies that affirmed the need to understand subjectivity in terms of historical, economic, and political conditions—in more general cultural terms—but that simultaneously documented psychology's apparent inability to incorporate these conditions into formal models or theories. Throughout the last century psychologists have explained certain psychological phenomena, occasionally gender-related ones, as partially (sometimes fully) caused by social structural forces. Yet few researchers have gone beyond simply naming these forces "culture," "society," or "social." One result of this truncated explanatory tendency is the lurking persistence of what in another context Mark Seltzer (1987) has referred to as a "double discourse" whereby realist and naturalist accounts of human action, the dominant discourse in psychology, are accompanied by accounts of human action as social, or constructed within social environments.

The introduction of feminist studies into psychology has neither resolved the inconsistencies of such double accounting nor generated a clearer concept of social structure. Feminist studies has a central interest in the structures of power, especially as they determine women's oppression. On this issue, however, feminist studies also bears the stamp of its multidisciplinary origins by employing what appears to be a hodgepodge of models on the structuring of power, from Marxism to psychoanalysis, and from semiotics to cultural studies (Franklin, Lury, and Stacey 1991).

The feminist psychological examination of social structure is thus twice complicated, by psychology's underdeveloped renditions and by the heterogeneity of feminist approaches. The complications further escalate once we address the status of subject consciousness and its articulation with, or relation to, social-structural conditions. To argue that subjectivity is a historical product, as was done earlier in the chapter, moves us beyond abstract individualism and mentalist formulas. To note that persons do not always report the full extent of their conscious experiences, as was proposed in the previous chapter, reminds us that experiences and the study of those experiences are complex undertakings. After these points, however, we are left with little guidance. Here again the last century of psychological science hardly brings clarity to the matter. Its double discourse has claimed, on the one hand, that whether observing behavior or mentation, subjects can not adequately report on their experiences and, on the other hand, specifically trained observers can make accurate accounts of that experience. This dualist claim is not necessarily contradictory, as shall be suggested in the following interchapter, but nevertheless poses more questions than answers about conscious experiences and about how to study them. Left unresolved is the matter, raised in the critical analyses of gender, of how a subjectivity can at once be constituted through particular cultural conditions, and be capable of refusing both that consciousness and those conditions. Also left unexplained are how varied structures of power, with their intersecting oppressions of racism, sexism, heterosexism, etc., result in differences in consciousness, both differences between subcultures and among members within those subcultures.

Despite the noted handicaps bestowed on feminist psychologists, we nevertheless remain in an opportune position to explore the workings of conscious experiences and articulate the constitutive influence of the structures of power, or culture. The conceptual confusion that is our legacy for contemplating consciousness and culture can be an advantage, and several investigative routes already taken begin to illustrate the kind of opportunities available. However, before noting some of these routes it is essential to note if it is not already apparent, that future work will demand theory choices, including decisions that have been suspended in much feminist psychology. Most important is first locating the dynamics of consciousness, specifically the degree of people's subjective awareness of the origins of their experiences and what constrains and enables them, and second, determining the constitution of the social world, notably how it structures or mediates those experiences. To date, feminist psychologists have largely defined these theoretical constructs by using the terms available through cognitive psychology and behaviorism; while these systems are insufficient to the tasks that lie ahead, we have yet to explore other systems, such as psychoanalysis and cultural studies, which may afford more comprehensive formulas.

The necessity of studying such theory options notwithstanding, researchers have pursued investigations that illuminate some of the conditions of subject consciousness and structural conditions. These include study of (1) the moments and contours of resistance and compliance; (2) characteristics of the oppressor's consciousness and not just the oppressed; and (3) the multiple forces playing in the conscious experiences of oppressed persons. The first line of investigation is a crucial step toward clarifying the aforementioned problem of understanding certain persons as oppressed and simultaneously assuming that they can or do have experiential grounds for challenging and changing that injustice. Work on this problem sometimes focuses on the situations in which women conform (Towson, Zanna and MacDonald 1989), or internalize dominant and oppressive ideologies (Crosby and Clayton 1990). Other studies have documented some of the factors affecting successful resistance to discriminatory forces in situations ranging from the attainment of feminist consciousness (Kalmuss, Gurin, and Townsend 1981) to recovery from sexist ordeals such as sexual abuse (Herman, Russell, and Trocki 1986). The second research route, examination of the subjectivity of oppressors, ranges from documenting real oppressive orientations, such as men's inclination to rape (Russell 1988), to simulating oppressors' behavioral tendencies (Frable, Blackstone, and Scherbaum 1990). The third avenue involves assessing the macro- and microstructures of oppression, identifying the multiple sites in which dominance is realized. As illustrated in the case of research on gay and lesbian experience, such investigations probe the experiences of everyday discrimination and its effects on self-awareness (Shuster 1991), and go further to locate historical and institutional forces, including psychology and psychological theorizing, which serve not simply to perpetuate bias but to create oppression and the experiences of the oppressed (Minton 1986; Sedgwick 1991; Terry 1990).

Such inclusive scrutiny provides the foundation for alternative theorizing of consciousness and resistance (Cohen 1991; Ellsworth 1988; Reiter 1989).

These three paths do not exhaust the investigative opportunities to deliberate central constructs surrounding consciousness and social structure. Yet they elucidate how, moving beyond the confines of gender categorization, we can explore the operations of consciousness and locate factors that mediate its expression.

A Note on Methods

The directives for reformulating gender categories and the discussion of several promising research ventures omit detailed consideration of methods. The shortcomings of orthodox research techniques (notably classic experimentation) as a means of interrogating the multidimensions, cultural conditions, and contradictions attending subjectivity have long been noted by psychologists both inside and outside the feminist community (Carlson 1972; Gergen 1973; Harré and Secord 1972; Lykes and Stewart 1986; Mishler 1979; Riger 1992; Wallston 1981). Critics and users of conventional methods alike have documented these limitations and advocated, at the least, an auxiliary program deploying other methods. The most common appeal has been for the increased use of qualitative methods, particularly those that are responsive to contextual features, realize the complexity of the subject's reasoning, and require greater participation of the researcher.

In most cases, the methods that are sensitive to the dynamics of subjectivity and the intersubjective relations of participant and investigator rely on an assumed complementarity of quantitative and qualitative research—of hard/soft, wet/dry, agentic/communal, and perhaps most importantly, objective/subjective. In other words, they argue that *both* types of research should be used (McHugh, Koeske, and Frieze 1986; Riger 1992; Wallston 1981). This methodological doubleness is a strategy, a tactic for altering normative practices while maintaining a respectable foothold in the dominant sites of research. Through this double mission, new, less acceptable practices are protected by those who conduct business-as-usual. Yet, given the ubiquity of the normative ideas about the subject and subjectivity, and given the dependence of a mixed-method agenda on oppositional distinctions between the objective and subjective worlds, this strategy may be only temporarily successful. The dual program might finally *reconfirm* rather than *test* the boundaries of objective science, especially the lines between the objective and subjective and the radically different notions of subjectivity accorded to researcher and participant respectively. In the end, it might well retain the subject as a "purely psychological entity" (Squire 1989). The dual program likewise reproduces the gendered quality of the boundaries that associates the hard and objective with male, and the soft and qualitative with female, and consequently tends to exacerbate gender stereotypes *and* perpetuate the field's history of relegating low-status work to women (Squire 1989).

The simple strategy of dual methods, then, unless accompanied by other critical work, sustains undesirable scientific tenets and restricts the reconstruction of gender and subjectivity. However, at this particular moment there are no viable alternatives, and unless this tactical route is taken, feminist psychology appears to be at an impasse. Nevertheless, rather than continue this work blind to its pitfalls, or relinquish all hope for feasible methods, we can proceed with critical awareness of when we must comply and when we can diverge. Feminist psychologists can proceed with a *politics of position* through which we remain alert to the specific historical place being occupied: Our interventions thus will depend on knowing "the strategies and spaces of its adversaries in order to undermine their positions within an overall system" (Gross 1986; 197). And by combining a politics of position with the sort of *identity positioning* discussed in the chapter on objectivity, we can continue a dual-faceted research strategy, staying ever mindful of where we stand and where we cannot afford to stand. As Toby Jayaratne and Abigail Stewart (1991) found, such mindfulness also highlights the procedures and objectives that are common to qualitative and quantitative methods.

An active politics of location and identity enables feminist psychologists to avoid the potentially freezing effects of the inconsistencies, contradictions, and paradoxes in our research. It also makes obvious the partiality of strategic practices: No single study or program of studies can erase the governing metaphysics of subjectivity or correct all the inadequacies of contemporary gender theory. But if seen as specific interventions operating to disrupt or displace one or another of these pervasive conventions, our studies are significant.

Experiments with revising how we think about subjectivity require small, repeated, and diverse undertakings. And although qualitative research remains marked as feminine and may reinforce the binary of objectivity/subjectivity, its use may shift, however minutely, the grounds for theorizing subjectivity. Several examples of such discerning expeditions into subjectivity illustrate their varied tactics and their emerging revisions of subjectivity.

Contours of Subjectivity

The overarching interest in this chapter, one curiously enough shared by poststructuralists, feminist scholars, and culture critics alike, is the desire to understand what constitutes subjectivity, how it is structured, and how we can talk about it. Once it is accepted that subjectivity can no longer be uncritically taken as an emergent, universal quality of human nature, but must be examined as a historically and culturally determined one, we still need specific knowledge about how subjectivity is determined and how that theory can accommodate human agency or self-making.

One promising approach to these questions lies with narrative studies, a cluster of investigations taking narrative to be a "cultural tool kit" (Bruner 1991) or "cognitive instrument" (Mink 1978) in the construction, representation, and interpretation of experience. Narrative studies warrant no single form of data or methodology. The materials available for analysis encompass (but are not limited to) autobiography, speeches, myths, and fictional and nonfictional texts, whereas viable methods range along a continuum from detailed quantification to descriptive interpretation. Narrative studies originated in no single discipline and with no single group of intellectuals, although most of its major proponents are self-identified skeptics of classical empiricism and realism.

Narrative studies present a bulky package of possibilities for the study of subjectivity. First and foremost, narratives can be the mediations between individual actions and material and social-structural conditions: Their analysis has enabled viewing the relation of individuals to society as a *dynamics* of ongoing constructions, negotiations, and interpretations. Narratives also are a means of constituting reality as well as a means of representing it, and therefore, permit investigation of how agents make and remake their world. However, narrative studies do not prefigure agency and social structure but rather illuminate the ongoing negotiations of their boundaries, specifically how identity is understood as an acceptance, suspiciousness, challenge, or refusal of societal norms and strictures. Although the subjectivities locatable through narratives are to some extent self-making, since it is argued that "some measure of agency is always present in narrative" (Bruner 1991, 7), agency can also be understood as a cultural product, one shaped by the available narrative forms themselves. Finally, narrative studies depend on a reconstructing of the relationship between investigator and participant, for they force consideration of the relative power of both parties, the ubiquity of reflection, and the essential partiality of any information. Narrative analysis reveals research relationships to be ones of coconstruction where, for instance, context is considered "from the standpoint of the subject of the personal narrative, as well as from the standpoint of the interpreter's analysis" (Personal Narratives Group 1989, 12). There now exists extensive literature that addresses these multiple features of narrative studies (Agar 1980; Bruner 1991; Mishler 1986; Personal Narratives Group 1989; Polkinghorne 1988; Riessman 1993; Sandelowski 1991; Sarbin 1986; White 1980).

Feminist investigators have long been interested in self-accounts, reports on reality produced by the participant, and have found in narrative studies a means of tracing the development of gendered self-identity. Because of the distinct cultural position of women as others, narratives by women usually are complicated by gender dynamics. The narratives "are, among other things, stories of how women negotiate their 'exceptional' gender status both in their daily lives and over the course of a lifetime" (Personal Narratives Group 1989, 5). Narrative studies of women's lives have articulated the culturally and specially gendered templates available for making sense of one's life (Quinn 1987; Wiersma 1988), and the complex ways in which one sometimes simultaneously accepts and rejects social norms (Ginsburg 1989; Helson 1989). In addition to generating dynamic concepts of subjectivity, narrative analysis has been employed to delineate gendered life structures and even to enhance classroom pedagogy (Howe 1989).

Two specific examples illustrate how narrative studies, broadly defined, enhance an understanding of subjectivity and focus on both the diversity of subjective forms and the less visible, sometimes subversive, dimensions of gendered lives. The first study locates the diversities and commonalities of gendered experience at a particular historical moment while maintaining critical reflection on the investigator's interpretations and forms of telling. Marcia Wright (1989) compared the biography of Christina Sibiya, a Zulu woman born in 1900 who married a tribal king, and the autobiography of Mary Leahey, a European woman, born in 1913 who married a celebrated archaeologist and lived most of her life in Africa. With scrupulous attention to the differences in these women's lives, Wright demonstrated how they negotiated their specific gender constraints and identity. Their connection with powerful men and "dynastic" families led both women "to become campaigners bent upon assuring the legitimacy and good name of the family," but who, nevertheless, were able to develop their own claims and forms of resistance late in life (169).

The narratives of Christina Sibiya and Mary Leahey tell of subjectivities formed within particular social-structural constraints and whose personal identities were claimed late in adulthood. However, in order to make this comparison the concept of dynasty "had to be brought from outside the texts and the consciousness of the narrators" (Wright 1989, 169). This analytic step permits seeing how women's views of their lives sometimes retain ideologically persisting ways "of framing their roles as reproducers of cultures as well as the biological sense" (169). Such analysis also underscores the difficulties of bringing new interpretations to the narratives that the investigator must do in order to delineate broader structural constraints on the formation of identities.

The second example is a study of ten women's written appraisals of satisfaction with their lives. Using an open-ended method of data collection, but one more systematic than most biographical or autobiographical studies, Abigail Stewart and Janet Malley (1989) first analyzed the "life structures" of these women and then enumerated the varying experiences of these structures. Life structures were defined as patterns of living that are "partly defined by women's choices themselves and partly defined by unintended consequences' of choices" (62). Stewart and Malley selected women whose life structures varied in terms of marriage, paid employment, and motherhood and used the conceptual categories of *agency* and *communion* to analyze the women's responses. However, these two constructs were found to be insufficient for studying these women's lives. Women may also enact *indirect* or *vicarious agency* where they work toward goals for others, feeling with it some gratification yet some misgivings, and they experience *asymmetrical communion* where one member of an intimate relationship, often the woman, provides more empathy and giving than the other. Stewart and Malley thus postulated that a balance of modalities is optimal for well-being, and they found that the analyzed life structures differed in the forms and amounts of agency and communion available through them. For instance, the reported experiences of single women without children reflected a dissatisfaction with the prevalence of the agentic modality while those of the married working women with children indicated difficulties in balancing multiple modalities.

Stewart and Malley (1989) applied distinct psychological categories to these women's accounts yet succeeded in demonstrating various structurings with varied effects on identity and personal experience. They altered the categories, and further indicated how other structural conditions, notably material resources and education, permitted these women a latitude of choice about their life structures that, in turn, shaped their experiences of satisfaction. The authors emphasized the need to study women who had fewer choices available, those for whom life structures are relatively determined. And although not part of the study, Stewart and Malley's analysis could be extended to explore how subjectivities are shaped not only by the specific sets of life structures but also by cultural expectations that force the realization of certain patterns at certain times, i.e., the cultural forces behind the ideal of "super-mom" or of the "career women" of the 1980s and 90s.

Agency and Subjectivity

Investigations of the historical, cultural, and psychological structures of subjectivity ultimately push toward the issues of agency, self-awareness, or identity. A sense of self may be a life-long endeavor, as illustrated in Wright's comparison, or it may be attached to experiences of satisfaction and choice, as seen in Stewart and Malley's analyses. Yet neither of those studies focuses on the specific connections between cultural conditions and subjective experience, particularly gendered experience. They need to be joined with accounts of how subjectivity, or identity, is formed within particular life worlds, and with determinations of how there can emerge agents capable of challenging or refusing (as well as conforming to) the very structures in which they are situated.

Given the aforementioned difficulties in developing a theory of subjectivity, the best approach may not be to hypothesize or theorize a single, monolithic theory. Instead, perhaps the only feasible purchase entails working from diverse concrete situations and with multiple techniques for visualizing subjectivity. Margaret Sandelowski's multilayered investigations of infertility in women stands as a notable example of this plural approach. In a series of studies viewing infertility from different experimental, social, historical, and economic angles, Sandelowski and her collaborators represent subjectivity as constructed through a variety of social relations and cultural conditions and which, at various moments, can be situated within the repetitions and cul-de-sacs of life's structures, or can act through and sometimes against those structures.

One facet of these studies of infertility involves the use of grounded theory and open-ended interviews. The technique of grounded theory requires a recursive process whereby investigators use initial data to construct theoretical propositions that then guide further data collection and so on; the process is a continuing one whereby assessment methods, data collection, verification, and theorizing are routinely modified (Sandelowski, Harris, and Holditch-Davis 1989). With these techniques, Sandelowski and her colleagues were able to document previously unknown features of identity and social processes and chart the complexities, changes, and contradictions in women's experiences of infertility. Women who confront the possibility or reality of infertility develop not a sense of changed or impaired identity as much as the sense of an *ambiguous* one: They are caught in a space of not knowing why not, or if, they could become pregnant, if the treatments they undertook would work or even should be attempted, and if they were responsible for their infertility (Sandelowski 1987). The ambiguity of self is not simply an internal experience of conflict and vacillating identity but is realized in the styles of decision making and social exchanges. Understanding the choices and perceptions of choices available to infertile women necessitates study of the social and material conditions that frame those choices and grant responsibility for them to the infertile woman.

That is, given the culturally produced association between infertility and women's liberation, and given the new medical technologies for assisting reproduction, infertility is coming to be seen in terms of freedom and choice, and infertile women are then placed in a dilemma of choice: "If women are now viewed as unconsciously or inadvertently choosing infertility and then regretting it, they are also, not surprisingly, viewed as choosing, even demanding to be cured of it" (Sandelowski 1986, 446). Their options are either to accept infertility, and with it a nonnormative social status in our culture, or to submit to treatments (if they can afford to), which are costly, time-consuming, and not guaranteed. Although these are presented as individual choices, ones attributing certain characteristics to the chooser's identity, in actuality they are structured by powerful social forces including pronatalism, technology and its costs, and the medicalization of life. Social exchanges as well as identity are affected because the infertile woman finds all her social exchanges different, especially with other women, and constructs new rules for social interaction as means to negotiate her sense of isolation and the ambivalence of the exchanges.

These studies of the experiences and choices of infertile women relocate identity not as *fixed* or somehow *damaged* (as is the case in most psychological studies where infertility is viewed as crisis, grieving, pathology, or a stressor) but rather as a *process*. Conception itself is not a fixed act or event; instead, for women undergoing medical treatment, it is a process of "dichotomous and continuous pregnancies with and without babies, embryos with and without pregnancies, in-body and out-of-body pregnancies, and pregnant-like bodies with and without either pregnancies or babies" (Sandelowski, Harris, and Holditch-Davis 1990, 279). Not all of these identity processes and choices are experienced alone; decisions about options are often done by couples, in which cases agency is collective, social relations are complex, and decision making is multilayered and sometimes in simultaneous pursuit of multiple goals (Sandelowski, Harris and Holditch-Davis 1989).

In studying the processes of identity formation and choice, Sandelowski's project attends to the cultural nature of infertility, not only the situation of infertile women as counter-culture and counter-nature, as standing outside cultural conventions and against some perceived natural state (Sandelowski 1988), but also as being situated within cultural contests over women's bodies and reproductive rights. Using historical analyses, Sandelowski (1990a) has charted a chronology of scientific understandings of infertility that, although varied in their causal explanations, nevertheless often attribute infertility to a failure of volition—to the shortcomings of female agency. Carrying this analysis forward to the present, Sandelowski also located vestiges of this volitional model in some feminist writings on infertility:

> When feminist critics argue that the infertile woman's motivation for a child is not really her own, they deny her autonomous will. When they suggest that she ought to fulfill her desire for children by adopting, they ignore the complex problems involved in adopting any kind of child. When they suggest that the infertile woman might be happier remaining child-free, they contradict the emphasis many feminists have increasingly placed on the importance of "natural" maternity. (1990b, 46)

If feminist examinations of infertility and reproductive technologies draw uncritically on individualistic notions of agency and crude ideas about biological and social determination, then infertile women will most likely continue to be seen as irrational and culpable agents fully responsible for their situations and decisions. The multiple methods employed by Sandelowski and her co-workers challenge the idea that subjectivity is either determined or fixed. These methods locate agency as emergent, transformative, and embedded in social processes that are as far ranging as intimate couplings, the construction of bodily experiences, relations between women, and the organization of medicine and technology.

Conclusion

Psychology has had everything to do with subjectivity: Its very existence has been to observe, describe and explain that peculiar element of the world. Although psychology has always been open to criticism from the outside, recent studies in various disciplines, from philosophy to cultural studies, have vigorously challenged its foundational tenets of subjectivity. Alongside these critiques has emerged speculative theorizing that casts subjectivity in a distinctly different light, replacing assumptions of autonomy, unity, and individualism with renderings of subjectivity as dynamic, multiple, fragmented, and sometimes contradictory.

Feminist investigators are especially committed to viewing subjectivity differently than as presupposed in the Western metaphysics that has bestowed psychology's model of the subject. Extensive studies of gender have indicated the need for a theory of subjectivity that not only accommodates pluralities and changeability but also captures the ways in which subjectivity is both structured through social practices and shaped by personal experiences. This theorizing also needs to make room for agency—whether in the form of compliance, reluctance, resistance, or subversion. Above all, these projects demand an appreciation of irony: as Kathy Ferguson has argued, "Irony allows contending thematizations of subjectivity to negotiate a political relationship that does not depend upon unanimity, consensus, or even majority agreement to any one metatheoretical stance" (1993, 157).

For feminist psychologists, forging a new theory of subjectivity can *never* be separated from constructing methods of inquiry. Just as conventional experimental methods both presume and impose certain claims about subjectivity, so will newer methods. Although the next interchapter addresses some of the connections between subjectivity and methods, it is at best a modest beginning. Feminist psychologists have opened not a Pandora's box but a vibrant if complex panorama of human relationships. Our progress depends on engaging, not avoiding, that complexity with all its identities, reflections, and entangled relations.

Interchapter

Reflexivity: Subject Positions

If only practical concerns continue to motivate the psychological research community, we may so alienate our current student subjects that as tax-paying adults they may simply stop supporting us.
—X. Coulter, "Academic Value of Research Participation by Undergraduates"

The fact is that people are agents . . . Until we accept the full implications of this conception of persons, our "subjects" will continue their gremlin-like behavior and so continue to bedevil our research efforts.
—R. O. Kroger and L. A. Wood, "Needed: Radical Surgery"

Philosophical and scientific renditions of subjects reviewed in the last chapter tell only part of the story about subjectivity and identity. The narrative of subjectivity or subjects in our science is always incomplete because modern psychology has proceeded with particular, and particularly foreclosed, notions of the subject. But the story is partial for another reason as well. Regardless of method or theoretical bent, psychologists are narrators and mediators of the psychological experiences of their objects of inquiry, their subjects, and this mediation of subjectivity gets revealed only selectively. Psychologists proceed not only with formal tenets of subjectivity but also with practical understandings of the subjects who do (or do not) enter the laboratories and who do (or do not) comply with instructions. Usually these understandings are tacit and rarely are they explicated in the official records of the science. As conveyed by the opening quotations, just as psychologists image subjects who are almost rational decision makers, so they also perceive subjects who have "tax-paying" or tuition-paying status and who can "bedevil our research efforts" in sometimes frustrating and even nefarious ways. We endow our subjects with considerably more attributes than those claimed in our theories and research reports. Because psychologists for the most part do not formally acknowledge such practical understandings, we know little about the ways in which they actually contribute to the more publicly visible accounts of subjectivity—investigative practices and products.

Reflexive analysis embraces the contents of both versions of subjects, the practical or parenthetical as well as the formal or public. For instance, once acknowledged, the comments on noncompliance reveal more than an objectified duality of subjectivity, they provide crude material for construing subjects and subjectivity in radically different ways. The capabilities of reactance, once removed from the shadows of scientific writing and instead seen as intrinsic to research relations, warrant a new dialogue about subjectivity. The preceding interchapter explored some of those very agentic and reflexive capabilities in observers; we turn now to extending those ideas to all research participants. Analyses of the observed and observers alike press the necessity of reappraising not only the *objective observer* and the *subjective object* of observation but also their very *relationships* and, hence, the arrangements of research practices. The last of these concerns is the major topic in this section, but the approach used is an intentionally indirect one. Instead of confronting, right off, the shortcomings of normative research arrangements, some practical representations of those arrangements must come first. Three rather ordinary accounts of the investigator-subject relationship are revisited in order to recover missing parts of the narrative of subjectivity, piece together more fully the relations of investigators and subjects, and then try to weave them back into the official and more public story. With this recovery, albeit itself partial, we can then move on to consider possible alternatives to or modifications of the social relations of research.

The Subject Speaks

Subject 1

When asked to participate in a psychological study of creativity, probably by psychologist Walter Dill Scott, the poet Amy Lowell promptly refused. She inscribed her *refusal* in poetic form unambiguously titled "To a Gentleman Who Wanted to See the First Drafts of My Poems in the Interest of Psychological Research into the Workings of the Creative Mind" (Lowell 1955). The poem proceeds, in equally unambiguous language, to condemn the incessant prying of research psychologists and to question their intentions. The first four stanzas are the most direct:

> So you want to see my papers, look what
>   I have written down
> 'Twixt an ecstasy and heartbreak, con
>   them over with a frown.
> You would watch my thought's green
>   sprouting ere a single blossom's blown.
>
> Would you, friend? And what should I
>   be doing, have you thought of that?
> It is pleasant, think you, being gazed
>   upon from feet to hat,
> Microscopically viewed by eyes com-
>   missioned just of that?
>
> Don't assure me that your interest does
>   not lie with me at all.
> I'm a poet to be dissected for the good
>   of science. Call
> It by any name, I feel like some old root
>   where fungi sprawl.
>
> Think you, I could make you see it, all
>   the little diverse strands
> Locked in one short poem? By no means
>   do I find your prying hands
> Pleasure bearing and delightful straying round
>   my lotus lands.
>
> (535)

Writing in the 1920s, Lowell borrowed the images, language, and emotion of science criticism of the period, thus charging psychology with invasiveness and destruction cloaked by the banner of "the good of science." Later in the poem Lowell probed the psychologist's intentions further: If he were to study a mad lover, to measure those foolish antics, would the psychologist not alter the lover's future and privilege scientific findings over the lover's close relations? In the end, Lowell refused the psychologist's request until death, and the poem concludes by inviting him to "come with spade and shovel when I'm safely in my tomb" (536).

Just as Lowell's proclamation borrows from an available cultural suspicion about science, so it also conveys a *wariness* commonly exhibited by those who are observed by expert others. In one sense, the poem stands as a rare instance where a psychological subject speaks without a scientist's editing or mediation. But in another sense, her refusal is already cast by prior understandings, both of science and of subjectivity, which she shares with the rebuffed psychologist. That is, Lowell readily placed the psychological subject in the role of object and plays on the tacit understandings of that role. She wrote, "If I did consent, to please you, I should tell you packs of lies" (Lowell 1955, 536). Although questioning the research relationship, the mutual understandings of observer and subject are not seriously endangered in Lowell's threat, rather, they are confirmed: It is because of shared cultural understandings that psychologists *and* their subjects can admit a tension between trust and deception in their roles. To announce a refusal to be vivisected likewise acknowledges the jointly known power inequities in psychologist-subject relations.

It needs to be remembered that Lowell was recalling the story not only as a subject, but perhaps more meaningfully from the position of a poet-narrator who stands somewhere *outside* the social tensions and confusions about which she wrote. Lowell's documentation does not make available the "raw voice" of subjectivity, yet it does represent one fairly common set of attitudes toward psychological research of the period. Early twentieth-century American psychology was one example of the new expertise that ordinary people simultaneously revered and doubted (Bledstein 1976; Haskell 1977) particularly as it introduced and institutionalized specific power differentials between psychologists and subjects. (One paradox of modern expertise is that this institutionalized relationship was frequently held suspect; for instance, the reliance on experts grew hand-in-hand with a distrust of that reliance.) Specifically, psychological research practices were "based on a profound differentiation of the roles of experimenter and subject. The former was supposed to have a monopoly on training and enlightenment, while the latter was to be untrained and naive" (Danziger 1979, 42). It was this unequal relation about which Lowell was wary and into which she ultimately refused to enter; in her account resistance is enacted rather than held in silence.

Subject 2

Another case of subject's accounting similarly reveals a subjectivity different from that officially represented in research records. As discussed in chapter 1, Josie's (the chimpanzee) response to the psychologists who studied her social behavior obviously was narrated by a human, Ruth Herschberger (1948). Thus, like Lowell's account, the Josie story is a self-consciously positioned narration by an outsider. In that story, the subject displays an awareness rarely granted to subjects in research situations. Josie was shown to be cognizant of experimental techniques, and this awareness is one that experimenters generally must remove or deny in order to perform their experimental operations and make claims about the subjectivity of the subject. Her detection of sloppy methods, her ability to render alternative interpretations, and her knowledge of the behavioral tendencies of humans intimate a subjectivity more rational and more learned than psychologists of the period generally acceded—to humans or nonhumans. Josie's account, or rather, Herschberger's essay, was in itself a form of *resistance* against the social relations of laboratory work and the knowledge it produced. And if the account were taken seriously, which at the time it was not, then the metaphysics of subjectivity attending most psychological research would need substantial revisioning as would the research methods and scientific authority. If Josie's telling (really a human's telling) reflected people's common knowledge about psychology, then it certainly would invalidate research as it is usually practiced. Herschberger's critique, like the early reports of experimental artifacts that (in a different way) also suggested that the subject's awareness was other than psychologists assumed it to be, was neglected; both kinds of reports indicated a *knowledgeability* and *resistance* of subjectivity that was disregarded for years afterward and often still goes unattended (Suls and Rosnow 1988).

Subject 3

In 1972 Sidney Jourard published a letter ostensibly written by a subject (S) to an experimenter (E). In that correspondence, S expressed a wariness and refusal (found in Lowell's poem) and a knowledgeability and resistance (recounted by Herschberger). S described how he/she was subjected to boring and possibly pointless tasks in experiments. S was perturbed about this subjugation that he/she recognized as coercion: "What's in it for me? Sometimes you pay me to serve. More often I have to serve, because I'm a student in a beginning psychology course, and I'm told that I won't receive a grade unless I take part in at least two studies . . ." (Jourard 1972, 11). Here S's distrust moves beyond that of Lowell: Not only is *coercion* an issue but so also is *deceit*.

> When I've asked what I'll get out of your studies, you tell me that, "It's for Science." When you are running some one particular study, you often lie to me about your purpose. You mislead me. It's getting so I find it difficult to trust you. I'm beginning to see you as a trickster, a manipulator. I don't like it. (11)

S is leery of E's ultimate interests, fearing that the line, "for the good of science" is really a cover and that E is "studying me in order to learn how to influence my attitudes and my actions without my realizing it" (12). S recounted enough technical information to indicate knowledgeability about experimental settings and relations, and he/she resisted both psychologists' experimental explanations of his/her behavior in a specific study, and post-experimental explanations as well. As he/she insisted, "Now look, Mr. *E.*, I'm not 'paranoid,' as you might say. Nor am I stupid" (12).

S's letter repeats the criticisms of the earlier two subject reports, but does so with a spirit of cynicism and conspiracy common to late 1960s social critiques. The letter also embraces a paradox of that period whereby conspiratory accountings often coincided with optimistic desires for freedom and personal enhancement. In keeping with that zeitgeist, S concluded the letter by proposing a new research contract that would be designed according to different concepts of subjectivity. And in that plan S renewed his/her dependence on expert knowledge: he/she asked to learn more about himself/herself, about ways to be freer and develop "potentialities." The request itself preserves certain canonical assumptions about subject and observer, notably about the subject's dependence on the observer. In essence, the contract is not so radical as one would imagine given S's social critique of psychologists and their practices.

> I'll make a bargain with you. You show me that you are doing your researches *for me*—to help me become freer, more self-understanding, better able to control *myself*—and I'll make myself available to you in any way you ask. And I won't play jokes and tricks on you. I don't want to *be controlled,* not by you or anyone else. And I don't want to control other people. I don't want you to help other people to understand how I am or can be "controlled," so that they can then control me. Show me that you are for me, and I will show *myself* to you. (13)

S resisted the standard investigative practices and interpretations, displayed knowledge that is not publicly taken to be part of his/her awareness, acted as an independent social agent capable of forming new contractual relations, and yet *could not or did not radically challenge* the social relations of experimentation that produce understandings of his/her subjectivity.

All three of these subject reports deployed some fictional form of narration: a poem, a literate chimp, and an apparently imaginary letter. The use of alternative (nonscientific) literary genres offers writers, scientists, and nonscientists alike, a conduit for reflexive thought that is proscribed in scientific writing (Oehler and Mullins 1986). These science fictions, whether written by psychologists or others, convey that which is not usually part of normal discursive practices. They enable the imparting of information that is not necessarily revolutionary, unthinkable, or novel, but that is *already present* at the margins or in the backstage of professional performances. To claim that the subject is wary, knowledgeable, distrusting, or capable of resistance, would surprise very few, if any, psychologists. However, to officially proclaim these subject attributes, or to earnestly entertain notions of subjectivity that are consistent with this tacit knowledge, would undermine standard methods and conflict with governing concepts of subjectivity. Even the technical procedures and ethical guidelines designed for detecting and responding to these subject positions at best lead to a simple acknowledgement of their appearance but most often yield no meaningful knowledge about subjects at all.

The Utility of Subject Dualities

Although these "extrascientific" writings cannot be and are not taken as critical interventions, when closely surveyed they do unsteady the normative structure of observer-subject relations along with the notions of subjectivity reproduced through that structure. And although these writings are merely three specific accounts, it is obvious that others like them can be found in written form and through anecdotal conversation. What does it mean that psychologists appear to accept two discrepant understandings of subjects? What are the implications of a dual-position for subjects or for ideas about subjectivity? At the least, it means that the accounts of subjects given in experimental or otherwise scientific writings are partial. The nature of that partiality then warrants examination: Are they partial in the sense that only certain dimensions of subjects' conditions or behaviors are recorded in research, that part of subject's cognitions or behaviors are being ignored or denied? Or are they partial in yet some other sense? These questions invite a further reflexive turn in suggesting the need to interrogate psychologists' motivations in their practices of observing and reporting in order to understand their partial representation of subjects—and to make sense of their occasional need to talk about those other omitted parts of subjects.

A traditional way of viewing this partiality of subjects (and the rare confessions) can be drawn from standard social-control theories. That is, psychologists, who are charged to generate knowledge that eventually serves the social control of human behavior, must ignore or bury those aspects of human subjectivity that would indicate that social control technologies are inadequate or unethical. However tempting because of its familiarity (and its concordance with liberal humanism), a social-control explanation may be too simple. Viewed somewhat differently, the two renditions of subjects, those made *in* and *outside* formal research scenes, may be more compatible than an initial comparison would indicate. The wary or knowing subject is one whom the psychologist must and can accommodate by developing sophisticated and agile methods. The disturbed (or disturbing) subject can be handled, and the consequential negotiations made through research methods, like informed consent and debriefing, apparently *both* settle problems of trust and augment the legitimacy of research claims. Similarly, the appearance of dual-subject perspectives may actually mask their interdependence. That is, if power relations, as Michael Foucault (1980) and others have proposed, function not simply as negative or repressive restraints but as productive forces in shaping certain social orders and subjectivities, then dual notions of subjects, and of subjectivity, might serve a productive network of power (even as aspects of them are talked about as negative or unwanted features of scientific life). Perhaps conceding the resistant, subversive, or knowledgeable qualities of subjects ultimately bolsters the legitimation of scientific reports of the other qualities of subjects. Finally, a dual perspective on subjects may be problematic only to those who retain a modernist view of individuals; from a postmodern perspective, the situation of subject multiplicity or nonunified subjectivity is no problem at all. Of this last issue more will be said later in the chapter.

Examination of subject accounts rendered outside formal scientific writing, whether in corridors or in fictions, introduces a different context for appraising conventional notions of subjectivity. If nothing else, such excursions suggest that there is more to subjects and subjectivity than that which is granted in the methods' sections of published reports. And if we are to take an interest in these purportedly sideline features of subjectivity, we need to determine how researchers participate with subjects in their making—how "we" and "they" are configured in relation to one another.

Making Subjects of Two Kinds, Twice

Up to this point the discussion has leaned on a dubitable language of parts and doubles, deploying terms that at once hint at some thwarted wholeness or fullness. The talk of partialities intimates some underlying whole, some real self mendable by stitching the parts or blending the dualisms. Such realist implications warrant clarification. The previous chapter scanned the varieties of subject theories, moving from Enlightenment and later positivist concepts of subjectivity as real, knowable, and independent, to critical appreciations of subjectivity as historically shaped, mutable, and sometimes multiple. Its comparisons offered no resolution to the vying theories of subjectivity and, hence, may have fostered realist conclusions. While intimating that the historical, constructionist theories provide escape from notions of the subject as asocial, unreflexive, a lesser being than the observer, and as gendered in disturbing ways, the previous chapter neglected to consider how those newer theories are themselves historical and constructed. While naming the virtues of theories that see subjectivity as invented, it did not articulate how those inventions transpired, and who executed them. To this unfinished business can be added the fact that the chapters on objectivity and subjectivity might appear to be retaining two kinds of subjects, one capable of critical positioning, vigilance, and reflexive monitoring, and the other a victim of the winds of time and whimsies of scientists who describe and inscribe it.

These gaps in theorizing left open in the previous chapters represent substantial problems of epistemology, but their greatness in the history of ideas does not mean that an adequate working solution to them is impossible. One approach and, I think, the only feasible one, is to take up a position in the space between these big ideas, deferring neither to the absolution of realism nor the relativism of constructionism. It is possible to appreciate the substance of subjective states while granting their historical origins, and to incorporate the activities of science and scientists into this making. Following Ian Hacking's proposal, we might adopt a "dynamic nominalism" claiming "not that there was a kind of person who came increasingly to be recognized by bureaucrats or by students of human nature, but rather that a kind of person came into being at the same time as the kind itself was being invented" (1986, 228). Accordingly, the actuality of persons and their psychological states need not be questioned, yet the matter of origins becomes more complex. The analyst is not prior to or privileged over the analyzed persons; both have bounded possibilities for personhood that are circumscribed by social and material conditions. And both sorts of persons can seize their possibilities such that sometimes "our classifications and our classes conspire to emerge hand in hand, each egging the other on" (228).

How do we account for persons and their actions according to something like a dynamic nominalist perspective? The approach, even Hacking's version, remains open to the use of a variety of theories about human action and methods of inquiry. What it insists upon is the fact that human actions, and scientific explanations of them, are interdependent and, thus, need to be understood in their mutual relations.

This mutuality and historical dynamism of person attributes and actions are illustrated in several studies whose orientation accords with dynamic nominalism. The first is a study of the making of child abuse done by Hacking (1991). This lucid survey reveals how social agencies, educational institutions, legal reforms, therapies, and new knowledge transformed the experience of child abuse over the last thirty years. Through an ongoing feedback process, new knowledge, once taken as true and disseminated, "will change the very individuals—abusers and children—about whom it was supposed to be the truth" (254). People are guided in their actions and sense of self by a culture of descriptions, and in altering their being in response to such descriptions, their changed behaviors eventually necessitate modification of that classificatory knowledge. Hacking found that through the recent tendency to analyze and code increasing forms of behavior into classes of deviant or normal, "people came to see themselves differently, choose different courses of action, and what is usual in human behavior itself changes, creating new phenomena to feed into an ever-changing concept such as child abuse" (287). Behavior is part of a perpetual system wherein morality, legality, and scientific knowledge are interconnected.

In a study surveying changes in the self and its voices in the modern era, John Gagnon (1992) explained the emergence of a "private protoself" that developed into a self that judged public events as the product of changes in public life. He abandoned a model of mental life as a mirror of culture for analysis "of the ways in which mental practices have a historically changing relationship with social and cultural practices, even though it takes its origins from them" (222). The formation of a distinctly private self with internal voices emerged along with the opportunities to hear many voices, namely through education and reading, and the cultural routines for practicing the voices of the self. Other institutional changes, including greater segmentation of individuals' roles, more diverse social interactions, along with scientific and professional knowledge about the self has fostered the problem of privileged but multiple internal voices of the self. The result is a permeable but complicated self wherein "external voices find their way more easily into the self, requiring acceptance or rejection or encapsulation. As the self becomes composed of more and more bits of what were once called ego-alien symbols and experience and desires, one comes to address more and more audiences but in increasingly limited ways" (239–40).

While Hacking and Gagnon's studies point out the interconnections of formal knowledge and human actions, Marcy Darnovsky (1991) analyzed knowledge in action in the specific form of advertising and marketing and charted its interdependence on audiences. Darnovsky investigated the media representation of the "new traditionalism," the (ideal) commodified woman who values tradition, truth and the family and who, in both using and rejecting feminism, can control the world foremost for the sustenance of intimate relations (the nuclear family). Advertising and marketing researchers engineered the new traditionalism by engaging the tensions and contradictions of contemporary women and by chronicling the life-historical experiences of consumers. Ultimately these professionals do not just manipulate people but articulate and respond to their "audiences' fears and desires far more clearly and sympathetically than do left intellectuals or activists" (87–88). They draw on existing emotions, cultural trends, moral questions, and ideologies to contrive new identities that, in turn, audiences attempt to emulate.

The prospects and limits of dynamic nominalism will only be known as studies proceed, but for the time being, that perspective answers to two immediate quandaries. It prevents conflating talk about partial selves with a presumption of some underlying wholeness or realness. But more importantly, dynamic nominalism offers a systematic means for considering the subjectivities of observers and subjects together in their social relations, and a framework for reconceptualizing those social arrangements as jointly lived, even if experienced differently by each kind of subject. With that framework of joined actions, we can try to make sense of the partial selves and representations of partial selves that have populated our practices and written accounts.

Relations

The cases reviewed at the outset of this section describe subjects who resist and sometime refuse, whereas formal writings, like journal articles, largely report on subjects who agree, comply, and assist. Both types of accounts are retrospectives that selectively report on the social relations on which they were based; what else occurred in those arranged meetings cannot be fully known. However, both accountings can be informative to redesigns of research arrangements once they are combined with thinking about subjectivity as culturally negotiated, changing, and reflexive.

There exists no alternative template for organizing research arrangements, although exemplary studies cited throughout this book testify to the existence of noncanonical practices. The absence of any standardized code outside the mainstream one does not mean that we must work without direction. In fact, there already exist numerous, ongoing conversations about different investigative practices. These conversations, although sometimes linked to concrete proposals or specific theories, nevertheless share at least five core interests: comprehension of (1) power in research; (2) problems associated with the study of experience and identity; (3) conceivable architectures for social arrangements in research; (4) status of the investigator; and (5) commitments to changing as well as explaining the subject. Each of these interests is expansive and interrelated to others, and each deserves extensive analysis in order to explicate its relevance to new psychological practices. For the time being, a brief cataloguing delineates these core interests and the experimental possibilities that attend them.

Power in Investigative Practices

The governing tenets of objectivity and subjectivity that have been appraised in this book are what give ideal form to our investigative practices. Among other things, these tenets inform regulative practices that mirror larger, nearly hegemonic arrangements of power. That is, what are taken to be orthodox arrangements and procedures, particularly those found in the laboratory, are not neutral relations in neutral environments but conform to larger bureaucratic structures with unequal distributions of authority and differential assumptions about personhood (Danziger 1990; Lave 1991; Sampson 1991; Walsh-Bowers 1992). Although feminists have been devoted to detecting social power, we have sometimes neglected the power relations constituting scientific practices. We are not always sensitive to the extent to which our middle-class understandings are congruent with scientific orderings of the world and, therefore, eclipse other cultural understandings of the world (Riessman 1987). Nor have feminist psychologists altered the relations between investigator and research participant in ways that diminish or eliminate the dominant structures of power in canonical research methods (Walsh 1989). We must, therefore, interrogate the power relations of investigative practices, and determine how subjects' actions in those practices relate (or do not relate) to other conditions in the world. Research relations need to be seen as real forces, such that, for instance, "experimenter and subject bias must be recognized as inevitable accompaniments of research and not as transient procedural contaminants" (Unger 1983, 27). Power is an inextricable condition and not a bias in all investigations.

As argued in the preceding chapter, power can be comprehended as productive, as well as restrictive, and hence, we must attend to its positive as well as oppressive effects (de Lauretis, 1990). Power relations are inscribed in psychology's texts (Lamb 1991; Lopes 1991; Morawski and Steele 1991) and are produced in methodological procedures and other institutional mechanisms. It is imperative that we work to locate those relations constituting investigative practices and identify how they both constrain and enable the realization of certain subjectivities. One model for such inquiry is offered by Henry Giroux (1992), who has called for the self-conscious examination of institutional forces operating in education. His description of the educational system is relevant to understanding power in social scientific inquiry.

> These institutions harbor in their histories, modes of scholarship, and disciplinary and pedagogical practices specific representations and practices regarding what it means to be a knowledgeable and informed citizen, how one might view the relationship between social identity and political agency, and how one responds to prevailing forms of cultural authority. Put another way, educating students and audiences in and out of schools is really an introduction to how culture is organized, a demonstration of who is authorized to speak about particular forms of culture, what culture is considered acceptable and worthy of valorization, and what forms of culture are considered invalid and unworthy of public esteem. (232)

Examining such modalities of power permits us to see the *relational* in power, and to trace how identities, experiences, and actions are formed or legitimated (or denied) through those relations. Research sites, like classrooms, are places for the transmission of culture and the rehearsal of certain relations of power.

Experience and Identity in Research Relations

Varied challenges to thinking about experience and identity have been raised in the previous chapters. The ideas that experience and identity originate within individuals and are available to observation and documentation, to operational descriptions, are unsteadied by several crucial arguments: that subjectivity is a historical product, the outcome of diverse practices; that transparency models of actors (their experiences and identities) foreclose on the play of meanings and interpretations, neglecting the limits of experience; and that psychological phenomena are made in the processes of investigating them. To take experience or identity as investigative givens reifies them, and in doing so, reproduces rather than examines the social structures and systems, including science, which operate in their making. As Joan Scott (1992) has asserted regarding constructs of identity and experience as they are employed in history (which is in this respect not unlike their uses in psychology), such talk "not only makes individuals the starting point of knowledge, . . . but also naturalizes categories such as man, woman, black, white, heterosexual, or homosexual by treating them as given characteristics of individuals" (27).

Even a reserved acknowledgement of the sociocultural origins of experience and identity raises two sorts of concerns: first, how investigators can come to know the dynamic forces in their making and, second, how relevant the investigative context itself is in those productions. The first concern requires that we cease taking the constructs of experience and identity for granted and design inquiries that seek to explain their sociocultural constitution. For instance, the aspiration to understand the experiences and identities of those persons involved in rape, assaultants and victims alike, necessitates analysis of the environments, social structures, and practices that enable rape and give it form and meaning (Martin and Hummer 1989).

The second concern, the relevance of particular investigative contexts, requires analyses that are not embedded in or derived from that context as it is usually understood by researchers. That is, the effort to understand how the dominant features of laboratories and other research settings are productive of some identities and experiences and not others, cannot simply use the language, spaces, and technical concepts that are part of those contexts to examine those contexts. Such uncritical reflection risks perpetuating the blindness of the determining forces of those contexts. And since psychology excels among the human sciences in its design of highly role-specific and action-controlled settings for observation, the consequential effects on identity and experience—of investigators and participants alike—are especially deserving of analysis.

New Investigative Practices

Just as critical analysis of research relations shows how our investigative practices are not neutral or innocent but actually enable (or mimic) particular subjectivities and actions, so those analyses can guide us, without the pretense of innocence, toward new practices. Once we comprehend the cultural ideals and practices of objectivity-subjectivity as they are routinely defined, and once we take experience and identity (in and out of investigative contexts) as needing exploration, then we can invent new forms of interacting in our investigations that challenge or change the prevailing cultural forms. Among the potential alterations are the inventions of new spaces and relations for researchers and subjects.

Constructing new research arrangements entails nothing less than audacious transformations of old ones. One approach, advocated by numerous feminist researchers, involves creating relationships "characterized by shared power between respondent and researcher" (Bograd 1988, 24). In this quest some feminist scholars have moved toward the design of "collaborative" or "participatory" science wherein the subjects actively engage in activities that ordinarily have been the jurisdiction of investigators. Subjects take part, for instance, in the collection, analysis, and interpretation of data or participate in the organizations charged with evaluating, permitting or censoring scientific research (Doell 1991; Fonow and Cook 1991a; Hoff 1988; Imber and Tuana 1988; Mies 1983).

To recruit subjects' active coparticipation does not mean an eradication of the differential positions of investigators and subjects for that would require obscuring power differences among them that are structured in and through scientific institutions. Therefore, the invention of new research relations must proceed hand in hand with systematic appraisals of institutional forms of power and how those forms are inscribed on the researcher, a task to be taken up shortly. Implementing such democratic research practices does not imply the neglect of cultural differences in power that exist prior to investigations, for they can remain salient within research contexts in yet unknown ways. There is now evidence that participants whose cultural background is less congruent with the dominant values embedded in conventional research arrangements, notably members of minority groups and lower socioeconomic classes, interpret the investigative setting differently (Fine 1989; Landrine et al. 1992; Patai 1991; Riessman 1987). Thus, establishing new arrangements among investigators and participants must include ongoing appraisal of the multiple power relations affecting inquiry.

In addition to feminist designs for collaborative or participatory research, several other new forms of research arrangements have been introduced. Plans for "democratic" arrangements, or the "democratization" of research involve replacing the bureaucratic and hierarchical model that reduces the participants' involvement to finite responses among a constrained number of options with a model that treats participants as citizens, respecting their dignity, welfare, and rights to voice in that research. Richard Walsh-Bowers (1992) has described such a democratic model as including investigators' responsibilities to values of "distributive justice, empowerment, and popular decision-making" (13). The model also proposes changes in standards of scientific writing that are consistent with the nature and ethics of that democratic research relationship. A related program for democratization involves learning about the world of participants, critically interrogating the social functions of psychological knowledge, and disseminating findings in ways that maximize their value to citizens (Sampson 1991). Yet another proposal for new research arrangements derives from recent work in socially shared cognitions, particularly its suggestions "that the social context in which cognitive activity takes place is an integral part of that activity, not just the surrounding context for it" (Resnick 1991, 4). Once taken seriously, the idea that cognitive activities are given form by social and physical structures, then the laboratory itself must be seen as a specific cite for producing specific cognitions. Following Jean Lave's (1991) claim that "learning, thinking, and knowing are relations among people engaged in activity, *in, with, and arising from the socially and culturally structured world*" the situated social practices that constitute psychological phenomenon can be modified in ways that produce not simply better knowledge but different phenomena (67). Although this research field is relatively new, and the conditions of research contexts are still relatively unexplored, its potential implications for the social relations of research are tremendous.

Investigating the Investigator

As one of its primary axioms, reflexivity "assumes that the study of human behavior necessarily includes the behavior of the psychologist" (Unger 1983, 27), and the preceding interchapter sketched some experiments in such self-interrogation. What needs a more intensive analysis are the specific positions and powers of the investigator. The realization of both gendered objectivity and the vicissitudes of feminist viewing complicates such analysis by pointing to bifurcations and contradictions in the experiences of feminist researchers themselves. The situation Dorothy Smith (1987b) described in regard to feminist sociologists holds for feminist psychologists:

> The relation between ourselves as practicing sociologists and ourselves as working women is continually visible to us, a central feature of experience of the world, so that the bifurcation of consciousness becomes for us a daily chasm which is to be crossed, on the one side of which is this special conceptual activity of thought, research, teaching, administration, and on the other the world of concrete practical activities in keeping things clean, managing somehow the house and household and the children, a world in which the particularities of persons in their full organic immediacy (cleaning up the vomit, changing the diapers, as well as feeding) are inescapable. (90–91)

As Smith argued, an alternative to the bifurcated and contradictory stance of feminist researchers is needed, one that

> involves first placing the sociologist where she is actually situated, namely at the beginning of those acts by which she knows

> or will come to know; and second, making her direct experience of the everyday world the primary ground of her knowledge. (91)

Self-reflection begins with examining that very specialized relationships between observer and object, complete with its typically normalized strangeness and authority. For instance, we need to examine how we as feminist psychologists embrace the paradox of "believing that humans are a product of their social reality, while at the same time asserting the ability of the individual to change that reality" (Unger 1989b, 26). Likewise, we need to understand how feminists (including ourselves?) can and do occasionally exempt themselves from feminist interpretations of daily life as, for example, is sometimes the case in the denial of personal (female) disadvantage (Crosby, Pufall, Snyder, O'Connell and Whalen 1989). And we need to understand how we inadvertently participate in producing objectified knowledge about women, as in the case of PMS research (Parlee 1991). We need to examine why we continue to write in a style of distanced authority, as I have done even while criticizing the dominant modes of scientific writing (Morawski and Steele 1991). In summary, we must attend to the minutiae of our actions and their meanings, remaining vigilant of the fact that our knowledge is at every stage mediated by symbols, terms, cultural traditions, and forms of communication.

The second step in this self-disclosure, as Smith described it, involves making our experiences "the primary ground" of knowledge. A much larger move than the first, this step is one that makes the personal scientific—and political. At its simplistic level, it demands "attention to the consciousness-raising effects of research on the researcher" as well as to those effects on the subjects under inquiry (Fonow and Cook 1991, 3). But this step of taking self as the primary ground of knowledge can advance much further, and Nancy Miller (1991) has suggested that personal or autobiographical studies exemplify this larger movement. Personal writing reframes the "subject's relation to itself and to authority, the authority in theory" (21). Personal writing emerged out of a resistance to the "self-conscious depersonalization" of feminist writing that accompanied its institutional acceptance as a legitimate professional activity. Personal or autobiographical work insists on recentering experience in intellectual activities, and rejecting the trend to exalt theory that "depended finally on the theoretical evacuation of the very social subjects producing it" (20). Miller speculated that the rise in autobiographical criticism may also have been an effect of a politics of identity whereby writing *"as a"* some kind of identity fosters an "anxiety over speaking *as* and speaking *for"* a particular identity (p. 20).

Personalizing inquiry (or personal writing) has long been known in psychology as introspection, a now nearly archaic method, but the modes of such self-interrogation, and of grounding knowledge through experience generally, need not be circumscribed by classical introspective techniques. Social scientists are exploring other modes including the narration of personal experience, performances of experiences, fiction, and self-reflective writings. These studies can focus on self as a specifically formed social identity or subject; they can extend that focus to engage and analyze cultural events or artifacts, as Nancy Datan (1989) did in her essay on breast surgery; or they can explore the self in relation to the production, reception, and defense of intellectual work—the lived experience of the research as Laurel Richardson (1991, 1992) has done in regard to her studies of mistresses and her novel experiments with interview techniques.

Other routes toward self-reflection in addition to critique and personalizing are conceivable. These may emerge specifically in response to reformulations of research relations. The aforementioned feminist and democratic models for investigative relations include shifts in the actions and responsibilities of investigators. New conceptualizations of thought, experience, and identity, particularly those that locate these phenomena as products of social interactions and structures, involve radical re-engineering of the idea of the personal. Whatever configurative of self-reflection and self-conscious inclusion are adopted, and whatever investigative practices are enacted, the researcher will no longer have the safe distance provided for in the predominant ideal type of investigator. Without that safety, the researcher's own agency and accountability will move into the foreground of scientific analysis.

Changing the Subject

Feminist studies are motivated by a commitment to social change as well as by an interest in delineating the conditions of women and the parameters of gender. Feminist psychology is no exception here (Fine

1985; Worell 1990). This political mandate includes the objective of *enhancing* the lives of our subjects by making them more self-aware of how gender structures their experiences, actions, and interpretations (Unger 1983). This objective also encompasses the search for ways to facilitate self-consciousness, or reflexivity, in others. Although subject enhancement or empowerment is regularly called for, and although it has been recommended by others besides feminist psychologists (Rosenwald 1985), few concrete measures for its realization have been taken. Outside psychology, several studies have attempted to generate consciousness-raising techniques (Fonow and Cook 1991, 4), but most routes to subject empowerment remain untried, and so many crucial questions remain unexplored. How would subject enhancement influence the researcher-subject relationship? How can researchers work to change subjects' perceptions without resorting to the existing hierarchy of that relationship and the authority of expertise generally? Can researchers overcome the historical reality of suspicion and disregard that has permitted their relationships with subjects? How enduring are various measures to increase self-consciousness or political awareness?

Despite a legacy of appeals for transforming or enhancing the lives of research subjects, several questions about this investigative objective remain. What cultural or political ideals should guide such emancipations? Who is to be responsible for identifying these ideals? Should that responsibility rest with investigators? Subjects? Or both? And if both investigators and subjects engage in the clarification of social ideals, how should we arbitrate the inevitable differences or conflicts? In other words, an aspiration to realize emancipation is not enough because, among other things, it neither directs nor guarantees social change. In fact, consciousness raising "has increasingly become a pretext for legitimating hegemonic forms of separatism buttressed by self-serving appeals to the primacy of individual experience" (Giroux 1992, 80).

These questions obviously have no simple answers, yet they must be addressed. As claimed in this interchapter and the preceding chapter on subjectivity, our own comprehension of alternative social goals will come partly from critically understanding the social order that is currently sustained in research, and partly from feminist analyses. Alternatives for guiding transformative efforts will also emerge if we truly enter marginal spaces, and meet those persons who serve as our subjects. It is a hope that, in entering into those spaces, and into new relationships, we will be better realizing our political aims at the same time as we create improved investigative techniques.

Recentering Research

There are now available assorted propositions for constructing different research arrangements, and although varying in their refinement and in their visions of subjectivity, they each deserve testing. These propositions share both a recognition of the distance between observer and other in normative research practices and a refusal to maintain that authoritative, and in the end, indefensible space. Originating in the margins of disciplinary activities, these propositions, if taken together, strive to eventually relocate the center. But even such a newly charted center contains boundary markers of its inside and outside, and we need to proceed cautiously with these demarcations. In writing about such spatial arrangements as they continually affect the work of minority scholars, bell hooks (1990) has appealed for a rethinking of marginal space as a site for enacting resistance as well as one of deprivation and repression.

> This "we" is that "us" in the margins, that "we" who inhabit marginal space that is not a site of domination but a place of resistance. Enter that space. Often this speech about the "Other" annihilates, erases: "No need to hear your voice. Only tell me about your pain. I want to know your story. And then I will tell it back to you in a new way. Tell it back to you in such a way that it has become mine, my own. Re-writing you, I write myself anew. I am still author, authority. I am still the colonizer, the speaking subject, and you are now at the center of my talk." Stop. We greet you as liberatories. This "we" is that "us" in the margins, that "we" who inhabit marginal space that is not a site of domination but a place of resistance. Enter that space. This is an intervention. I am writing to you. I am speaking from a place in the margins where I am different, where I see things differently. I am talking about what I see. (151–52)

Hooks self-consciously used politicized language to underscore the transformative potential of speaking and trying new social practices, and to remind us that a move into that marginal space, as a location of understanding, resistance, and transformation, must be taken by dominant members in the arrangement. Hers is an invitation not for investigators to hear and then translate the voices of those at the margins, somehow appropriating them as our own. Her invitation is to enter the space and disrupt previous relations.

Hooks has spoken primarily about literary and artistic practices, but her depiction of margins, of the ones and the others, are appropriate for investigative practices in psychology. If we, the orchestrators of investigative arrangements, are to move into those margins where everyone's relations would be different, we can best start by appreciating what might be or must be involved in that move. First, in refashioning objective practices, it was proposed that a "critical positioning" or "strong objectivity" permits an observer to accommodate the perspective of those others, but to do so critically and tentatively. Upon considering reflexivity in more detail, it also became apparent that, at some point, the observer or investigator will confront limits to a fixed politics of identity or location. At this crucial point, at least two very different (although not necessarily incompatible) directions can be taken, toward further exploration of the *personal,* on the one hand, and toward the collective, on the other hand. At various moments in this section it has been suggested that writers and researchers push beyond identity politics in order to reconfigure the personal as political, and to endow subjectivity with historical and cultural specificity. This crossover into the personal and historically specific violates the ultimate rule of empiricist and positivist inquiry, and this fact alone might well justify its happening. Yet, it is important to recall that the canonical rule has functioned finally to protect investigators, not the inquiry or subject, and that its transgression at once endangers the inquirer even as it carries the potential to enhance her experience in viewing. Bringing the personal to inquiry, then, is a risk perhaps worth taking. As Miller has discovered in personal writing,

> The embarrassment produced in readers is a sign that it is working. At the same time the embarrassment blows the cover of the

> impersonal as a masquerade of self-effacement—at least by indirection—and points to the narcissistic fantasy that inheres in the poses of self-sufficiency we identify with Theory; notably, those of abstraction. (1991, 24)

Returning to the personal is not about embarrassment, although that experience may attend the venture. Rather, it is about the latitude of visions and understandings that are enabled. It is about *re*-seeing, *re*-hearing, *re*-thinking, and *re*-writing.

I offer an instance of the advantages that can be accrued by recalling the personal. In a study of narrative accounting, Elliot Mishler (1986) analyzed and interpreted a series of interviews with a single individual. Systematic analysis led him to conclude that the individual's narrative conformed to a structure through which a distinct social identity was routinely claimed and validated. Mishler's interview methods incorporate an astute awareness of the possible effects of interview style on the story being narrated, and numerous techniques have been deployed to reduce these influences. Nevertheless, at the study's termination Mishler felt he had failed to achieve solidarity with the interviewee and that "it would not be too far off the mark to say that we had an adversary relationship in that we were struggling for control of the interview" (246). His personal reflection did not end there; instead, Mishler went on to confess that he completely failed to learn that the interviewee was an alcoholic, a fact he later learned from his wife who had interviewed the man's wife. The failure is reexamined in terms of the power relations and personal styles of both participants in the interview, and this reanalysis led to a refashioning of the methods: "If we wish to hear respondent's stories then we must invite them into our work as collaborators, sharing control with them, so that together we try to understand what their stories are about" (249). In this instance, considering the personal motivated reanalysis, or more precisely, it permitted a rehearing of the multivocal nature of the narrative account thus producing a new interpretation that could incorporate the previously neglected or unheard voices.

The second direction toward critical positioning and away from the hazards of reifying identity politics, of speaking as we and them, requires thinking beyond embodied selves and identities. It consists of admitting communities and collectivities themselves as potential sites for new actions and interactions. Donna Haraway (1985) recommended that feminists with diverse backgrounds and commitments form affinity projects or groups that are "related not by blood but by choice, the appeal of one chemical nuclear group for another, avidity" (72). Although our work transpires in local contexts and our imaginings are shaped by the specifics of our selves as marked by our gender, race, and social status, we can seek to subvert these partial locations by affinity projects as responses "through coalition, not identity" (73). Such projects can take hold in the scientific world where we can locate collectively shared aspirations often looming in the margins, as hooks suggested; disrupt hegenomic practices of science; and build new social relations. The actions of such larger collectives, sometimes not maintained through direct contacts, elude ready identification. I offer a modest and micro example of a more local grouping that is drawn from my own research on infertility and conceptive technologies. Through the unpredictable circumstances of educational institutions, several students and research associates signed on to a project (on infertility) that had been designed before their arrival. As such, members of this "lab group" varied considerably in their attitudes toward reproductive technologies and motherhood, and they represented a cacophony of positions regarding the issues. They included women and men for whom motherhood was impossible (due to physical impairments as well as gender), undesirable, as yet unimagined, or already achieved; individuals who varied greatly in family background, age, sexual preference, and professional status. It appeared to be a recipe for investigative disaster. Over time and through continued interactions, our group coalesced and our study was transformed into a project that grasps, sometimes with difficulty, the variations and contradictions of medical technology and of childbearing, and that seeks to include as reproductive issues not only the physical limitations to reproduction but culturally produced ones as well (such as sexualities, economics, and minority-group membership). Our microcoalition is now better prepared to enter the margins and, as we begin interviewing a diverse group of participants, to engage the different sorts of voices speaking (not always harmoniously or consistently) about their reproductive experiences, choices, barriers, and undetermined influences.

To summarize, the relations of research comprise a complex matter that is yet barely even recognized as a concern. Even with such amorphous beginnings, it is clear that the mobilization of practices engaging reflexive subjectivities (of researchers and subjects alike) demands multiple, sometimes even incompatible tactics. We need to revisit our representations of the identities involved, remaining wary although not intolerant of the splits and dualisms that have formed (or have been formed in) these selves. By fashioning tentative investigative frameworks, we can explore how these selves and social arrangements are coconstructed in their realities as well as in their illusions. Most importantly, we can experiment with new relations and yet unimagined experiments, transforming our investigative practices in order to invent and discover that which has been overlooked or thwarted in the prevailing techniques. The transformation of research arrangements will mean deploying all our resources, from the personal to the collective.

Chapter 4

Validity

One of our earliest lessons learned as students of psychology could be readily recalled to contest the title of this chapter: With just a skimming of its subheadings, we might well find that most of the chapter has nothing to do with validity as it is routinely defined in the discipline. And this textual discrepancy is no small matter because validity is taken to be the ultimate criterion of psychological inquiry, the standard by which findings are evaluated as truthful or not. Psychologists have fashioned elaborate *conceptualizations* of validity which, in their totality, comprise an equally complicated set of *procedures* for evaluating scientific knowledge. Validity has been transmuted into a seemingly ever-expanding typology, with detailed versions such as construct, discriminate, convergent, face, internal, external, predictive, concurrent, content, and so on. In this procedural typology, validity pertains to methodology as well as to epistemic ideals of what counts as truth, as valid knowledge. In other words, validity is all about investigative practices, and the norms for those practices, just as it is all about ascertaining the adequacy of our utmost ambition—knowing the world (Cherryholmes 1988).

This chapter has no section titles conforming to any regular typology of validity, yet it remains concerned with knowing the world better and with what we do to attain credible knowledge. The strangeness of this chapter, in the eyes of the many trained psychologists, derives from the fact that it departs from the reigning model of what comprises accurate knowledge. Allied with positivist philosophy, that model takes accounts of reality to be true to the extent that they *correspond to* or *reflect* in a one-to-one manner certain features of reality.

Departure from that positivist tradition, however significant, is not entirely radical since a growing number of social scientists are abandoning epistemological claims to a correspondence theory of truth, the separation of values or ideology from research, and the valorization of a single set of appropriate methods (Bernstein 1983; Gergen 1982; Rabinow and Sullivan 1979; Reason and Rowan 1981). This recent enterprise is sometimes called "postpositivist," "postempiricist," or "interpretive," and is frequently connected with other intellectual endeavors, including feminism, neo-Marxism, and radical pedagogy. Despite their diverse agenda, these movements share some core tenets: (1) that claiming knowledge represents or corresponds to the world might no longer be an accurate portrayal of knowing; (2) that research originating with explicit value premises "is neither more nor less ideological than is mainstream positivist research" (Lather 1986a, 64); and (3) that evaluating or warranting knowledge claims consists not of formal rule following but of ongoing, revisable, social activities that "depend, irremediably, on the whole range of linguistic practices, social norms and contexts, assumptions and traditions that the rules had been designed to eliminate" (Mishler 1990, 418).

Even prior to the arrival of these more-or-less systematic options to positivism, some investigators had criticized the technical procedures of validity for their circular and basically psychological properties. As early as 1957, Jane Loevinger demonstrated the inadequacy of validity techniques due to their dependence on social and psychological conditions created by psychologists themselves. Although not addressing matters of validity per se, Howard Gadlin and Grant Ingle (1975) analyzed the inherent limitations in psychologists' routinized tendency to evaluate the adequacy of experimental techniques with those very experimental techniques. The evaluation of the validity of psychological knowledge claims is no exception to such a circular tendency because the technical procedures for examining validity consist largely of techniques adopted from experimental practices. In the end, the same model of science and its relation to the world used for investigations are deployed to test the adequacy of that model of science and its relation to the world.

The present chapter joins with these long-standing critiques and with more recent epistemic enterprises that are proposed to replace positivism; it therefore transfigures many psychologists' cherished assumptions about validity specifically and about the generation of knowledge claims more generally. This refiguring transgresses the regular boundaries that bracket what is usually taken to be the procedures for ascertaining validity. Among the boundaries that are dismantled are those that separate knowledge about the world (in this case about persons who are the subject of study) from the world (the persons who are the subject of study) and those that divide expert and presumedly reliable information from nonexpert and avowedly unreliable information. Overall, this refiguring steps out of the closely regulated bounds of taking validity as the sum of so many technical skills and into the more expansive and dynamic if messier realm of investigative practices. This move from tool-driven validity to the practices of validity, admittedly merely sketched in this chapter, fits with appraisals of science as a endeavor. It returns questions of accountability to scientists themselves (not to data, instruments, and technologies) and to all other individuals involved in the relations of scientific work. Validity, then, is both a cluster of practices that pertains to more actors then previously presumed and an investigative situation in which a wide variety of social and political actions become possible.

The audacity as well as the opportunities inherent in refiguring validity are displayed in the chapter by three challenges to the formal boundaries separating what are taken to be the legitimate expectations for sound knowledge and other demands and interests typically considered extraneous to knowledge making. These challenges are then connected with reappraisals that take science to be a social practice, and its products, including its own criteria of truth, to be the result of local and contextually meaningful rituals, linguistic traditions, and accidents. This social epistemological perspective on science is compatible with the feminist transmutations of objectivity and subjectivity and, once understood, kindles new expectations for generating credible, or valid knowledge. The final sections of the chapter review several of these expectations, from subverting institutional structures to affirming social action, and offer several exemplars of transfiguring validity.

Some Challenges

Normal science, the dominant mode of inquiry in a discipline, has often been accompanied by challenges to it and, from a Kuhnian standpoint, these contests sometimes (although infrequently) succeed in upsetting the dominant worldview. Most often, challenges to normative practices either eventually recede into the obscurity of antiquarian memory, as was the case in a controversy between Thomas Hobbes and Robert Boyle over the nature of experiments (Shapin and Schaffer 1985), or they pass undocumented rarely to be recovered in the historical records, as is the case of a pragmatic, natural-history model for social psychology that was devised in the 1930s (Pandora 1991). In fact, quelling dissent from prevailing scientific commitments is an ongoing and important (albeit generally unobtrusive) chore in the maintenance of scientific order. The task cannot always be completed discretely, and some contentions of scientific belief demand visible, sustained, and ornate efforts to dismiss or assimilate (for example, note the extensive work committed to quell or assimilate or uphold Carol Gilligan's contestation of several cherished ideas in psychology).

The three challenges to be enumerated here are less like Kuhn's scientific anomalies that are life threatening to a scientific paradigm and more like persistent irritants, reminding practitioners that something is not quite right. For the more conventional researcher, the challenges comprise distinctly unpalatable positions. For others who are less sanguine about or committed to the dominant practices, they are temptations that represent, even if in inchoate form, alternatives for scientific inquiry. Although the exemplars presented here are not all drawn from psychology or feminist work, they each signify a challenge that has surfaced in feminist psychology.

Enhancing selves through science

In 1985, George Rosenwald proposed an amendment to the scientific mission of personality and social psychology. Describing in detail the field's mounting knowledge about how individuals, even psychologists themselves, go about their daily lives perplexed and self-deceived, he called for research that would help individuals transcend such prevalent perplexities and self-deceptions, asserting that "if we wish to aid people in clarifying their interests, we must address the reversibility, not the mere description or analysis of acquired perplexity" (685). The appeal is fueled simultaneously by an empiricist logic that points to the obvious incompleteness of an investigative program that stops short of comprehensive inquiry, and a postempiricist logic that charges empiricism with the dual failure to reflect on the interests behind inquiry and to scientifically engage such interests for the betterment of social life. With this multifaceted logic, Rosenwald further argued that it is necessary to make substantive revisions in methodology since "perplexity is not a state to be alleviated solely from outside, that is, by the conveyance of knowledge. The approach must be made from the subject's side as well. Subjects must come to the point of recognizing their own participation in maintaining perplexities" (686).

Rosenwald's challenge is not a solitary one. It coheres with "generative" research that would sensitize the public through theories having "the capacity to challenge the guiding assumptions of the culture, to raise fundamental questions regarding contemporary social life, to foster reconsideration of that which is 'taken for granted,' and thereby to generate fresh alternatives for social action" (Gergen 1982, 109). It resonates with educational researchers' call for illuminative evaluation and for "catalytic" validity or "the degree to which the research process reorients, focuses, and energizes participants toward knowing reality in order to transform it" (Lather 1986b, 272). The challenge also connects with feminist psychologists' appeals for research that is *for* women and that uses the implications of research findings as a criterion for evaluating knowledge claims (Fine 1985; Striegel-Moore 1993; Worell 1990). Aside from the work of feminist psychologists, which is discussed later in the chapter, this challenge has proven to be barely even a temptation, and a scan of the *Journal of Personality and Social Psychology*, where Rosenwald's recommendation appeared seven years ago, yields no evidence whatsoever that it was taken up.

Extending Accountability

In assessing the ascendancy of theory in literary studies, especially as it affects the understanding of literature by black women, Barbara Christian (1989a, 1989b) enumerated what that theorizing omits, eclipses, and diverts by not being grounded in practice. The "race for theory" is found to be incomplete when submitted to the question, "For whom are we doing what we are doing when we do literary theory?" Christian answered the question for herself: "What I write and how I write is done in order to save my own life" (1989b, 235). But her reply extends further:

> My readings do presuppose a need, a desire among folk who like me also want to save their own lives. My concern, then, is a passionate one, for the literature of people who are not in power has always been in danger of extinction or of cooperation, not because we do not theorize, but because what we can even imagine, far less who we can reach, is constantly limited by societal structures. For me, literary criticism is promotion as well as understanding, a response to the writer to whom there is often no response, to folk who need the writing as much as they need anything. (235)

In an earlier essay, Christian (1985) posed the question somewhat differently:

> Can one theorize about an evolving process? Are the labels informative or primarily a way of nipping the question in the bud? What are the philosophical assumptions behind my praxis? I think how the articulation of a theory is a gathering place, sometimes a point of rest as the process rushes on, insisting that you follow. I can see myself trying to explain those tiers of books to my daughter as her little foot taps the floor. (xi)

By insisting that the *for whom* questions are intrinsic to the validation of knowledge claims, Christian challenged not only the language of elite theory or its exclusion of particular people or groups, but also the grounds of accountability. Accountability then becomes a criterion for evaluating theories, and accountability is expanded inward—to the self—and outward—to those represented in theories, even her daughter. This heterogeneous version of accountability contrasts with the conventional social scientific one in which workers are accountable to a restricted and protected community of peers and sometimes to the third parties supporting their research, typically to funding agencies. It demands that accountability be extended (Bevan 1976), and democratized in ways consistent with the calls for the democratization of research arrangements that were entertained in the previous chapter (Sampson 1991; Walsh-Bowers 1992).

Refusing Institutionalization

All intellectual work, even the nonconventional, transpires within institutional structures. Dorothy Smith (1987a) has warned about the dangers of "institutional capture" as an inadvertent consequence of feminists' participation in institutions that are structured by the relations of ruling: "We find, whether we want it or not, that somehow the practices of our art come to take on the distinctive character that they do as we participate in relations that are not fully within the scope of our knowledge and certainly not fully within the scope of our control" (218). Constraints on feminist practice derive from the divergent (often conflicting) functions of institutions *and* from the feminist who is a professional within those institutions. The complex networking of structures means that

> Her standing in the academic setting she works in, her capacity to get grants to do research, and so forth depend to a large degree upon her standing in professional discourses external to her work setting. Her individual standing in her profession contributes to the overall standing of the institution of which she is a member. These relations interlock and support each other. Awareness of and responsibility to them are what makes a professional. Awareness of and responsibility to them contain one's work as a researcher within the relations of ruling." (219)

Thus, Smith observed, as feminist work "becomes institutionalized, it is built upon exclusions that it has not produced but takes for granted" (222). These exclusions happen when we delimit phenomena for study, and when we select certain words to describe, categorize, and give abstract meanings to those phenomena. Smith advocated the use of strategies that subvert such institutionalization, namely the continual explication of what aspects of the world are outside as well as inside our scientific texts, and the creation and maintenance of relations with "women who do not participate in the relations of ruling and the discourses that impenetrate them" (225).

The challenge to subvert institutionalized relations, then, becomes one means to acquire more accurate knowledge of the social world. Whereas Smith's strategies concentrate on ensuring relations by working *outside* the text and dominant institutions, allied recommendations have been made for altering relations *within* them as well. These latter strategies involve altering the usual communication systems by, for instance, establishing new journals or changing older ones; creating informal and formal networks among women professionals; and modifying the local, immediate relations with co-workers. Whether large or small, local or extended, challenges to unsteady institutionalized relations at once are checks against unrecognized blinders in scientific vision and guides for evaluating the credibility of research findings.

Beyond Classical Science Stories

Textbooks and manuals in psychology typically present validity as a cluster of rules or procedures for ascertaining the extent to which a given description of reality corresponds with that segment of reality that it is intended to explain or describe. A variety of ways for testing that correspondence inhere in the many forms of validity currently available to psychologists. Multiple "truth" tests, then, function to demonstrate the extent to which empirical findings about reality match the set of abstract constructs or "nomological net" of theoretical terms. In this sense, then, validity is a formal set of scientific procedures or rules. At the same time, it is an epistemic claim about the relation between reality and accounts or representations of reality (a schematic depiction of this claim is given in fig. 1).

This model of representation is but one feature of science (as commonly conceived) that is undergoing reappraisal. It is cited here because, as it will become apparent in the following pages, the representation model not only serves to portray how science operates but, probably more importantly, it obscures the active and moral roles of agents who produce scientific knowledge (Woolgar 1988b, 1989). The model also operates to keep validity and the technical tools of validity separate from the objects in the world that are examined through those technical practices. In other words, it sustains the questionable beliefs that first, validation procedures do not influence or determine objects in the world (a belief Loevinger contested in 1957) and, sec-

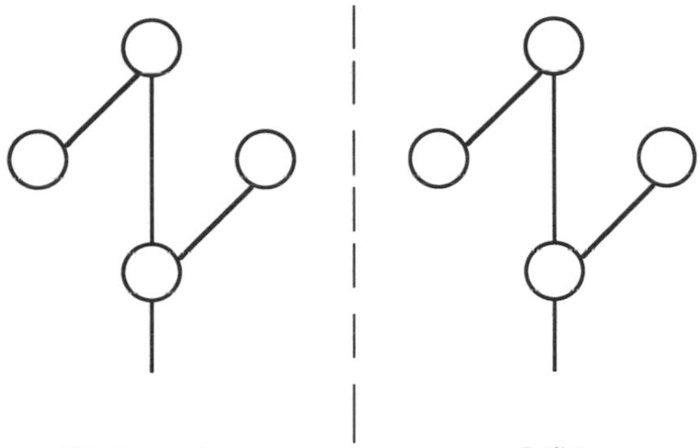

Nomological net
of theoretical
constructs/empirical
statements

Reality
(the world)

Fig. 1.

ond, objects in the world cannot (and should not) affect the making of representations.

Psychology's routines of validating, its expansive assemblage of validity tests, along with the representational episteme axiomatic to those routines, are among the features of science that have been betrayed in the history and sociology of science. Historical and social studies have repeatedly found that science does not proceed in the same manner as the textbooks and investigative reports say it should or does. The written accounts of scientific work are mythic, recounting the ideal forms of research rather than the messier, contingent, and context-specific practices that really occur in the making of scientific claims. Social studies of science, beginning with the work of Fleck (1979) and Kuhn (1962) and evolving into refined investigations of research practices (Collins 1985; Latour 1983, 1987; Gilbert and Mulkay 1984; Latour and Woolgar 1979; Mulkay and Gilbert 1982), have upturned idealist accounts of scientific behaviors by revealing the diverse and unorthodox social practices that comprise actual science. They demonstrate the shallowness of these myths, known even to the actors: Scientists "tell parables about objectivity and scientific method to students in the first years of their initiation, but no practitioner of the high scientific arts would be caught dead *acting on* the textbook versions" (Haraway 1988, 576). No one, with the possible exception of science novitiates and nonscientists, believe that science as practiced conforms at all closely to science as depicted in its rule-bound texts and manuals.

Psychologists whose research concentrates on issues of validity are, with increasing frequency, correcting the view of validity propounded in the discipline. As Lee Cronbach (1988) described it, "Validation was once a priestly mystery, a ritual performed behind the scenes, with the professional elite as witness and judge. Today it is a public spectacle combining the attractions of chess and mud wrestling" (3). Cronbach's attention to science as practiced (rather than science as idealized) is not merely descriptive for he has rendered a new understanding of what it means to seek validity in inquiry. He has found that "although the swarm of doctrines and rulings buzzing about us is chaotic, one dominant note is heard. Validation speaks to a diverse and potentially critical audience; therefore, *the argument must link concepts, evidence, social and personal consequences, and values*" (4). Validation thus is redefined as a persuasive practice within a community, and is extended to incorporate assessment of the consequences of research for individuals and institutions (Cronbach 1986). Elliot Mishler (1990) has noted how such redefinitions being fashioned by "the principal architects" of our governing concepts of validity converge with the (previously cited) accounts of scientific practice being revealed in the social studies of science. Although they originate in distinct scholarly communities, both programs concur that no abstract rules are (or can be) heeded and that the prescribed "rules," in fact, "are not universally applicable, are modified by pragmatic considerations, and do not bypass or substitute for their non rule-governed interpretation of their data." (418)

There is now an emerging consensus among those researchers who have abandoned the textbook ideology of validity. The newer view, consistent with the social studies of science, sees research as "forms of life" (a complex of social practices) and validation as a widespread set of activities whereby claims are appraised. Validation, in this sense, is "functional" rather than a structured map of truth finding; it is about conditional truths, about trustworthiness and about an active and changing world. Therefore, the social contexts, values, and consequences of research are pertinent since "truth claims and their warrants are not assessed in isolation, but enter a more general discourse of validation that includes not only other scientists but many parties in the larger community with different and often conflicting views." (Mishler 1990, 420)

These revisions of validity, despite how they appear to more conventional practitioners, are neither an anarchist deconstruction nor a substitute set of rules eventually to be reified and abstracted. Rather, the revisions delineate new guideposts for scientific work. Donna Haraway (1988) has aptly asserted how stopping with deconstructive techniques leaves feminist critics of science only with excuses for not engaging in scientific ideas since "they're just texts anyway, so let the boys have them back" (578). Similarly opposed to such a dead-end scenario, researchers advocating the reformulation of validity have rejected neither the need for procedures for making scientific claims credible nor the belief that something lies beyond the texts, that there is something about the world that can be credibly told. They are neither anarchists nor dilettante relativists, but are committed to producing knowledge that recasts the world. For practitioners committed to value-based research, as many feminists are, knowledge is essential to transforming our hold on the world, and investigative procedures remain essential to getting the work done. As Patti Lather (1986a) has shown, workable ways for assessing credibility are needed for multiple reasons: "Agreed-upon procedures are needed to make empirical decision-making public and, hence, subject to criticism. Most importantly, if we fail to develop these procedures, we will fail to protect our work from our own passions, and our theory-building will suffer" (78).

Workable means for evaluating knowledge claims—means that presume both the historically contingent nature of inquiry and its social dimensions linking communities of practitioners, subjects, and users—is the first of two necessary conditions for going beyond inaccurate accounts and restrictive practices. The second condition involves reevaluating the overarching epistemology of representation that legitimates truth statements about the world. The interchapters in this book have inched toward such reevaluation by refusing many of the common divisions of the world made in science (see "Betwixt and Between") including psychology's cherished separations between the experimenter and her self ("Reflexivity 1") and the experimenter and her subjects ("Reflexivity 2"). These explorations contest a schematic rendering of science that isolates the work of describing objects in the world from those objects (the separation depicted in fig. 1) and that erases the moral and political interests motivating that work. In order to fully sever the line drawn between representations and reality, we need to see the world as dynamic (a suggestion made in the last interchapter). The reality we seek to know better is active and generates meanings. Haraway has described this reality in a way that I believe is consistent with the dynamic nominalist approach introduced in the last interchapter. The objects of that reality are generative and relational: "Their *boundaries* materialize in social interaction. Boundaries are drawn by mapping practices; objects do not preexist as such. Objects are boundary projects. But boundaries shift from within; boundaries are very tricky. What boundaries provisionally contain remains generative, productive of meanings and bodies" (1988, 595).

Transcending classical stories about science, and transcending even science that shuns these out-of-date tales, depends on a far-reaching understanding of how knowledge claims are appraised and warranted. Our consequently expanded evaluation practices need to simultaneously look back on the social origins and consequences of those claims, and forward toward viewing objects in the world as dynamic forces in scientific projects.

Feminist Debates

What constitutes the appropriate methods for feminist psychology is proving to be a question of protracted debate. Although not unique to psychology, that debate has its own peculiar history in our discipline. At one level it has taken form in a disagreement between two simply defined factions: those researchers advocating adherence to orthodox procedures (or eschewing unconventional ones) and those proposing augmentation of existing procedures with other less-canonical or entirely new ones. The contours of this debate are traced on several occasions in this book. However, understanding the "controversies" at this level alone elides the deeper issues at stake in creating methods amenable to feminist interests. At another level, those controversial issues can be seen to be precisely about validation as it has just been reformulated. They are about whether or not there is need for evaluation procedures that explicate the *full* extent of the scientific appraisal process, thus making it accessible to criticism, including self-criticism, and incorporating all its components and participants (including the objects of inquiry).

To frame the method debate in feminist psychology by distinguishing between "traditional" and "nontraditional," or "quantitative" and "qualitative," methods misses the crucial, more interesting stakes in the dialogues over appropriate procedures for the generation and evaluation of knowledge. The multidimensionality of these stakes is illustrated in a debate in which both parties in the conflict are members of the same methodological camp, if you will. The case to be described exemplifies how the perception of validation as adjudication through agreed-upon technical operations is illusory. Instead, the case reveals how validation fits Cronbach's description as an ongoing argument about truth claims that "must link concepts, evidence, social and personal consequences, and values." The claims made by the protagonists in this debate demonstrate the functional and conditional nature of validation, and attest to the instability and continued revision of what is taken as consensus. It is not the specific type of method or the quality of data that is ultimately being negotiated but more general and serious questions about what we should know about the world, who is able to know it, and how they should claim it to know it.

The debate coalesced around a specific methodological question: whether or not the analysis of research data should *routinely* test for gender differences whenever males and females are used as subjects. In their guide for nonsexist research, Maureen McHugh, Randi Koeske, and Irene Frieze (1986) offered a "moderate" reply to the question, submitting that sex-related differences that have not been replicated or have not been predicted by or grounded in a theoretical model may not be appropriate content for published research" (883). The rationale for their solution was simply that, without reasonable bases for suspecting or expecting sex differences in the phenomenon under study, there is no need to routinely test for such differences. Further, the authors recommended that when analyzing for sex or gender differences, investigators should provide the percent of variance explained by sex that would, in turn, allow readers of the study to assess the meaningfulness of the findings. The suggestions of McHugh et al. was probably the first gesture to regularize the systematic testing for sex differences. Until then, most feminist researchers had primarily voiced concerns about the failure of many investigators to include women or conduct *any* test of sex differences (sometimes even when claims about sex differences were made in research reports), or about the unsystematic fashion in which sex differences were analyzed and recorded. Given these unruly conditions, the nonsexist guide seemed to render a system for regulating research.

Soon afterward, Alice Eagly (1987a) responded to the task force's guide by taking issue with both the recommendation that sex-difference analyses need not be done routinely but only if warranted, and that when differences are interrogated, reporting the percentage of variance explained by sex served as sufficient analysis. Instead, she proposed an alternative guide whereby researchers "(a) routinely report sex comparisons, regardless of whether these findings are replicated, hypothesized, or theoretically relevant and (b) report these findings precisely, in the same metrics that they apply to their reports of other findings" (756). The justification of these alternative guidelines and for rejecting the McHugh et al. (1986) recommendations was based on a standard understanding of the verification model in psychology. According to Eagly the exclusion of findings that are not "theoretically meaningful" essentially meant suppressing new data that then "would tend to lie buried in file drawers" (756). In turn, such suppression would hamper, if not violate, the process of scientific verification because it would make it impossible to submit those findings to replication (there would be no publicly known findings to replicate). Perhaps most importantly, this exclusion of data would eliminate reports of null findings, thus short-circuiting the normal procedure of hypothesis testing. For all these reasons, the decisions *not* to test routinely for sex differences function, however inadvertently, to protect sexist myths:

> In fact, there is little gender-relevant theory about some behaviors, because neither psychologists nor laypersons believe that such behaviors are sex-typed and therefore predictable in terms of any theories that take sex and gender into account. It is probably just such theory-irrelevant sex comparisons that are most likely to yield null findings. (756)

In summary, Eagly described how our warranting rules must ensure the possibility of generating null findings because such findings correct false beliefs about gender. Her recommendation for including more precise metrics also fits this end because they enable investigators to "more readily convey the practical meaning of sex comparisons" (757) and to compare this data with findings from other studies (in order to ascertain the cumulative impact of the sex difference). Eagly's alternative recommendations apparently are designed to serve the reduction of sexist biases both inside and outside the scientific community, although they might be seen as eliminating just one kind of bias from research (Rothblum 1988).

An altogether different stance, one supporting the original directive of McHugh et al. (1986), was taken by Roy Baumeister (1988) who especially agreed with its caveat that "findings of sex differences might be used to justify discrimination and oppression" (1093). Baumeister acknowledged that sex difference analyses have been a necessary corrective to the "masculinist bias that had led researchers to study only men and to generalize recklessly to women . . ." but he also believed that "initial goal has been achieved" (1093). In terms of verification, routine testing for sex differences actually might render research "scientifically suspect" by corrupting the idea of experimental manipulation as a test of *specific* hypotheses. The scientific adequacy of sex difference analyses is further shaken by the fact that sex or gender are easily confounded by other variables including physical stature, hormones, social oppression, flirtation with the experimenter, and personal ideas. In making this point, Baumeister challenged the validity of using sex as a variable, suggesting that "one might profitably start by focusing on the true causal variable, bypassing the initial demonstration of gender differences. Sex differences may be a source of hunches, but they do not seem satisfactory as scientific explanation" (1094). Further, Baumeister's defense of the nonsexist guide was explicitly phrased in political as well as scientific terms. Rather than liberating science and society from social biases, he warned that sex-difference research "perpetuates the distinctions and contributes to the persistence of stereotypes and discrimination" (1093). Even the search for gender similarities is implicated in these politics: The entire research program "endorses a way of looking at the world in which men and women are fundamentally different. The hope that people will be surprised when there are no differences itself acknowledges that differences are to be expected" (1094). In summary, Baumeister claimed that psychology is part of the realization of sex differences, and hence, continuing its current preoccupation with gender categories not only endangers valid scientific work, but *validates* those very categories.

This debate, played out in the back pages of the *American Psychologist,* resurrects basic questions about the evaluation of psychological claims about the world. Both Eagly and Baumeister disrupt the task force's comfortable presumptions about "value-free, repeatable methods," despite their own sustained efforts to hold fast to a conventional form of objectivity. Yet, what is much more important and interesting about this debate is its demonstration of scientific procedures as contingent, negotiated, and context-dependent—not fixed, regular, and universal. The arguments of Eagly and Baumeister exemplify how the appropriate techniques for validating knowledge claims are adjudicated, and decisions about them are dependent on *theoretical, political,* and *personal* commitments. This illustration of the negotiation of validation procedures is all the more convincing once it is noted that the protagonists are not members of separate methodological camps, say, qualitative and quantitative or experimental and nonexperimental, but are both earnest proponents of canonical methods: They are both experimental social psychologists who apparently subscribe to the reigning notions of scientific verification.

The two researchers grounded their stances on differing theoretical commitments to gender: Eagly on a belief that sex is a variable corresponding to a meaningful category of reality and Baumeister on doubts about this correspondence and about the causal properties of gender categories. They defended their warranting procedures with slightly different interpretations of scientific verification but, more importantly, they both molded their interpretations to include conditions outside the laboratory. Here their relative comprehensions of (and commitments to) politics further differentiate their retrospective recommendations. Eagly's world is one where science and the rest of it all are similar in some respects and dissimilar in others: Like ordinary people, researchers hold sex-biases, but unlike ordinary people, they are better situated to check them and have obligations to do so. In addition, this is a world where the relations between psychologists and others are straightforward ones consisting largely of one-way messages, in the form of research findings, sent by researchers to the public. And given the persistent sexism of that public, psychologists have to organize and conduct their research in order to combat it. Although Baumeister also distinguished between scientists and everybody else, he depicted different boundaries and described a different social climate outside the scientific community. Researchers, like all the rest, are susceptible to sexism, yet they appear to be well on the way toward ridding themselves of it. However, in Baumeister's world the lines of communication between researchers and others is far more permeable than in Eagly's: Not only do psychologists send signals when they merely speak about gender, but the public can be significantly affected by those signals, and thus, produce a different reality of gender. In the end, psychologists are responsible for *what* they study, *how* they study it, and *what then* happens to the world that they study. Despite this complex system and the consequential obligations bestowed on researchers, Baumeister was more sanguine about sexism, and apprehended its dissolution in the world as well as the laboratory (where he suggested that it might be nearly eradicated already).

As typified by this debate, the procedures for producing and appraising knowledge are not agreed on beforehand, nor are they always resolved in the end. Rather, there is no end to these procedures for they are continually negotiated via investigators' interpretations of the "rules," their expectations for the functioning of those rules, and their understandings of the consequences of research—or the world and not just for scientific logic. The dynamics underlying these negotiations would be further illuminated if the personal realms of the two parties were addressed: their own genders, personal histories, and respective research programs. Additional complications would ensue if we compared, say, these two apparently divergent views of the world and of psychologists' political commitments with yet another view that does not share the first two's assumptions about the superiority of the expert's position, the inevitability or ease of social change, or about the existence of science as a liberal, change-inducing institution. Even without adding these complicating features, the dispute over the analysis of sex differences exemplifies how validation, specifically the malleable rules for validation, comprises a far more expansive activity than our textbooks indicate.

The Vicissitudes of Warranting

To acknowledge the essential sociality or even the multiple dynamics lying behind the creation of valid knowledge is not to conclude that anything goes. Nor is it to imply that all knowledge claims are equal in those processes, for there is a dominant institution of validation that, despite being unlike the textbook accounts and more like an interpretative process, does impose boundaries on what knowledge claims can count as credible. This validation system is part of what Dorothy Smith (1987a) has referred to as the "institutional capture" that feminists risk whenever they undertake inquiry. However, in psychology, as other disciplines, not all feminists locate themselves or get located *outside* the prevailing system for warranting their work. Some, like Letita Peplau and Eva Conrad (1989), caution against identifying feminist research as being of one type, and thus they oppose "the view that nonexperimental methods are *inherently* more feminist than experimental ones" (388). Although their refusal to separate investigative practices according to old typologies corresponds with a general claim of this chapter, their position differs from the present one in its relative confidence in existing methods and in the feminist opportunities inherent in them. Their faith is sustained, in part, by seeing methods and validation routines as relatively benign—in other words, by embracing the rule-book view of scientific activity.

There are at least two reasons why such confidence in science-as-described might lead feminist researchers into uncomfortable, constrictive corners. First, as discussed at length, benign portraits of science as orderly and ordered do not mirror what actually occurs in scientific practices, and feminists as well as all other practitioners are impeded if not imperiled without understanding science as it is practiced. For instance, by not recognizing how normal processes of validation extend to negotiation of political and social values and how they remain open to revision, as illustrated in the Eagly-Baumeister correspondence, we lack the language and conceptual tools to settle such differences of belief. Second, because feminists operate with political commitments that diverge from the politics of routine science, we are handicapped if these politics remain tacit. Inclusive analyses of moral and political values, and the negotiation of differences regarding these values, require seeing the full range of practices constitutive of science. This "seeing" depends on a reconstructed portrayal of science. It is further clarified by comprehending just what feminism is and how it takes form in practice. It is true that "there is no real boundary between feminism and what is external to it; no boundary separates or insulates feminism from other social practices or makes it impervious to the institutions of civil society" (de Lauretis 1986, 4). But this being the case, there are certain assumptions, inferences, and interpretations that distinguish feminist work, and these are always needing to be recalled, analyzed, and extended. These distinguishing elements help illuminate the field on which scientific activities transpire. In a moment we will consider how this seeing and recommitting might proceed—what possible forms it can take—but for now it is necessary to consider briefly the immediate vicissitudes, the downsides as well as upsides, of revisioning validation to serve the political commitments of feminism.

First, the downsides. The obvious and most fatal risk to feminist psychologists who operate with noncanonical standards of scientific inquiry is that their work will not be admitted into the scientific community, and hence, that they will fail both in their projects and in their professional careers. Although feminists who publicly discuss such risks are not infrequently accused of paranoid thoughts, the history of feminist scholarship is replete with evidence that such thoughts are hardly unwarranted. And it is for this reason (and for assuring the avoidance of such failures in the future) that we must talk about and deploy carefully charted strategies in conducting research, remaining conscious of the fact that even these tactical measures may not work.

There are two other downside matters that, although less threatening to survival, are crucial to the "quality of life" of our research. Both of these are matters of identity, but they are very different: whereas one matter concerns identity imposed *on* and *around* us as we inhabit the scientific community, the other concerns those *preexisting* features of identity that influence who we are before we enter the scientific environment. The configurations of identity imposed on feminists once we enter science are multiple. Feminist psychologists who adopt revised validation procedures, whether they entail such practices as the warranting of claims by collaborating with subjects or the employing of action-oriented methods, risk a professional identity that is marginal and suspect. We are susceptible to the label "applied" psychologists along with all the inferior status that label conveys: Applied research is thought to be not just derivative but also polemic and, hence, dubitable (Parlee 1979; Reinharz 1992). More critical to feminist psychologists' identity is a chain of associations conflating feminists with women, and the unconventional procedures used by some feminists with the feminine (Squire 1989). Thus, alternative-appraisal techniques are not simply suspect because they are challenges to the status quo, but because they are feminine—"soft," "tender," "communal," "subjective," and finally, unscientific. However vigorous or rigorous the work may be, in the end it is discounted.

The second identity issue is a thornier one that pokes out mainly in the course of reflexive analysis, especially when we comprehend that identity is conditioned through gender-relations long before a researcher enters the doors of scientific institutions. Once we acknowledge that our methods and warranting procedures must take into account the gender relations saturating our scientific practices, from the simple idea that the genders of subject and experimenter are relevant to the more complicated realization that our hypothetical constructs and discourses are gendered, then in good faith we need to consider the gender dynamics of our own identity as it gets articulated in scientific activities. Feminist inquiries are not free from the cultural and personal inscriptions of gender and, therefore, "as in any form of social analysis, the study of gender relations will necessarily reflect the social practices it attempts to understand" (Flax 1987, 632). Jane Flax has pointed out several ways in which feminist analysis is tied to historically specific gender relations: the tendency of feminist studies to ironically position males as less determined by gender; the heavy focus on child-rearing practices as causes of gender relations when they are actually also effects of gender structures; or the manner in which this child-rearing focus rarely considers children as persons or "fathering" as part of children's or men's consciousness. There undoubtedly are many ways in which feminist analysis "may partially reflect a mode of thinking that is itself grounded in particular forms of gender (and/or other) relations in which domination is present" (633). In the first chapter I suggested that the concept of androgyny, while correcting all sorts of sexist presuppositions in psychology, must be critically appraised in terms of its meaningfulness to the life structures of feminist psychologists (specifically to the importance of "passing" in a man's world of science while retaining core features of feminine gender identity). Feminist psychologists also must consider how their own gendered experiences are reflected in their concepts of women's relational selves, concepts that stop short of asking what sorts of relations and what social hierarchies are sustained through relational selves, or what sorts of difficulties women have in these relations. We similarly must learn how our own gender relations figure into or prefigure our explanations of sexual preference as "chosen" without calculating how prevailing gender relations structure those choices. Thus, feminist research, like all other research, bears the prints of our identities and risks the blindnesses of those identities just as it is enhanced by them. Sandra Harding reaffirmed the "need to eliminate the politics of the garden of Eden which have been constituent factors in modern science." But in doing so, she also warned that "we need simultaneously to give up the notion that the processes of modern science can be meaningfully understood in isolation from the processes of daily social relations" (1987b, 135).

There are upsides or special benefits to revisioning our system of scientific appraisal, not the least of which are those occasional victories, however local or minor, like persuading major journals to adopt gender-sensitive language or removing a category from the *Diagnostic and Statistical Manual of Mental Disorders*. These little victories point to the *transformative* potential residing in the newer understandings of valid knowledge. Untethered from correspondence theories of truth or positivist aspirations to describe reality, new concepts of scientific practice engender commitments to changing the world. Although the governing scientific worldview, especially in psychology, is couched in a liberal ideology of progress, it contains predetermined ideas of what specifically constitutes progress and how it should occur. Briefly stated, that ideology assumes that objects in the world conform to linear, often mechanical, and universal patternings. Progress is equated first with the discovery of the laws explaining the patterns, and second with technical knowledge that can be utilized to maximize control over these avowedly natural patterns. The generalizations made about objects in the world are taken as relatively unproblematic templates for engineering the best possible functioning of those objects; that is, what is found in that natural order is uncritically assumed to be a guide for what is optional.

The very postulate that this worldview itself can be transformed is a large step beyond specific ideas about progress that are embedded in current science, precisely because it is believed to be a neutral, apolitical view. Replacing this worldview with a comprehension of science as inherently political necessarily means transforming the world through new appreciations of its very participation in the making of scientific knowledge. Once no longer believed to abide by linear and mechanistic patternings, and no longer held as passive phenomena in the procedures of representation, objects in the world are immediately altered. But also changed are our own responsibilities as scientific agents committed to the tasks of knowing those objects. Validation, along with the other duties of scientific labor, explicitly encompasses decisions about change as well as the implications ensuing from those decisions. Transformation of scientific practice, ourselves and the world is but one task in feminist psychology. Others include description of the social world, critiques of that world and the dominant modes of "knowing it," and self-correcting criticism. Transformation is a galvanizing task and a promise, one rarely if ever available through conventional science.

Validity as Challenge

The chapter opened with three challenges to validity as it is usually practiced, and each pushed against the boundaries of some facet of validation. The challenge of enhancement pressed a commitment beyond the obligation to describe or map the world. The challenge of multiple accountability moved thinking beyond restricted accounting practices. And the challenge of socially active change expanded work outside the rule-following ethos of scientific institutions. These challenges *to* canonical practices translate into challenges *for* new practices; just as they stand as oppositions so they are interpretable as opportunities. This section briefly explores what these challenges, when translated into opportunities, might mean for the validation of research. However, if we take the new enterprise of validation to mean workable ways of gathering data, and if we recognize that those ways are value-based and are inclusive of the entire range of social relations and settings that constitute science, then no exhaustive enumeration of its implications for research can be set forth in advance.

Enhancement and Generativity

In his challenge to conventional research practices, Rosenwald (1985) contended that they fail to complete their scientific task of understanding phenomena as fully as possible and do not take seriously the ideas of socially beneficial or "emancipatory" knowledge. He went on to propose how these shortcomings could be corrected through other investigative techniques, and described three such approaches: phenomenology, psychoanalytic interpretation, and life history. Each approach permits the investigator to move from the description of perplexing experiences to more rigorous examination of the motives behind those experiences. And each affords ways for the subject to personally explore his or her involvement in perplexity. Yet some approaches are better than others in making way for transformative action, and on this ground Rosenwald favored the life-history one. Rosenwald meticulously contrasted these techniques with conventional criteria for research, and distinguished enhancement from the mere reliance on subject reporting: "Interventions which enhance the subject do not consist, as critics might suppose, of the participants' collaboration in a new, possibly delusive ideology. Rather, they aim at the removal of barriers that have kept the subject from recognizing its actuality and exploring its potentiality in the world" (697). The search for appropriate techniques is open ended and might extend beyond the dialogic ones that he surveys, for "the aim is to legitimate the enhancement of the subject as a methodological criterion. Whether any particular research method meets this criterion is an empirical question" (701).

Two other proposals for assessing knowledge claims with the criterion of enhancement or transformation demonstrate the vastness of methodological possibilities. Patti Lather (1986a) has described a set of validity criteria that might attend "openly ideological research." Included in those guidelines is "catalytic validity" or "the degree to which the research process re-orients, focuses, and energizes participants in . . . 'conscientization,' knowing reality in order to better transform it" (67). Lather illustrated these alternative guidelines by drawing on examples from feminist research, neo-Marxist critical ethnography, and Freirian educational research. These research programs use varied procedures to ensure catalytic validity, but they also depend on other (similarly reformulated) measures of validity, notable triangulation of methods, and revised conceptualization of construct and face validity (Lather 1988). Although borrowing well-known terms, the examples forwarded by Lather differ in two ways from the technical operations generally associated with them: first, in the absence of any notion of a neutral standpoint in evaluation and, second, in an explicit commitment to altering reality and/or experiences of reality. The idea of investigative neutrality, a premise corroborated in many technical operations of validation, is replaced by reflexive awareness of investigative positions, thereby returning the investigator to an active stance in inquiry. Thus, for instance, construct validity is reconceived to include "ceaseless confrontation with the experiences of people in their daily lives in order to stymie the tendency to theoretical imposition" (Lather 1986a, 67). Construct validity, therefore, is social and dialogical, connected at once to the investigator, participants, and the ultimate commitment to social enhancement. As similarly redefined, triangulation extends beyond the use of multiple measures and provides means for more honestly dealing with counterpatterns by considering multiple data sources and theoretical models as well as methods.

Another proposal ensues from Kenneth Gergen's (1982) model for generative theory. Focusing not on methodological but on metatheoretical commitments, Gergen enumerated several routes toward more generative theorizing. Hampered by metatheoretical obligations to objectivity, empirical demonstration, and naive realism, psychologists are unable to construct theories that "can provoke debate, transform social reality, and ultimately serve as a stimulus to reordering social conduct" (109). In contrast, generative theorizing can be motivated through a variety of exercises including articulation of the interpretative stance of minorities; recontextualization of the referent (by examining it in a radically different context of usage); extension of commonplace assumptions to the point of absurdity; elaboration of antitheses to commonly held explanations; and deployment of novel metaphors.

These recommendations do not in themselves comprise a code for validation, yet they do cohere in a general expectation that research should entail accounts of the world, or of people in that world, which provide *avenues to see that world or those people differently,* as an initial step in generating active change. Whether called catalytic, transformative, enhancing, illuminative, or generative validity, this expectation is instrumental to the vigor of feminist psychology. To date, feminist psychology has not transcended certain ideologies that constrain our perceptions of our subject matter and restrict our engagement with emancipatory aims. Most often our research continues to harbor notions of subjectivity compatible with the dominant view in psychology (as examined in chapter 3). As Arnold Kahn and Janice Yodor (1989) found, studies of the psychology of women frequently subscribe to a focus on the individual as source and cause of psychological conditions (and thus as the primary vehicle for change), along with a complacency about the social order as it currently exists (Parlee 1979; Prilleltensky 1989; Sampson 1977, 1981). Michelle Fine (1985) detailed these dominant premises in the psychology of women, finding that most of that research clings to assumptions of individual determinism, individual-focused remedies, and the imminent amelioration of social injustice. Kahn and Yodor offered two investigative remedies for the status quo state of affairs in the psychology of women: "(a) becoming aware of the various external forces that shape the behavior of women, and (b) having an image of the kind of society that would maximize women's well-being" (428). Their recommendations are just the threshold from which we can enter into an investigative world where transformative practices are a criterion for appraising the adequacy of our knowledge claims—and are an investment in the future.

Accountability

To inquire about the relation of theory (or research findings) to the lives of daughters, cohorts, and self, as Barbara Christian did, is to contest the traditional assumptions about *for whom* we must be accountable when making knowledge claims. The normative tradition sharply distinguishes between experts and nonexperts, and validity is foremost an issue of accountability within a community of experts. Even efforts to attain "face" validity are usually taken to mean assessing the extent to which a trained group of "experts" agrees with the measures under scrutiny (Judd, Smith and Kidder 1991, 54). However, these are idealized representations of what actually transpires in scientific work since "truth claims and their warrants are not assessed in isolation but enter a more general discourse of validation that includes not only other scientists but parties in the larger community with different and often conflicting views" (Mishler 1990, 420).

In order to rethink the validation process to incorporate this larger community and, hence, to diversify accountability practices, we need to release a constricted notion of face validity, enlarging it to include individuals in a variety of roles related to scientific practice. Kersti Yllö (1988) has argued that doing research *for* women, as opposed to research *of* or *about* women, "involves accountability for how those findings are used by others" (42). This accountability has two distinct implications. First, it means that researchers sense their part in the entire life of their research, monitoring its later interpretations and uses by other experts and by nonexperts. The need and the responsibility to do so is based on simultaneous awareness of science as an extended social practice as well as the consequences of not being aware: "Feminists do not release findings into the 'marketplace of ideas' assuming that truth will (win) out. They know that the marketplace is not free. Caution must be taken to prevent damaging use of information." (42) Second, accountability for the life course of research means that researchers continuously attend to the power relations of science, and especially to how those relations privilege certain experts, like scientists and related professionals, over others, like ordinary recipients of scientific findings and even social activists. These relations of power are made more visible when we recall that "somehow the mainstream researchers' commitments to vague goals such as social justice are not seen as subjective or problematic, whereas feminist goals to end patriarchy are" (42). New guides for accountability, then, demand vigilance over the demarcation of workers, of experts and nonexperts. They also require the inclusion of those whose participation is denigrated (through that demarcation) yet who also know the phenomena at hand and produce knowledge, like those in the case Yllö cited—activists and shelter workers who work with battered women.

Another contingent about whom accountability needs to be reconsidered is the participants in investigations. Here face validity is radically redefined in terms of "recycling description, emerging analysis, and conclusions back through at least a subsample of respondents . . ." (Lather 1986b, 270). In reviewing forms of participatory research, Lather found that the active inclusion of participants serves as a critical check against invalid or irrelevant findings. It affords an additional check against the investigator's interests: "Research designs can be more or less participatory, but dialogic encounter is required to some extent if we are to involve the reflexivity needed to protect research from the researcher's own enthusiasms" (268). Described as a process of reciprocity, participatory or collaborative practices also feed the aims of emancipatory or generative inquiry by illuminating the worldview of participants—inclusive of its contradictions, ideological tropes, and partial understandings.

Reciprocal research techniques take the scientist as a "major shareholder" in the scientific enterprise rather than a sole owner (Lather 1986b), and as such, promote research that can be evaluated and modified by varied parties both within and outside the scientific communities. The specific techniques for such an accountable or reciprocal practice are numerous (Sampson 1991; Walsh-Bowers 1992). Lather (1986b) has described some techniques that maximize subject participation: interactive and dialogic interviews; involving subjects in the negotiation of meanings at each stage of research; revised debriefing practices; and creating a scientific language that is accessible to all parties. Mishler (1986, 1990) suggested other techniques connected with interactive interviews, arguing that interview transcripts, as documents accessible to others, increase opportunities for appraising the trustworthiness of research.

In the end, the governing view of accountability, and even of face validity, is sustained by and simultaneously sustains the dualist distinctions of objectivity and subjectivity, knowers and objects to be known. Just as this restricted system of accountability maintains a certain order of the world and of people in that world, so too, does it truncate all sorts of possible corrective measures and, not the least, more innovative and transformative theorizing. The redesign of accountability as an expectation for sound research and as an investigative practice insists on, and finally realizes, the dissolution of the old borders of objectivity and subjectivity.

Social Action

When Dorothy Smith (1987a) spoke of feminists' need to undertake institutional subversion, she identified one (but only one) way of viewing research as social action. Yet, although psychology has a long history of calling for social-action research, for directing research at and through social change, rarely have these rallying cries included mandates to subvert the institution of psychology. A notable exception is to be found among feminist psychologists who have found the means to protect the work and livelihood of other feminist psychologists against a system that denigrates or even rejects their participation: Many feminist psychologists have honed their skills of mentoring and defending junior workers, and of networking to increase the visibility and recognition of feminist scholars. We usually stop short of taking legal measures against institutions, boycotting prestigious journals that shun feminist research or noncanonical methods, or advertising the names of great psychologists who are widely known as harassers of women.

In other words, feminist psychologists have gone about their subversions mostly in private and not public, informal and not formal, ways. In one sense, that is what subversion is generally about. Yet it is important that we occasionally take the time to analyze our social activism at this institutional level, assessing what works and what does not, and ascertaining what features of the scientific structure must be tackled next. And we need to evaluate how we sometimes let our institutions off the hook, as it were, by being too gentle, nice, and not hysterical, and by looking outside the institution of psychology for our audiences and alliances (Fine and Gordon 1989).

But social action, in tradition and in reality, includes more than those subversions. It also means taking seriously one of the working premises of feminism to change the social order—to create new systems, better laws, and different social relations (Reinharz 1992). The techniques and settings for doing so are far ranging, and they absolutely depend on new relationships between researchers, research participants, activists, other professionals, and government workers (Schecter 1988). One technique is known to many psychologists as "action research": studies conducted in lived contexts with the participation of its inhabitants and aimed at initiating agenda for change as well as performing systematic evaluation. Besides that specific tradition (which has been underused by feminist psychologists), there are others. Sulamit Reinharz (1992) has prepared a roster of available techniques for conducting action research and the list includes collaborative research, needs-assessment studies, evaluation research, and methods of demystification or "consciousness raising."

How to do it

Framed as opportunities rather than oppositions, the three challenges for validity involve investigative practices that are far more extensive, complex, and multidimensional than do our prescribed, mythic accounts of scientific conduct. The challenges intimate a fundamental, from-the-ground-up restructuring of research. Yet, if viewed as a collection of strategies from which any single investigator must select, refine, and fit to her respective investigation, they appear less daunting. This book contains many examples of realizable strategical decisions, all of which work in their own ways to unsettle normative practices, but none of which in themselves are sufficient. Following are two case examples wherein validation is presented, and reflected upon, more as a substantive enterprise than as one or several independent technical maneuvers. These cases are distinctive but not unprecedented explorations. They represent a growing movement toward mobilizing a more comprehensive and accurate rendition of validation.

Case 1

Validation, whether defined conventionally or otherwise, is an investigative practice transpiring through a historically constituted language. Following this point, Cleo Cherryholmes (1988) has argued that validity, specifically construct validity, is a discursive production that, therefore, needs to be analyzed in terms of the power relations inherent in that discourse. Such interrogation is especially important given the ahistorical and acontextual grounding of validation in the positivist worldview. In a connected set of projects, Leonore Tiefer has initiated such a historical and political interrogation of sexuality research. She began by tracing the specific investigative techniques (and the language they imposed) that, over time, came to guide what is taken to be sexuality. The techniques include medical terminology, biological reductionism, and professional self-interests, all of which imposed a language and categories that informed the idea of sexuality as universal, individualized, and physicalized. These techniques, and the discourse they imposed, emerged not because they were the most valid, in the routine sense of best representing the real world, but because of their "usefulness" in various communities (1987). Tiefer (in press) proceeded to recover the history of sexuality discourses by examining the history and language of formal classifications of sexual dysfunction (1991a, 1991c, in press); by analyzing the dominant metaphors and rhetoric behind one of the field's central tenets, the "human sexual response cycle" (1991c); and by measuring the constitutive force of professional legitimation of scientific knowledge (1991a, 1991b, 1991c).

Tiefer's historical studies indicate that "out of human potentials for consciousness, behavior, and human experience, sociocultural forces of definition and regulation shape the perceptions and experience of sexuality which then become 'naturalized' and feel unlearned" (1991a, 597). From the onset of scientific investigation, understandings of the phenomenon are regulated by technical routines just as they are influenced by sociocultural conditions. Tiefer's studies trace the effects of these regulative forces on the eventual scientific knowledge about the phenomenon, and ultimately, on the common understandings of sexuality that are produced and disseminated in culture.

Tiefer's historical project has also generated material for imagining new language, metaphors, and methods in sexuality research. These provisions begin with self-consciousness about where the sexologist stands when she gazes on sexuality, and about how her "facts" will be circumscribed in various ways by the context of their production. Through such reflexive techniques, the investigator moves toward a critical positioning, permitting her better visualization of other sexualities as well as the sociocultural maintenance of sexualities. These examinations thus augment historical analysis with exemplary alternatives, untread avenues of research, and imaginary projects (Tiefer 1991b). Such options for investigative practice and metatheory integrate accountability, transformation, and subversion into the project of scientific validation.

One additional feature of Tiefer's projects deserve note, and that is her decision to speak *in, through,* and *for* multiple communities of professionals. Her work appears in literature specifically designated for medical researchers, sexologists, psychologists, and feminists. In these forums she has positioned herself as both advocate and critic, as member and betrayer, and has strategically but subtly varied her language and style. This is part of what accountability and generativity is about. It also reaffirms feminists' need to furnish positive as well as critical programs. Tiefer's project is localized and her methodological innovations are limited to several techniques, yet her findings carry the potential to challenge and change diverse audiences.

Case 2

A common stance of feminist psychologists, one noted earlier in the chapter, is the appeal for multiple methods in feminist studies. This recommendation usually implies the augmentation of quantitative and experimental techniques by qualitative and nonexperimental ones, and tends to preserve the polar opposition of two techniques with its inevitable privileging of the more orthodox one. Kersti Yllö (1988) recognized the dangers of such "triangulation of methods" in its consistency with positivism and its consequential favoring of mainstream methods over feminist ones (48). The operations she and her colleagues deployed to avoid such undesired favoritism make manifest new routes toward validation.

In her research on wife abuse, Yllö has replaced the metaphors of distrust and dissension built into classic triangulation approaches with that of "dialogue," and a volume edited with Michele Bograd, *Feminist Perspectives on Wife Abuse* (1988), reflects such dialogic investigative practices. The text is unique in its inclusive coverage of the subject and in the manner in which the varied parts of wife-abuse research are knitted together. The contents include studies of the experiences of wife abuse, in men as well as women; the relationships between battering and other psychological conditions and experiences; and clinical implications for all persons involved. These more-or-less expected research topics are interspersed with essays considering other professionals involved with spousal abuse, such as members of the medical community (Kurz and Stark 1988) and activists (Schechter 1988). Also incorporated are chapters elaborating on feminist methods, such as social action (Dobash and Dobash 1988) collaborative research (Hoff 1988), and the integration of theory and practice (Pence and Shepard 1988). These contributions cohere to make the volume multimethodological—to realize an altered sense of triangulation:

> Feminist descriptions of multimethod research express the commitment to thoroughness, the desire to be open-ended, and to take risks. Multiple methods enable feminist researchers to link past and present, "data gathering" and action, and individual behavior with social frameworks. In addition, feminist researchers use multiple methods because of changes that occur to them and others in a project of long duration. Feminists describe such long projects as "journeys." Sometimes multiple methods reflect the desire to be responsive to the people studied. By combining methods, feminist researchers are particularly able to illuminate previously unexamined or misunderstood experiences. Multiple methods increase the likelihood of obtaining scientific credibility and research utility. (Reinharz 1992, 1987)

The mere accumulation of studies employing distinct and distinctly feminist techniques and covering the interstices of battering in its cultural context is a significant advance but does not fully account for the force of the book. Essays by the two editors are the touchstone in its radical reformulation of validation. Bograd (1988) detailed the framework undergirding feminist perspectives on wife abuse, and her succinct review captures the theoretical as well as the political necessity of "collaboration of the wide variety of feminists who are dedicated to understanding and eradicating wife abuse" (25). The chapter elucidates validation as the practices of an elaborate community of knowers and details the dynamic forms of accountability that are constitutive of collaborative work. Yllö (1988) went on to illustrate the limits of methodological debates by sharing a reflexive inspection of her own research program on wife abuse. She recalled how one product of her researches, a quantitative study correlating women's inequality and wife abuse, was rejected by a feminist journal for its "inherently patriarchal" methodology. She then recounted how her ventures into qualitative interview methods unsettled her satisfaction with that earlier study by making it

> clear to me that I am a part of what I am studying. As a woman in this society, I am vulnerable to such violence. Being aware of this makes a difference in how I understand the problem. This research was far more emotional and painful than my previous

> research. It had more impact on my personal life and my own relationships. The connection I felt to the women could not be simulated by the computer. Moreover, this subjective understanding was not an impediment to my work; rather, it was an important component of my analysis. (34–35)

At this point, Yllö refused to duck the dilemma that was surfacing in her own investigative career. She did not concede to the "simple, happy ending" that she had finally discovered "real" feminist methods. Rather, she rejected that common and all-too-comfortable narrative of closure, seeing it as truncating conversations and necessary epistemological analyses. Instead, she went on to explore the political, gender-structured terrain whereby what is feminist is subordinated to orthodox inquiries. In refusing to take this route toward reinstating a positivist worldview, Yllö proposed a dialogic model that transforms debates into collaboration, and embraces self-reflection as well as cultural analysis.

The validation process exemplified in the selection and arrangement of the volume's chapter is enunciated, not merely assumed, in the essays by Bograd and Yllö. Collaboration, as an essential of accountability and empowerment, is rendered a self-conscious and conscientious project, one that cannot be taken for granted in the course of scientific work. Dialogic practices, whether part of a single investigator's decision making or the conversations among a heterodox and perhaps discordant group of investigators, is shown to afford means (also requiring self-conscious monitoring) for circumventing common but ineffective remedies to methodological problems and transcending dilemmas that have previously thwarted feminist inquiry.

Conclusion

The story-book renditions of validity, although long-standing, continue to misrepresent the actual practices of validation. Yet among those researchers who stand as "experts in the field" are some who are redefining validity to more accurately match those practices. Validation is coming to be seen as a collective and collaborative task, not an individual one, and as comprised of many more parties, including the participants in investigations, than merely an elite community of psychological experts. Validation likewise is beginning to be comprehended as relevant to *investigation in its entirety* and not as a technical afterward, a final procedural treatment of the data.

Both within and outside psychology, feminist researchers are experimenting with newer practices of validation. These experiments tie validity with political commitments to describing how gender structures the world and our interpretations of that world, and to devising means to transform those gendered arrangements into more equitable, democratic, and life-sustaining ones. Sometimes these commitments demand subversive measures, particularly within intellectual communities that are themselves the products and reproducers of gender relations. At other times, these commitments need more public, more explicitly collaborative tactics in order to realize a comprehensive vision of validation. As the challenges and examples in this chapter indicate, no single route can be taken and no finite typology of techniques can be neatly compiled because validation depends on historically specific practices, languages, and organizations of work. Validation is a pragmatic objective, and for that reason alone, we need to be vigilant in our critical reflections on that objective and in selecting the tools we use to reach it.

Conclusion

Feminist psychology is transpiring in a vibrant space, one affording advantages not normally available to those relying on canonical procedures: plurality, audacity, and novel experimentation. Despite (or perhaps because of) resistances to unconventional and certainly to feminist contributions, feminist psychologists face opportunities for ingenuity. Our genuine experiments consequently often contain more than fresh data, they fashion new holds on the world that psychologists study and sometimes they even present new worlds. If the conversations developed in the book convey these advantages, even as they register accompanying complications and tensions, then something crucial has been accomplished. The canonical conception of science represents its practices as rational and programmatic, as methodically progressing toward better knowledge about the world. It accordingly depicts the agents of science as passive, distanced, and in the end, not too relevant. This portrayal of science fosters deprivations. Science practitioners who heed that worldview are cognitively primed to see only parts of the amazing processes that constitute their work, and hence, miss innumerable opportunities to extend or alter scientific visions—and possibly to transform science and the rest of the world. Further, those abiding scientists are invited, even required, to manifest identities that reduce their responsibilities as well as their opportunities.

Social epistemological concepts of science, as normative, descriptive projects, instill none of these deprivations. According to many feminist philosophers, a social epistemology of science is necessary to comprehend the gender politics of modern science, including its effects on both knowledge about gender and the gender relations of scientific work. A social epistemology does more than explain discriminatory practices, it offers a perspective that explicitly and systematically embodies the full range of activities that make up science. With such breadth of vision, it becomes possible to regard the interdependence of cognition and social relations, probe the dynamics of consensus making and dissent, and critically analyze the taken-for-granted categories and distinctions used to describe the world and our study of it. Finally, a social epistemology takes science as constituted through relations of power, both productive and regulative, thereby revealing how science, through its technologies, languages, and practices, transforms the world and our place in it.

A social epistemology, in itself, does not demand a rejection of science: It simply brings to light the norms or politics that are embedded in science's languages, procedures, and technologies and in the foundational distinctions of science—distinctions such as objectivity and subjectivity, the natural and the social. The rules of modern science are political because they ultimately cannot be separated from decisions about who we are, what differences are perceived among us, and how our relations with the world and each other should be conducted. Beyond these epistemic concerns about politics in science, feminists have raised a second and more specific form of political questioning, particularly through critical analyses of how sexism is perpetuated through science and how those structural inequities might be eliminated.

Feminist psychology has been largely, although not solely, interested in the second form of politics in science, and its practitioners have concentrated on the difficult task of locating the means for terminating gender oppression while preserving the objectives of science. This task of repairing science has not required social epistemology in any formal sense, and has largely been advanced through critiques of isolated methods or biases underlying specific theories. By interposing the perspective of social epistemology, the long-term efficacy of much of this feminist work in psychology becomes questionable. The first chapter of this book utilizes this perspective to chronicle the tensions and obstacles (as well as the successes) in such remedial politics, particularly those advanced by feminist empiricists. That initial chapter also documents feminist psychology as a long-standing movement, present in one or another form throughout the life of modern psychology. In revisiting the history of feminists' subsistence within psychology it becomes apparent that just as psychology (as a cultural activity) is dependent on the circumstances governing the larger culture, so too is the viability of feminist psychology dependent on larger cultural trends and happenings. Feminist psychology has been able to move into a marginal, liminal space that affords more substantive and generative opportunities because of other changes in culture, especially because of widespread challenges to dominant gender relations, shifts in women's participation in the paid labor force, and not insignificantly, critical reformulations of scientific knowledge.

Taking science as social practices raises doubts about the mainstream efforts of feminist psychology, but it also poses alternatives for that science. The advantages of a social perspective are threefold. It provides a descriptive model of science that accommodates the full range of scientific practices, including both productive and oppressive relations not generally taken into account in evaluations of science. Second, it offers a comprehension of science as constitutively involved in politics and power and not as incidentally corrupted (or occasionally biased) by dominant power relations. Finally, this perspective gives a concept of science as practice that returns us to questions about agents and actions and supplies us with conceptual tools to reconfigure those practices and agents. In other words, a social epistemological stance not only provides a more inclusive, detailed map for comprehending how gender is an inextricable part of science, and for self-critically analyzing our own efforts to remedy its sexist manifestations, but also creates new space for rethinking the subject matter of psychology, including the observer herself.

Before entertaining the investigative potentials that emerge from taking science as a social practice, a caveat is in order. An alternative episteme that comprises not merely a descriptive instrument for evaluating scientific productions but also a liberatory, transformational apparatus, costs its adherents the privileges of the dispassioned stance usually taken in the philosophy of science (and in science). Further, that alternative stance affords none of the cognitive faith in the workings of science that is available to feminists who subscribe to empiricism. Therefore, those who realize the social nature of science participate *unconditionally* in liminal science; but they do so with the undeniable advantages of new languages and techniques and, ultimately, new possibilities for human understanding.

In the previous chapters, I have attempted to use different language and techniques to locate the differences that some feminist psychology is making. Many of the innovations in this domain of inquiry, however modest they may appear, are nevertheless making meaningful alterations in the overarching ideals of research. Once objectivity is dislocated, no longer equated with some distanced and abstracted neutrality, then new positions of objectivity can be articulated—positions that both realize and critically reflect upon the agency of investigators and experiment with new, even subversive, standpoints. Once objectivity and subjectivity are seen not as oppositions but as an interdependent and hierarchical relation that organizes the social relations of research, then new identities and relations can be explored. And once the social relations of investigation are accessible to critical rethinking, it then becomes apparent how techniques of observation, evaluation, and dissemination also can be transformed.

Through strategical and local gestures, feminist psychologists are establishing new investigative practices that at once transmute epistemic commitments and generate new theories of human action. These new practices are everywhere challenging old ones, from the distanced, impersonal stance of the investigator whose moral connections with participants have been deferred to a formal ethics code, to the varied techniques for validating knowledge that rarely, if ever, permit any means for participants to have voice in that validation. Feminist innovations are likewise supplanting theories that assume the autonomy of individuals' thoughts and actions and that explain mental life as the end product of so many mechanical causal forces. In their stead, feminist work is producing fertile ground for comprehending cognition and action as constructed through (and as actively constructing) complex interactions within the human and nonhuman world.

Given the emergent, still liminal state of feminist practices, it would be premature if not illogical to enumerate their core tenets. Nevertheless these investigative practices share several themes that have been characterized in the book. First, feminist psychologists' operative concept of psychological science resonates with social epistemological interpretations: Psychology, as other sciences, does not exist apart from culture but is constituted through historically contingent social relations and interests—through culture. The knowledge produced reflects and usually maintains those arrangements and interests, among which are certain normative gender relations. Second, feminist psychologists, in diverse ways, are refusing the classic distinctions (notably differentiations between observers and those who are observed and between objectivity and subjectivity) that undergird conventional investigative techniques. These classes of actors and actions are no longer being taken as consisting of two kinds, except that psychology has made them so through the extended, repeated, and routinized technologies of research. The making and finding of human nature are seen as inextricably linked events in the production of knowledge. Third, with the two working premises listed above, feminist psychologists are returning to remake and relocate psychological phenomena through significantly altered investigative practices. This refiguring is necessarily local, piecemeal, and intermittent, and it requires interrogation of the myriad assumptions previously made about investigators, participants, and the knowledge-making process itself. The resultant reappraisals and refashionings are leading to complex, sometimes even contradictory, notions of human nature (notions that will be settled, to the extent that settlement is ever certain, through further experimentation with research practices). For instance, we have already come to realize that subjectivity is not always transparent to observers, yet the subjective voice cannot be dismissed as entirely unreliable. Subjectivity is an outcome of sustained relations within a particular social order, yet it nevertheless contains capacities to resist those determining relations. Finally, feminist psychologists' working assumptions about science take knowledges as power and scientific accomplishments as more than merely representing the world. We have begun a revision of science that returns attention to the political and moral work that it does, and as one consequence of this revisioning, feminist psychologists are reappraising the investigator and her expert community as one of the sources (and consequences) of those ethics and politics.

Some of these themes have been eloquently charted by feminist analysts working in psychology, and I have generously and gratefully drawn on these analyses. For the most part, however, the themes are yet emergent and are detectable only through scrutiny of experimental reports, texts, and review articles. Above all, they must be taken as tentative and incomplete for such instability is characteristic of a liminal science.

Even as I have asserted that restructuring scientific work necessitates that we also change our style of scientific writing, I still cannot resist the narrative convention in psychological writing that expects, as an epilogue, summary of the limitations as well as implications of the project being reported. This book has aimed to describe and synthesize the accomplishments of feminist psychology, yet that rather global objective is a recipe for making exclusions. Insomuch as the book is intended for an audience conversant with both psychology and feminism, it does not provide introductory surveys. Such omissions are intentional and necessary, but others warrant comment. In writing about the need to create new relations in research, especially to see and interact with participants in radically different ways, I said little about these participants who are the coproducers, recipients, and oftentimes the practitioners of psychological knowledge. As such, the chapters do not give a substantive (re-)introduction to these persons, their life circumstances, differences, and possibilities. And, although the project regards the labors of feminist psychologists, it omits important details—notably about the concrete circumstances within which they work and the microrelations that shape their lives.

Perhaps the vague representation of the varied voices populating the text parallels my reluctance to make the project candidly performative, to engage in reflexive experimentation by visibly writing in my own self. Two dedicated readers of my chapters-in-progress noted this reluctance. "I think there is a missing space where your own voice should be" (Mary Gergen). And more critically, "Given . . . your inexplicable passion for reflexivity why is it that we enjoy so little of you in this book? . . . You appear to be yourself liminal when it comes to the question of a performative notion of the subject versus (I assume experimentally compelled) notion of agency" (Kareen Ror Malone). Against my rallies for an outdoor psychology, a performative subjectivity, I have tended to narrate with a privatized, indoor psychology of authorship. Even as I write about how our selves are at once constituted through scientific activities and affect those activities, I have relied on the dominant logic of the authorial eye and voice, a logic that buries and often effaces much of my experience. The astuteness of these faithful readers bestows on me an auspicious challenge for future experimentation with psychological writing.

A second omission deserves mention because it points ahead to work remaining to be done. Presenting feminist psychology as a viable, indeed vital, domain of new experimental practices implies a shift away from the usual talk of theories, but that strategic move leaves some uncomfortable lacuna. Although the book is not a thesis on what are the best theories, it would be ridiculous to pretend that theories and theory talk are not central to our work. (In fact, I have generously borrowed from various theories). It is necessary, therefore, to take the advances, rehearsed in the book, back to questions about theory, evaluating not only systems that are commonly used in North American feminist psychology but also those deriving, for instance, from cognitive psychology and psychoanalysis. Our evaluations should attend to the psychological as it is theorized in other disciplines—especially fields like anthropology, history, and cultural studies where psychological phenomena are more explicitly taken to be connected with varied material and cultural conditions. We need to revisit all feasible theories, thinking about ways to integrate, revise, or transcend them, and always remaining aware of how theories function as cognitive instruments that construct the world and observers in the world in particular ways. These sorts of theory reassessments are part of the galvanizing work that lies ahead for feminist psychology; they signal a future of continued provocation and discovery.

It is my hope that the chapters underscore such lacuna and omissions, indicating what remains to be done. The liminal space that is feminist psychology is filled with unfinished work, and that is but one of its virtues. Feminist psychology has taken a variety of forms over the last century, at times enduring in most inhospitable environments. Even in the best of times, feminist inquiry has entailed a double labor consisting first, of making a place for research to be done, and second, accomplishing the investigative work that is normally thought of as the doing of science. As a relatively stable space for working is established, we can concentrate more on investigating and making knowledge claims, although we are hardly exonerated from confronting possible rebounds and backlashes in the future. Yet even as we stand ready for difficulties, a new world is already in the making, a world where we have earnestly participated in (among other changes) the transformation of gender, knowledge, and knowledge makers.

References

Acker, J., K. Barry, and J. Esseveld. 1983. Objectivity and truth: Problems in doing feminist research. *Women's Studies International Forum* 6 (4):423–35.

Addelson, K. P. 1983. The man of professional wisdom. In *Discovering Reality*, 165–86. *See* Harding and Hintikka 1983.

Agar, M. 1980. Stories, background knowledge and themes: Problems in the analysis of life history narrative. *American Ethnologist* 7:223–39.

Agronick, G. 1988. "Feminist Psychologists, 1915–1930: Personal, Political and Professional Constraints." B.A. thesis, Wesleyan University.

Alcoff, L. 1988. Cultural feminism versus post-structuralism: The identity crisis in feminist theory. *Signs* 13:405–36.

Archibald, W. P. 1978. Dangers in applying results from experimental psychology. *American Psychologist* 30:469–85.

Arnott, C. 1972. Husbands' attitude and wives' commitment to employment. *Journal of Marriage and the Family* 34:673–84.

Ashmore, M. 1989. *The Reflexive Thesis: Wrighting the Sociology of Scientific Knowledge*. Chicago: University of Chicago Press.

Ayres, I. 1991. Fair driving: Gender and race discrimination in retail car negotiations. *Harvard Law Review* 104(4):817–72.

Bart, P. 1977. Review of Chodorow's *The Reproduction of Mothering*. *Contemporary Psychology* 22:834–35.

Baumeister, R. 1987. How the self became a problem: A psychological review of historical research. *Journal of Personality and Psychology* 52:163–76.

———. 1988. Should we stop studying sex differences all together? *American Psychologist* 43:1092–95.

Bayer, B. 1993. "Passing Notes and Pressing Buttons: Investigative Technologies in Small Group Research." Department of Psychology, Hobart and William Smith Colleges, March.

Bayer, B., and J. G. Morawski. 1992. "Experimenters and Their Experimental Performances: The Case of Small Group Research." Paper presented at the annual meeting of the Canadian Psychological Association, Quebec City, June.

Bazerman, C. 1988. *Shaping Written Knowledge: The Genre and Activity of Experimental Article in Science*. Madison: University of Wisconsin Press.

Belenky, M. F., B. M. Clinchy, N. R. Goldberger, and J. M. Tarule. 1986. *Women's Ways of Knowing: The Development of Self, Voice, and Mind*. New York: Basic Books.

Bem, S. 1974. The measurement of psychological androgyny. *Journal of Clinical and Consulting Psychology* 42:155–62.

Berg, D. N., and K. K. Smith. 1988. *The Self in Social Inquiry: Researching Methods.* Newbury Park: Sage.

Bernstein, R. J. 1983. *Beyond Objectivism and Relativism: Science, Hermeneutics and Praxis.* Philadelphia: University of Pennsylvania Press.

Bevan, W. 1976. The sound of the wind that's blowing. *American Psychologist* 31:481–91.

Billig, M. 1990. Rhetoric of social psychology. In *Deconstructing Social Psychology,* 47–60. *See* Parker and Shotter 1990.

Birke, L. 1991. "Life" as we have known it: Feminism and the biology of gender. In *Science and Sensibility: Gender and Scientific Enquiry, 1780–1945,* ed. M. Benjamin, 243–63. Oxford: Basil Blackwell.

Bledstein, B. J. 1976. *The Culture of Professionalism: The Middle Class and the Development of Higher Education in America.* New York: Norton.

Bleier, R. 1984. *Science and Gender: A Critique of Biology and Its Theories on Women.* New York: Pergamon.

Bleier, R. 1986a. Sex differences research: Science or belief? In *Feminist Approaches to Science,* 147–64. *See* Bleier 1986b.

———, ed. 1986b. *Feminist Approaches to Science.* New York: Pergamon.

Bograd, M. 1988. Feminist perspectives on wife abuse. In *Feminist Perspectives on Wife Abuse,* 11–26. See Yllö and Bograd 1988.

Bordo, S. 1986. The Cartesian masculinization of thought. *Signs* 11(3):439–56.

———. 1987. *The Flight to Objectivity: Essays on Cartesianism and Culture.* Albany: State University of New York Press.

———. 1990a. Feminism, postmodernism, and gender-skepticism. In *Feminism/Postmodernism,* 133–56. *See* Nicholson 1990.

———. 1990b. "Material girl": The effacements of postmodern culture. *Michigan Quarterly Review* 29:653–77.

Bradley, B. S. 1993. *Darwin's Intertextual Baby: Erasmus Darwin as Precursor in Child Psychology.* Unpublished manuscript, James Cook University, Townsville, Australia.

Bronfenbrenner, U., J. Kessel, W. Kessen, and S. White. 1986. Toward a critical social history of developmental psychology: A propaedeutic discussion. *American Psychologist* 41 (11):1218–30.

Bruner, J. 1991. The narrative construction of reality. *Critical Inquiry* 18:1–21.

Brush, S. G. 1974. Should the history of science be rated X? *Science* 183:1164–72.

Buss, A. R. 1978. The structure of scientific revolutions. *Journal of the History of the Behavioral Science* 14:57–64.

———, ed. 1979. *Psychology in Social Context.* New York: Irvington.

Butler, J. 1990a. *Gender Trouble: Feminism and the Subversion of Identity.* New York: Routledge.

———. 1990b. Gender trouble, feminist theory and psychoanalytic discourse. In *Feminism/Postmodernism,* 324–40. *See* Nicholson 1990.

Capshew, J. H., and A. C. Laszlo. 1986. "We would not take no for an answer": Women psychologists and gender politics during World War II. *Journal of Social Issues* 42 (1):157–81.

Carlson, R. 1972. Understanding women: Implications for personality research. *Journal of Social Issues* 28(2):17–32.

Cherryholmes, C. H. 1988. Construct validity and the discourses of research. *American Journal of Education* 96:421–57.

Chorover, S. L. 1985. Psychology in cultural context: The division of labor and the fragmentation of experience. In *A Century of Psychology as Science*, 870–79. *See* Koch and Leary 1985.

Christian, B. 1985. Black feminist process: In the midst of . . . In *Black Feminist Criticism*. New York: Pergamon.

———. 1989a. But what do we think we're doing anyway: The state of black feminist criticism(s) or My version of a little bit of history. In *Changing Our Words*, ed. C. A. Wall, 58–74. New Brunswick: Rutgers University Press.

———. 1989b. The race for theory. In *Gender and Theory: Dialogues on Feminist Criticism*, ed. L. Kauffman, 225–37. Oxford: Basil Blackwell.

Code, L. 1993. Review of Impure thoughts, is women's philosophy possible? and Who knows: From Quine to a feminist empiricism. *Signs* 18 (3):711–16.

Cohen, A. G., and B. A. Gutek. 1991. Sex differences in the career experiences of members of two APA divisions. *American Psychologist* 46:1292–98.

Cohen, E. 1991. Who are we? Gay identity as political (e)motion (a theoretical rumination). In *Inside/out: Lesbian Theories, Gay Theories*, ed. D. Fuss, 71–92. New York: Routledge.

Collins, H. M. 1985. *Changing Order: Replication and Induction in Scientific Practice*. Beverly Hills: Sage.

Collins, P. H. 1989. The social construction of black feminist thought. *Signs* 14(4):745–73.

———. 1990. *Black Feminist Thought: Knowledge, Consciousness, and Politics of Empowerment*. Boston: Unwin Hyman.

Constantinopole, A. 1973. Masculinity-femininity: An exception to a famous dictum. *Psychological Bulletin* 80:389–407.

Cott, N. F. 1986. Feminist theory and feminist movements: The past before us. In *What Is Feminism?* ed. J. Mitchell and A. Oakley, 49–62. Oxford: Basil Blackwell.

———. 1987. *The Grounding of Modern Feminism*. New Haven: Yale University Press.

Coulter, X. 1986. Academic value of research participation by undergraduates. *American Psychologist* 41:317.

Cozzens, S. E., and T. F. Gieryn. 1990. Putting science back in society. In *Theories of Science in Society*, ed. S. E. Cozzens and T. F. Gieryn, 1–14. Bloomington: Indiana University Press.

Crawford, M. 1989. Agreeing to differ: Feminist epistemologies and women's ways of Knowing. In *Gender and Thought*, 128–45. *See* Crawford and Gentry 1989.

———. 1992. Identity, "passing" and subversion. *Feminism and Psychology* 2:429–31.

Crawford, M., and M. Gentry, eds. 1989. *Gender and Thought: Psychological Perspectives*. New York: Springer-Verlag.

Cronbach, L. J. 1986. Social inquiry for and by earthlings. In *Metatheory in Social Science: Pluralities and Subjectivities*, ed. D. W. Fiske and R. A. Shweder, 83–107. Chicago: University of Chicago Press.

———. 1988. Five perspectives on the validity argument. In *Test Validity*, ed. H. Wainer and H. I. Braun, 3–18. Hillsdale, N.J.: Laurence Earlbaum.

Crosby, F., and S. Clayton. 1990. Affirmative action and the issue of expectancies. *Journal of Social Issues* 46:61–79.

Crosby, F. J., A. Pufall, R. C. Snyder, M. O'Connell, and P. Whalen. 1989. The denial of personal disadvantage among you, me, and all the other ostriches. In *Gender and Thought*, 79–99. *See* Crawford and Gentry 1989.

Cushman, P. 1990. Why the self is empty: Toward a historically situated psychology. *American Psychologist* 45:599–611.

Danziger, K. 1979. The social origins of modern psychology. In *Psychology in Social Context*, 27–45. *See* Buss 1979.

———. 1990. *Constructing the Subject: Historical Origins of Psychological Research*. New York: Cambridge University Press.

Darnovsky, M. 1991. The new traditionalism: Repackaging Ms. Consumer. *Social Text* 29:72–94.

Datan, N. 1989. Illness and imagery: Feminist cognition, socialization, and gender identity. In *Gender and Thought*, 175–87. *See* Crawford and Gentry 1989.

Deaux, K., and B. Major. 1987. Putting gender into context: An interactive model of gender-related behavior. *Psychological Review* 94(3):369–89.

Deegan, M. J. 1988. *Jane Addams and the Men of the Chicago School, 1892–1910*. New Brunswick, N.J.: Transaction.

de Lauretis, T. 1986. Feminist studies/critical studies: Issues, terms, and contexts. In *Feminist Studies/Critical Studies*, ed. T. de Lauretis, 1–19. Bloomington: Indiana University Press.

———. 1990. Eccentric subjects: Feminist theory and historical consciousness. *Feminist Studies* 16:115–50.

Dempewolf, J. A. 1974. Development and validation of a feminism scale. *Psychological Reports* 34:651–57.

Diehl, L. A. 1986. The paradox of G. Stanley Hall: Foe of coeducation and educator of women. *American Psychologist* 41(8): 868–78.

Dobash, R. E., and R. P. Dobash. 1988. Research as social action: The struggle for battered women. In *Feminist Perspectives on Wife Abuse*, 51–74. *See* Yllö and Bograd 1988.

Doell, R. G. 1991. Whose research is this? Values and biology. In *(En)Gendering Knowledge: Feminists in Academe*, ed. J. E. Hartman and E. Messer-Davidow, 121–39. Knoxville: University of Tennessee Press.

Dreyer, N. A., N. F. Woods, and S. A. James. 1981. ISRO: A scale to measure sex-role orientation. *Sex Roles* 7:173–82.

Eagly, A. H. 1987a. Reporting sex differences. *American Psychologist* 42:756–57.

———. 1987b. Sex differences in influenceability. *Psychological Bulletin* 85:86–116.

———. 1990. On the advantages of reporting sex comparisons. *American Psychologist* 45:560–62.

Eccles, J. S. 1989. Bringing young women to math and science. In *Gender and Thought*, 36–58. *See* Crawford and Gentry 1989.

Edwards, R. 1990. Connecting method and epistemology: A white woman interviewing black women. *Women's Studies International Forum* 13:477–90.

Ellis, C., and M. G. Flaherty, eds. 1992. *Investigating Subjectivity: Research on Lived Experience*. Newbury Park: Sage.

Ellsworth, E. 1988. Illicit pleasures: Feminist spectators and *Personal Best*. In *Becoming Feminine: The Politics of Popular Culture*, ed. L. G. Roman, L. K. Christian-Smith, and E. Ellsworth, 102–19. London: Falmer.

Fausto-Sterling, A. 1985. *Myths of Gender: Biological Theories about Women and Men*. New York: Basic Books.

Fee, E. 1981. Is feminism a threat to scientific objectivity? *International Journal of Women's Studies* 4:378–92.

———. 1983. Women's nature and scientific objectivity. In *Women's Nature and Scientific Objectivity*, ed. M. Lowe and R. Hubbard, 9–28. New York: Pergamon.

———. 1986. Critiques of modern science: Relationship of feminism to other radical epistemologies. In *Feminist Approaches to Science*, 42–56. *See* Bleier 1986b.

Ferguson, K. E. 1993. *The Man Question: Visions of Subjectivity in Feminist Theory*. Berkeley: University of California Press.

Fine, M. 1985. Reflections on a feminist psychology of women. *Psychology of Women Quarterly*, 9:167–83.

———. 1989. Coping with rape: Critical perspectives on consciousness. In *Representations*, 186–200. *See* Unger 1989c.

Fine, M., and S. M. Gordon. 1989. Feminist transformations of/despite psychology. In *Gender and Thought*, 146–74. *See* Crawford and Gentry 1989.

Fitzpatrick, E. 1990. *Endless Crusade: Women, Social Scientists, and Progressive Reform*. New York: Oxford University Press.

Flanagan, O. J., Jr. 1981. Psychology, progress, and the problem of reflexivity: A study in the epistemological foundations of psychology. *Journal of the History of the Behavioral Sciences* 17:375–86.

Flax, J. 1983. Political philosophy and the patriarchal unconscious: A psychoanalytic perspective on epistemology and metaphysics. In *Discovering Reality*, 245–82. *See* Harding and Hintikka 1983.

———. 1987. Postmodernism and gender relations in feminist theory. *Signs* 12:621–43.

———. 1990. *Thinking Fragments: Psychoanalysis, Feminism, and Postmodernism in the Contemporary West*. Berkeley: University of California Press.

Fleck, L. 1979. *Genesis and Development of a Scientific Fact*. Chicago: University of Chicago Press.

Fonow, M. M., and J. A. Cook. 1991a. Back to the future: A look at the second wave of feminist epistemology and methodology. In *Beyond Methodology*, 1–15. *See* Fonow and Cook 1991b.

———. 1991b. *Beyond Methodology: Feminist Scholarship as Lived Research*. Bloomington: Indiana University Press.

Foucault, M. 1980. *Power/Knowledge: Selected Interviews and Other Writings, 1972–1977*. Trans. Colon Gordon, Leo Marshall, John Mepham, and Kate Soper. New York: Pantheon.

Frable, D.E.S., T. Blackstone, and C. Scherbaum. 1990. Marginal and mindfuls: Deviants in social interactions. *Journal of Personality and Social Psychology* 59:140–49.

Franklin, S., C. Lury, and J. Stacey. 1991. Feminism and cultural studies: Pasts, presents, futures. In *Off-Centre: Feminism and Cultural Studies,* ed. S. Franklin, C. Lury, and J. Stacey, 1–19. New York: HarperCollins.

Fraser, N., and L. J. Nicholson. 1990. Social criticism without philosophy: An encounter between feminism and postmodernism. In *Feminism/Postmodernism,* 19–38. *See* Nicholson 1990.

Fuller, S. 1988. *Social Epistemology.* Bloomington: Indiana University Press.

Funder, D. C. 1992. Psychology from the other side of the line: Editorial processes and publication trends at JPSP. *Personality and Social Psychology Bulletin* 18:493–97.

Furman, E. R., and K. Oehler. 1986. Discourse analysis and reflexivity. *Social Studies of Science* 16:293–307.

Furner, M. O. 1975. *Advocacy and Objectivity: A Crisis in the Professionalization of American Social Science,* 1865–1905. Lexington: University of Kentucky Press.

Furumoto, L. 1988. Shared knowledge: The experimentalists, 1904–1929. In *The Rise of Experimentation in American Psychology,* 94–113. *See* Morawski 1988c.

———. 1992. Joining separate spheres–Christine Ladd-Franklin, woman-scientist (1847–1930). *American Psychologist* 47(2):175–82.

Gadlin, H., and G. Ingle. 1975. Through a one-way mirror: The limits of experimental self-reflection. *American Psychologist* 29:1003–9.

Gagnon, J. H. 1992. The self, its voices, and their discord. In *Investigating Subjectivity,* 221–43. *See* Ellis and Flaherty 1992.

Genova, J. 1988. Women and the mismeasure of thought. *Hypatia* 3(1):101–17.

Gergen, K. J. 1973. Social psychology as history. *Journal of Personality and Social Psychology* 26:309–20.

———. 1982. *Toward Transformation in Social Knowledge.* New York: Springer-Verlag.

———. 1991. *The Saturated Self: Dilemmas of Identity in Contemporary Life.* New York: Basic Books.

Gergen, M. M. 1990. Finished at forty: Women's development within the patriarchy. *Psychology of Women Quarterly* 14:471–93.

Gerson, J. M., and K. Peiss. 1985. Boundaries, negotiation, consciousness: Reconceptualizing gender relations. *Social Problems* 32(4):317–31.

Giddens, A. 1979. *Central Problems in Social Theory.* Berkeley: University of California Press.

Gieryn, T. F. 1983. Boundary-work and the demarcation of science from non-science: Strains and interests in the professional ideologies of science. *American Sociological Review* 48:781–95.

Gieryn, T. F., and A. E. Figert. 1986. Scientists protect their cognitive authority: The status degradation ceremony of Sir Cyril Burt. In *The Knowledge Society: The Growing Impact of Scientific Knowledge on Social Relations,* ed. G. Bohme and N. Stehr, 67–86. Boston: Reidel.

Gigerenzer, G. 1991. From tools to theories: A heuristic of discovery in cognitive psychology. *Psychological Review* 98:254–67.

Gilbert, G. N., and M. Mulkay. 1984. *Opening Pandora's Box: A Sociological Analysis of Scientists' Discourse.* New York: Cambridge University Press.

Gilligan, C. 1982. *In a Different Voice: Psychological Theory and Women's Development.* Cambridge: Harvard University Press.

Ginsburg, F. 1989. Dissonance and harmony: The symbolic function of abortion in activists' life stories. In *Interpreting Women's Lives*, 59–84. *See* Personal Narratives Group 1989.

Giroux, H. 1992. *Border Crossings: Cultural Workers and the Politics of Education.* New York: Routlege.

Glazer, P. M., and M. Slater. 1987. *Unequal Colleagues: The Entrance of Women into the Professions, 1890–1940.* New Brunswick: Rutgers University Press.

Goldschmidt, J., M. M. Gergen, K. Quigley, and K. J. Gergen. 1974. The women's liberation movement: Attitudes and action. *Journal of Personality* 42:601–17.

Goodenough, F. 1946. Semantic choice and personality structure. *Science* 104:451–56.

Gouldner, A. 1970. *The Coming Crisis in Western Sociology.* New York: Basic Books.

Grady, K. E. 1981. Sex bias in research design. *Psychology of Women Quarterly* 5:628–36.

Green, C. D. 1992. Of immortal mythological beasts: Operationism in psychology. *Theory and Psychology* 2:291–320.

Gross, E. 1986. Conclusion: What is feminist theory? In *Feminist Challenges: Social and Political Theory*, ed. C. Pateman and E. Gross, 190–204. Boston: Northeastern University Press.

Gruenberg, B. 1978. The problem of reflexivity in the sociology of science. *Philosophy of Social Science* 8:321–43.

Gubar, S. 1981. Blessings in disguise: Cross-dressing as re-dressing for female modernists. *Massachusetts Review* 22:477–508.

Haaken, J. 1988. Field dependence research: A historical analysis of a psychological construct. *Signs* 13:311–30.

Hacking, I. 1986. Making up people. In *Reconstructing Individualism: Autonomy, Individuality, and the Self in Western Thought*, ed. T. C. Heller, M. Sosna, and D. Wellberry, 222–36. Stanford: Stanford University Press.

———. 1991. The making and molding of child abuse. *Critical Inquiry* 17:253–88.

Haraway, D. 1985. A manifesto for cyborgs: Science, technology, and socialist feminism in the 1980's. *Socialist Review* 15:65–107.

———. 1986. Primathology is politics by other means. In *Feminist Approaches to Science*, 77–118. *See* Bleier 1986b.

———. 1988. Situated knowledges: The science question in feminism and the privilege of partial perspective. *Feminist Studies* 14(3):575–99.

———. 1990. *Primate Visions: Gender, Race and Nature in the World of Modern Science.* New York: Routledge.

Harding, S. 1986a. The instability of the analytical categories of feminist theory. *Signs* 11(4):645–64.

———. 1986b. *The Science Question in Feminism.* Ithaca: Cornell University Press.

———. 1987a. The garden in the machine: Gender relations, the process of science, and feminist epistemological strategies. In *The Process of Science*, ed. N. J. Nersessian, 125–37. Dordrecht: Martinus Nijhoff Publishers (Kluwer Academic Publishers).

———, ed. 1987b. *Feminism and Methodology.* Bloomington: Indiana University Press.

———. 1991. *Whose Science? Whose Knowledge? Thinking from Women's Lives.* Ithaca: Cornell University Press.

Harding, S., and M. B. Hintikka, eds. 1983. *Discovering Reality: Feminist Perspectives on Epistemology, Metaphysics, Methodology, and Philosophy of Science.* Boston: Reidel.

Hare-Mustin, R. T., and J. Marecek. 1988. The meaning of difference: Gender theory, post modernism and psychology. *American Psychologist* 43:455–64.

———. 1990a. Beyond difference. In *Making a Difference,* 184–201. *See* Hare-Mustin and Marecek 1990c.

———. 1990b. On making a difference. In *Making a Difference,* 1–21. *See* Hare-Mustin and Marecek 1990c.

———, eds. 1990c. *Making a Difference: Psychology and Construction of Gender.* New Haven: Yale University Press.

Harré, R., and P. F. Secord. 1972. *The Explanation of Social Behavior.* Oxford: Basil Blackwell.

Harris, B. 1984. Give me a dozen healthy infants: John B. Watson's popular advice on childrearing, women and the family. In *In the Shadow of the Past,* 126–54. *See* Lewin 1984.

———. 1988. Key words: A history of debriefing in social psychology. In *The Rise of Experimentation in American Psychology,* 188–212. *See* Morawski 1988c.

Harris, B., and J. Morawski. 1979. "John B. Watson's Predictions for 1979." Paper presented at the Eastern Psychological Association Meetings, Philadelphia, April.

Hartmann, H. I. 1981. The family as the locus of gender class, and political struggle: The example of housework. *Signs* 6 (3):366-93.

Hartsock, N. 1984. *Money, Sex, and Power.* Boston: Northeastern University Press.

———. 1987. The feminist standpoint: Developing the ground for a specifically feminist historical materialism. In *Feminism and Methodology,* 157–80. *See* Harding 1987b.

———. 1990. Foucault on power: A theory for women? In *Feminism/Postmodernism,* 157–75. *See* Nicholson 1990.

Haskell, T. L. 1977. *The Emergence of Professional Social Science: The American Social Science Association and the Nineteenth-Century Crisis of Authority.* Urbana: University of Illinois Press.

Hawes, S. E. 1993. "Reflexivity and Collaboration in the Supervisory Process: A Role for Feminist Poststructural Theories in the Training of Professional Psychologists." Paper presented for the National Council of Schools of Professional Psychology Conference, Las Vegas.

Helson, R. 1989. E. Nesbit's forty-first year: Her life, times, and symbolizations of personality growth. In *Representations,* 29–44. *See* Unger 1989c.

———. 1992. Women's difficult times and rewriting of the life story. *Psychology of Women Quarterly* 16:331–48.

Henriques, J. 1984. Social psychology and the politics of racism. In *Changing the Subject,* 60–89. *See* Henriques et al. 1984.

Henriques, J., C. Hollway, C. Urwin, C. Venn, and V. Walkerdine, eds. 1984. *Changing the Subject: Psychology, Social Regulation and Subjectivity.* London: Methuen.

Herman, E. 1993. "Psychology as Politics: How Psychology Experts Transformed Public Life in the United States, 1940–1970." Ph.D. diss. Brandeis University, Waltham, Mass.

Herman, J., D. Russell, and K. Trocki. 1986. Long-term effects of incestuous abuse in childhood. *American Journal of Psychiatry* 143:1293–96.

Herschberger, R. 1948. *Adam's Rib*. New York: Pellegrini and Cudahy.

Higginbotham, E. B. 1992. African-American women's history and the metalanguage of race. *Signs* 17:251–74.

Higgins, E. T. 1992. Increasingly complex but less interesting articles: Scientific progress or regulatory problems? *Personality and Social Psychology Bulletin* 18:489–92.

Hinkle, B. M. 1920. On the arbitrary use of the terms "masculine" and "feminine." *Psychoanalytic Review* 7:15-30.

———. 1978. Why feminism? *The Nation*, 1927. In *These Modern Women: Autobiographical Essays from the Twenties*, 137– 41. *See* Showalter. 1978.

Hirsch, M., and E. F. Keller, eds. 1990. *Conflicts in Feminism*. New York: Routledge.

Hoff, L. A. 1988. Collaborative feminist research and the myth of objectivity. In *Feminist Perspectives on Wife Abuse*, 269–81. *See* Yllö and Bograd 1988.

Hollingworth, L. S. 1918. Comparison of the sexes in mental traits. *Psychological Bulletin* 15:427–32.

———. 1940. *Public Addresses*. Lancaster: Science Press.

Hollis, M., and S. Lukes. 1984. *Rationality and Relativism*. Cambridge, Mass.: MIT Press.

Hollway, W. 1989. *Subjectivity and Method in Psychology*. London: Sage.

hooks, b. 1990. *Yearning: Race, Gender, and Cultural Politics*. Boston: South End Press.

Hornstein, G. A. 1988. Quantifying psychological phenomena: debates, dilemmas, and implications." In *The Rise of Experimentation in American Psychology*, 1–34. *See* Morawski 1988c.

Howe, K. G. 1989. Telling our mother's story: Changing daughters' perceptions of their mothers in a women's studies course. In *Representations*, 45–60. *See* Unger 1989c.

Hronszky, I., M. Feher, and B. Dajka, eds. 1988. *Scientific Knowledge Socialized*. Budapest: Akademiai Kiodo.

Hurtado, A. 1989. Relating to privilege: Seduction and rejection in the subordination of white women and women of color. *Signs* 14:883–85.

Hyde, J. S. 1991. *Half the Human Experience: The Psychology of Women*. Lexington, Mass.: Heath.

Imber, B., and N. Tuana. 1988. Feminist perspectives on science. *Hypatia* 3(1):139–44.

Jaggar, A. M. 1990. Sexual difference and sexual equality. In *Theoretical Perspectives on Sexual Difference*, ed. D. L. Rhode, 239–54. New Haven: Yale University Press.

———. 1983. *Feminist Politics and Human Nature*. Totowa, N. J.: Rowman & Allenheld.

Janich, P. 1988. Truth as success of action. The constructive approach in the philosophy of science. In *Scientific Knowledge Socialized*, 313–26. *See* Hronszky et al. 1988.

Jayaratne, T. E., and A. J. Stewart. 1991. Quantitative and qualitative methods in the social sciences: Current feminist issues and practical strategies. In *Beyond Methodology*, 85–106. *See* Fonow and Cook 1991b.

Johnson, R. 1986. What is cultural studies anyway? *Social Text* 16:38–80.

Jourard, S. M. 1972. A humanistic revolution in psychology. In *The Social Psychology of Psychological Research*, ed. A. G. Miller, 10–13. New York: Free Press.

Judd, C. M., E. R. Smith, and L. H. Kidder. 1991. *Research Methods in Social Relations*. Fort Worth: Holt, Rinehart, & Winston.

Kahn, A. S., and J. D. Yoder. 1989. The psychology of women and conservatism: Rediscovering social change. *Psychology of Women Quarterly* 13:417–32.

Kalmuss, D., P. Gurin, and A. L. Townsend. 1981. Feminist and sympathetic feminist consciousness. *European Journal of Social Psychology* 11:131–37.

Keller, E. F. 1985a. *Reflections on Gender and Science*. New Haven: Yale University Press.

———. 1985b. The gender/science system: Or, is sex to gender as nature is to science? *Hypatia* 2:33–44.

Keller, E. F., and H. Moglin. 1987. Competition and feminism: Conflicts for academic women. *Signs* 12(3):493–511.

Kelly-Gadol, J. 1987. The social relation of the sexes: Methodological implications of women's history. In *Feminism and Methodology*, 15–28. *See* Harding 1987b.

Kessen, W. 1983. The child and other cultural inventions. In *The Child and Other Cultural Inventions*, ed. F. S. Kessel and A. W. Seigel, 26–39. New York: Praeger.

Kessler, S. J., and W. McKenna. 1978. *Gender: An Ethnomethodological Approach*. New York: Wiley.

Kihlstrom, J. F., and N. Cantor. 1983. Mental representations of the self. In *Advances in Experimental Social Psychology*, vol. 15, ed. L. Berkowitz, 1–47. New York: Academic Press.

Kimmel, E. B. 1989. The experience of feminism. *Psychology of Women Quarterly* 13:133–46.

Kipnis, D. 1987. Psychology and behavioral technology. *American Psychologist* 42:30–36.

Kirkpatrick, C. 1936. The construction of a belief-pattern scale for measuring attitudes toward feminism. *Journal of Social Psychology* 7:421–37.

Kitzinger, C. 1991a. Feminism, psychology and the paradox of power. *Feminism and Psychology* 1:111–30.

———. 1991b. Politicizing psychology. *Feminism & Psychology* 1(1):49–54.

Koch, S. 1992. Psychology's Bridgman vs. Bridgman's Bridgman: An essay in reconstruction. *Theory and Psychology* 2:261–90.

Koch, S., and D. E. Leary, eds. 1985. *A Century of Psychology as Science*. New York: McGraw-Hill.

Kohout, J. 1991. "Changes in Supply: Women in Psychology." Paper presented at the annual meeting of the American Psychological Association, San Francisco.

Kroger, R. O., and L. A. Wood. 1986. Needed: Radical surgery. *American Psychologist* 41:317–18.

Krohn, W. 1988. Social change and epistemic thought (reflections on the origins of the experimental method). In *Scientific Knowledge Socialized*, 165–78. *See* Hronszky et al. 1988.

Kuhn, T. S. 1962. *The Structure of Scientific Revolutions*, Vol. 2. International Encyclopedia of Unified Science. Chicago: University of Chicago Press.

Kurz, D., and E. Stark. 1988. Not-so-benign neglect: The medical response to battering. In *Feminist Perspectives on Wife Abuse*, 249–66. *See* Yllö and Bograd 1988.

Lamb, S. 1991. Acts without agents: An analysis of linguistic avoidance in journal articles on men who batter women. *American Journal of Orthopsychiatry* 61(2):250–57.

Landrine, H., E. A. Klonoff, and A. Brown-Collins. 1992. Cultural diversity and methodology in feminist psychology: Critique, proposal, and empirical example. *Psychology of Women Quarterly* 16:145–63.

Lather, P. 1986a. Issues of validity in openly ideological research: Between a rock and a soft place. *Interchange* 17(4):63–84.

———. 1986b. Research as praxis. *Harvard Educational Review* 56:257–77.

———. 1988. Feminist perspectives on empowering research methodologies. *Women's Studies International Forum* 11 (6):569– 81.

Latour, B. 1983. Give me a laboratory and I will raise the world. In *Science Observed,* ed. R. Knorr-Cetina and M. Mulkay, 141–70. Newbury Park: Sage.

———. 1987. *Science in Action: How to Follow Scientists and Engineers through Society.* Cambridge: Harvard University Press.

———. 1991. The impact of science studies on political philosophy. *Science, Technology, and Human Values* 16:3–19.

Latour, B., and S. Woolgar. 1979. *Laboratory Life: The Social Construction of Scientific Facts.* Newbury Park: Sage.

Lave, J. 1991. Situating learning in communities of practice. In *Perspectives on Socially Shared Cognition,* ed. L. B. Resnick, J. M. Levine, and S. D. Teasley, 63–82. Washington: American Psychological Association.

Lawson, H. 1985. *Reflexivity: The Post-Modern Predicament.* La Salle, Ill.: Open Court.

Leahey, T. H. 1980. The myth of operationism. *Journal of Mind and Behavior* 1:127–43.

Leary, D. E. 1980. The intentions and heritage of Descartes and Locke: Toward a recognition of the moral basis of modern psychology. *Journal of General Psychology* 102:283–310.

Lewin, M., ed. 1984. *In the Shadow of the Past: Psychology Portrays the Sexes.* New York: Columbia University Press.

Levine, N., C. Worboys, and M. Taylor. 1973. Psychology and the "psychology" textbook: A social demographic study. *Human Relations* 26(4):467–78.

Linden, R. 1990. "Threshold Ethnography: Life Histories as Liminal Texts." Paper presented at the Qualitative/Interactionist Research Conference, Toronto, May.

Loevinger, J. 1957. Objective tests as instruments of psychological theory. *Psychological Reports* 3:635–94.

Longino, H. E. 1988. Review essay: Science, objectivity, and feminist values. *Feminist Studies* 14(3):561–74.

———. 1990. *Science as Social Knowledge: Values and Objectivity in Scientific Inquiry.* Princeton: Princeton University Press.

Lopes, L. L. 1991. The rhetoric of irrationality. *Theory and Psychology* 1:65–82.

Lott, B. 1985. The potential enrichment of social/personality psychology through feminist research and vice versa. *American Psychologist* 40(2):155–64.

Lowell, A. 1955. *The Complete Poetical Works of Amy Lowell.* Boston: Houghton Mifflin.

Lubek, I. 1979. A brief social psychological analysis of research on aggression in social psychology. In *Psychology in Social Context,* 259–306. *See* Buss. 1979.

Lubove, R. 1965. *The Professional Altruist: The Emergency of Social Work as a Career, 1880–1930.* Cambridge: Harvard University Press.

Lykes, M. B. 1989. Dialogue with Guatemalan Indian women: Critical perspectives on constructing collaborative research. In *Representations,* 167–85. *See* Unger 1989.

Lykes, M. B., and A. J. Stewart. 1986. Evaluating the feminist challenge to research in personality and social psychology: 1963–1983. *Psychology of Women Quarterly* 10:393–412.

Lyotard, J. F. 1984. *The Post-modern Condition: A Report on Knowledge.* Minneapolis: University of Minnesota Press.

Maccoby, E. E., and J. W. Jacklin. 1974. *The Psychology of Sex Differences*. Stanford: Stanford University Press.

McHugh, M. C., R. D. Koeske, and I. H. Frieze. 1986. Issues to consider in conducting nonsexist psychological research: A guide for researchers. *American Psychologist* 41(8):879–90.

MacIntyre, A. 1985. How psychology makes itself true–or false. In *A Century of Psychology as Science*, 897–903. *See* Koch and Leary 1985.

McLoyd, V. C., and S. M. Randolph. 1986. Secular trends in the study of Afro-American children: A review of *Child Development*, 1936–1980. In *History and Research in Child Development: Monographs of the Society for Research in Child Development*, ed. A. B. Smuts and J. W. Hagen, 211, nos. 4–5. Chicago: University of Chicago Press.

Mahoney, M. A., and B. Yngvesson. 1992. The construction of subjectivity and the paradox of resistance: Reintegrating feminist anthropology and psychology. *Signs* 18:44–73.

Mann, S. A. 1989. Slavery, sharecropping, and sexual inequality. *Signs* 14:774–98.

Martin, E. 1987. *The Woman in the Body: A Cultural Analysis of Reproduction*. Boston: Beacon.

Martin, P. Y., and R. A. Hummer. 1989. Fraternities and rape on campus. *Gender and Society* 3:457–73.

Mednick, M. T. 1989. On the politics of psychological constructs: Stop the bandwagon, I want to get off. *American Psychologist* 44:1118–23.

Merchant, C. 1980. *Death of Nature: Women, Ecology and the Scientific Revolution*. New York: Harper & Row.

Mies, M. 1983. Toward a methodology for feminist research. In *Theories of Women's Studies*, ed. G. Bowles and R. D. Klein, 117– 39. London: Routledge & Kegan Paul.

Miller, N. K. 1991. *Getting Personal: Feminist Occasions and Other Autobiographical Acts*. New York: Routledge.

Mink, L. O. 1978. Narrative form as cognitive instrument. In *The Writing of Literacy: Literacy Form and Historical Understanding*, ed. R. H. Canary and H. Kozicki, 72–93. Madison: University of Wisconsin Press.

Minnich, E. K. 1990. *Transforming Knowledge*. Philadelphia: Temple University Press.

Minow, M. 1990. Adjudicating Differences: Conflicts among feminist lawyers. In *Conflicts in Feminism*, 149–63. *See* Hirsh and Keller 1990.

Minton, H. L. 1986. Femininity in men and masculinity in women: American psychiatry and psychology portray homosexuality in the 1930s. *Journal of Homosexuality* 13:1–21.

———. 1988. *Lewis M. Terman: Pioneer in Psychological Testing*. New York: New York University Press.

Mishler, E. G. 1979. Meaning in context: Is there any other kind? *Harvard Educational Review* 49:1–19.

———. 1986. *The Discourse of Medicine: Dialectics of Medical Interviews*. Norwood, N.J.: Ablex.

———. 1990. Validation in inquiry-guided research: The role of exemplars in narrative studies. *Harvard Educational Review* 60:415–42.

Mohanty, C. T. 1991. Cartographies of struggle: Third world women and the politics of feminism. In *Third World Women and the Politics of Feminism*, ed. C. T. Mohanty, A. Russo, and L. Torres, 1–47. Bloomington: Indiana University Press.

Morawski, J. G. 1984. Not quite new worlds: Psychologists' conceptions of the ideal family in the twenties. In *In the Shadow of the Past*, 97–125. *See* Lewin 1984.

———. 1985. The measurement of masculinity and femininity: Engendering categorical realities. *Journal of Personality* 53:196–223.

———. 1987. The troubled quest for masculinity, femininity, and androgyny. *Review of Personality and Social Psychology* 7:44–69.

———. 1988a. Impasse in feminist thought? In *Feminist Structures of Knowledge*, ed. M. M. Gergen, 182–94. New York: New York University Press.

———. 1988b. Impossible experiments and practical constructions: The social bases of psychologists' work. In *The Rise of Experimentation in American Psychology*, 72–93. *See* Morawski 1988c.

———, ed. 1988c. *The Rise of Experimentation in American Psychology*. New Haven: Yale University Press.

———. 1990. Toward the unimagined: Feminism and epistemology in psychology. In *Making a Difference*, 150–83. *See* Hare-Mustin and Marecek 1990c.

———. 1992. Self regard and other regard: Reflexive practices in American psychology, 1890–1940. *Science in Context*, 5 (2):281–308.

Morawski, J. G., and G. Agronick. 1991. A restive legacy. *Psychology of Women Quarterly* 15:567–79.

Morawski, J. G., and B. Bayer. 1991. "Stirring Trouble and Making Theory." Report to the Task Force on Cultural Diversity, Division 35 of the American Psychological Association.

Morawski, J. G., and G. Hornstein. 1991. Quandary of the quacks: The struggle for expert knowledge in American psychology, 1890–1940. In *The Estate of Social Knowledge*, ed. J. Brown and D. VanKeuren, 106–33. Baltimore: Johns Hopkins University Press.

Morawski, J. G., and R. S. Steele. 1991. The one and the other: Textual analysis of masculine power and feminist empowerment. *Theory and Psychology* 1:107–31.

Moulton, J. 1983. A paradigm of philosophy: The adversary method. In *Discovering Reality*, 149–64. *See* Harding and Hintikka 1983.

Mulkay, M., and G. N. Gilbert. 1982. Accounting for error: How scientists construct their social world when they account for correct and incorrect belief. *Sociology* 16:165–83.

Nagel, T. 1979. *Mortal Questions*. London: Cambridge University Press.

National Science Foundation. 1992. *Women and Minorities in Science and Engineering: An Update*. Washington, D.C.

Nicholson, L. J., ed. 1990. *Feminism/Postmodernism*. London: Routledge & Kegan Paul.

Oakley, A. 1981. Interviewing women: A contradiction in terms. In *Doing Feminist Research*, ed. Helen Roberts, 30–61. London: Routledge & Kegan Paul.

O'Connell, A., and N. Russo. 1983. *Models of Achievement*. New York: Columbia University Press.

Oehler, K., and N. C. Mullins. 1986. "Mechanisms of Reflexivity in Science: A Look at Nontraditional Literary Forms." Paper presented at the meeting of the Society for the Social Studies of Science, Pittsburgh, October.

Pandora, K. 1991. "Dissenting from Pure Experimentalism: The Natural History Model and Pragmatic Psychologists During the 1930s." Paper presented at the Cheiron Meetings, Slippery Rock, Pa.

Parker, I., and J. Shotter, eds. 1990. *Deconstructing Social Psychology*. New York: Routledge.

Parlee, M. B. 1973. The premenstrual syndrome. *Psychological Bulletin* 80:454–65.

———. 1979. Psychology and women. *Signs* 5:121–33.

———. 1982. Changes in moods and activation levels during the menstrual cycle in experimentally naive subjects. *Psychology of Women Quarterly 7:119–31.*

———. 1991. Happy birthday to *Feminism & Psychology*. *Feminism & Psychology* 1:39–48.

Patai, D. 1991. U.S. academics and Third World women: Is ethical research possible? In *Women's Words: The Feminist Practice of Oral History*, ed. S. B. Gluck and D. Patai, 137–54. New York: Routledge.

Pence, E., and M. Shepard. 1988. Integrating feminist theory and practice: The challenge of the battered women's movement. In *Feminist Perspectives on Wife Abuse*, 282–98. *See* Yllö and Bograd 1988.

Peplau, L. A., and E. Conrad. 1989. Beyond nonsexist research: The perils of feminist methods in psychology. *Psychology of Women Quarterly*, 13:379–400.

Personal Narratives Group, eds. 1989. *Interpreting Women's Lives: Feminist Theory and Personal Narratives*. Bloomington: Indiana University Press.

Pfister, J. 1991. The Americanization of cultural studies. *Yale Journal of Criticism* 4:199–229.

Philipson, I. 1992. The new no-man's land: The changing face of psychotherapy. *Tikkun* 6(5):9–12, 86.

Pinch, T. T. The externalization of observation: An example from modern physics. In *Scientific Knowledge Socialized*, 225–44. *See* Hronszky, Feher, and Dajka 1988.

Polkinghorne, D. E. 1988. *Narrative Knowing the Human Sciences*. Albany: State University of New York Press.

Poovey, M. 1988. Feminism and deconstruction. *Feminist Studies* 14:51–65.

Pratt, C. C. 1939. *The Logic of Modern Psychology*. New York: Macmillan.

Prilleltensky, I. 1989. Psychology and the status quo. *American Psychologist* 44:795–802.

Quinn, N. 1987. Convergent evidence for a cultural model of American marriage. In *Cultural Models in Language and Thought*, ed. D. Holland and N. Quinn, 173–92. Cambridge: Cambridge University Press.

Rabine, L. W. 1988. A feminist politics of non-identity. *Feminist Studies* 14:11–31.

Rabinow, P., and W. M. Sullivan. 1979. *Interpretive Social Science: A Reader*. Berkeley: University of California Press.

Reason, P., and J. Rowan, eds. 1981. *Human Inquiry: A Sourcebook of New Paradigm Research*. New York: John Wiley & Sons.

Reinharz, S. 1992. *Feminist Methods in Social Research*. New York: Oxford University Press.

Reis, H. T., and J. Stiller. 1992. Publication trends in JPSP: A three-decade review. *Personality and Social Psychology Bulletin* 18:465–72.

Reiter, L. 1989. Sexual orientation, sexual identity, and the question of choice. *Clinical Social Work Journal* 17:138–50.

Renzetti, C. M. 1987. New wave or second stage? Attitudes of college women toward feminism. *Sex Roles* 16:265–77.

Reskin, B. F. 1988. Bringing the men back in: Sex differentiation and the devaluation of women's work. *Gender and Society* 2:55–81.

Resnick, L. B. 1991. Shared cognition: Thinking as social practice. In *Perspectives on Socially Shared Cognition*, ed. L. B. Resnick, J. M. Levine, and S. D. Teasley, 1–20. Washington: American Psychological Association.

Richards, G. 1987. Of what is history of psychology a history? *British Journal of the History of Science* 20:201–11.

Richardson, L. 1991. Sharing feminist research with popular audiences: The book tour. In *Beyond Methodology*, 284–95. *See* Fonow and Cook 1991b.

———. 1992. The consequences of poetic representation: Writing the other, rewriting the self. In *Investigating Subjectivity: Research on Lived Experience*, 125–37. *See* Ellis and Flaherty 1992.

Riemer, R. 1986. Political thought: A re-visioning. *Women and Politics* 6(1):57–67.

———. 1993. *Narrative Analysis*. Newbury Park: Sage.

Riessman, C. K. 1987. When gender is not enough: Women interviewing women. *Gender and Society* 1(2):172–207.

———. 1991. When gender is not enough: Women interviewing women. In *The Social Construction of Gender*, ed. J. Lorber and S. A. Farrell, 217–36. Newbury Park: Sage.

Riger, S. 1992. Epistemological debates, feminist voices: Science, social values, and the study of women. *American Psychologist* 47(6):730–40.

Riley, D. 1988. *"Am I That Name?" Feminism and the Category of "Women" in History*. Minneapolis: University of Minnesota Press.

Robinson, E. A., and D. R. Follingstad. 1985. Development and validation of a behavioral sex-role inventory. *Sex Roles* 13:691–706.

Rorty, R. 1979. *Philosophy and the Mirror of Nature*. Princeton: Princeton University Press.

———. 1989. *Contingency, Irony and Solidarity*. Cambridge: Cambridge University Press.

Rose, A. M. 1982. "Vision of a New Profession: Annie Fisher and Educational Reform." B.A. thesis, Wesleyan University, Middletown, Conn.

Rose, H. 1983. Hand, brain and heart: A feminist epistemology for the natural sciences. *Signs* 9(1):73–90.

———. 1986. Beyond masculinist realities: A feminist epistemology for the sciences. In *Feminist Approaches to Science*, 57–76. *See* Bleier 1986b.

Rose, N. 1985. *The Psychological Complex: Psychology, Politics and Society in England* 1869–1935. London: Routledge & Kegan Paul.

———. 1989. Individualizing psychology. In *Texts of Identity*, ed. J. Shotter and K. Gergen, 119–31. London: Sage.

———. 1990a. *Governing the Soul: The Shaping of the Private Self*. London: Routledge & Kegan Paul.

———. 1990b. Psychology as a "social" science. In *Deconstructing Social Psychology*, 103–16. *See* Parker and Shotter 1990.

Rosenberg, R. L. 1982. *Beyond Separate Spheres: Intellectual Origins of Modern Feminism*. New Haven: Yale University Press.

Rosenberg, S., and M. A. Gara. 1985. The multiplicity of personal identity. In *Review of Personality and Social Psychology,* vol. 6, ed. P. Shaver, 87–113. Newbury Park: Sage.

Rosenwald, G. C. 1985. Hypocrisy, self-deception and perplexity: The subject's enhancement as methodological criterion. *Journal of Personality and Social Psychology* 49:682– 703.

Rossiter, M. W. 1982. *Women Scientists in America: Struggles and Strategies to 1940.* Baltimore: Johns Hopkins University Press.

Rothblum, E. D. 1988. More reporting on sex differences. *American Psychologist* 43:1095.

Rouse, J. 1987. *Knowledge and Power: Toward a Political Philosophy of Science.* Ithaca: Cornell University Press.

———. 1992. What are cultural studies of scientific knowledge? *Configurations* 1:1-22.

Russell, D.E.H. 1988. Pornography and rape: A causal model. *Political Psychology* 9:41–73.

Russo, N. F., and F. L. Denmark. 1987. Contributions of women to psychology. *Annual Review of Psychology* 38:279–98.

Samelson, F. 1978. From "race psychology" to "studies in prejudice": Some observations on the thematic reversal in social psychology. *Journal of the History of the Behavioral Sciences* 14:265–78.

Sampson, E. E. 1977. Psychology and the American ideal. *Journal of Personality and Social Psychology* 36:1332–43.

———. 1981. Cognitive psychology as ideology. *American Psychologist* 36:730–43.

———. 1991. The democratization of psychology. *Theory and Psychology* 1(3):275–98.

Sandelowski, M. 1986. Sophie's choice: A metaphor for infertility. *Health Care for Women International* 7:439–53.

———. 1987. The color gray: Ambiguity and infertility. *IMAGE: Journal of Nursing Scholarship* 19 (2): 70–74.

———. 1988. Without child: The world of infertile women. *Health Care for Women International* 9:147-61.

———. 1990a. Failures of volition: Female agency and infertility in historical perspective. *Signs* 15 (3): 475–99.

———. 1990b. Fault lines: Infertility and imperiled sisterhood. *Feminist Studies* 16:33-52.

———. 1991. Telling Stories: Narrative approaches in qualitative research. *IMAGE: Journal of Nursing Scholarship* 23:161–66.

Sandelowski, M., B. G. Harris, and D. Holditch-Davis. 1989. Mazing: Infertile couples and the quest for a child. *IMAGE: Journal of Nursing Scholarship* 21(4):220–26.

———. 1990. Pregnant moments: The process of conception in infertile couples. *Research in Nursing and Health* 13:273–82.

Sarbin, T. R., ed. 1986. *Narrative Psychology: The Storied Nature of Human Conduct.* New York: Praeger.

Sass, L. A. 1988. The self and its vicissitudes: An "archaeological" study of the psychoanalytic avant-garde. *Social Research* 55(4):551–607.

Sayers, J. 1986. *Sexual Contradictions: Psychology, Psychoanalysis, and Feminism.* New York: Tavistock.

Scarborough, E., and L. Furumoto. 1987. *Untold Lives: The First Generation of American Women Psychologists.* New York: Columbia University Press.

Schecter, S. 1988. Building bridges between activists, professionals and researchers. In *Feminist Perspectives on Wife Abuses*, 299–312. *See* Yllö and Bograd 1988.

Scheman, N. 1983. Individualism and the objects of psychology. In *Discovering Reality*, 225–44. *See* Harding and Hintikka 1983.

———. 1991. How to question authority. *Women's Review of Books* 9:19–20.

Schneider, D. J. 1992. Publication games: reflections on Reis and Stiller. *Personality and Social Psychology Bulletin* 18:498–503.

Scott, J. W. 1986. Gender: A useful category of historical analysis. *American Historical Review* 91(5):1053–75.

———. 1988. Deconstructing equality-versus-difference: Or the uses of poststructuralist theory for feminism. *Feminist Studies* 14(1):33–50.

———. 1992. Experience. In *Feminists Theorize the Political*, ed. J. Butler and J. W. Scott, 22–40. London: Routledge & Kegan Paul.

Sears, D. O. 1986. College sophomores in the laboratory: Influences of a narrow data base on social psychology's view of human nature. *Journal of Personality and Social Psychology* 51:515–30.

Sedgwick, F. 1991. How to bring your kids up gay. *Social Text* 29: 18-27.

Seltzer, M. 1987. Statistical persons. *Diacritics* 17:82–98.

Seward, G. H. 1946. *Sex and the Social Order*. New York: McGraw-Hill.

Shapin, S., and S. Schaffer. 1985. *Leviathan and the Air Pump: Hobbes, Boyle and the Experimental Life*. New Jersey: Princeton University Press.

Sherif, C. W. 1979. Bias in psychology. In *Feminism and Methodology*, 37–56. *See* Harding 1987b.

———. 1982. Needed concepts in the study of gender identity. *Psychology of Women Quarterly* 6(4):375–98.

Shields, S. A. 1975. Functionalism, Darwinism and the psychology of women: A study in social myth. *American Psychologist* 30:739–54.

Shields, S. A., and M. E. Mallory. 1987. Leta Stelter Hollingworth speaks on "Columbia's legacy." *Psychology of Women Quarterly* 11:285–300.

Showalter, E. ed. 1978. *These Modern Women: Autobiographical Essays in the Twenties*. Old Westbury, Conn.: Feminist Press.

Shuster, R. 1991. Beyond defense: Considering the next steps for bisexual liberation. In *Bi Any Other Name: Bisexual People Speak Out*, ed. L. Hutchins and L. Kaahumanu, 266–74. Boston: Alyson.

Silver, B. R. 1991. The authority of anger: Three guineas as case study. *Signs* 16(2):340–70.

Small, M. F., ed. 1984. *Female Primates: Studies by Women Primatologists*. New York: Alan R. Liss.

Smith, D. E. 1987a. *The Everyday World as Problematic: A Feminist Sociology*. Boston: Northeastern University Press.

———. 1987b. Women's perspective as a radical critique of sociology. In *Feminism and Methodology*, 84–96. *See* Harding 1987b.

Smith, E. R., M. M. Feree, and F. D. Miller. 1975. A short scale of attitudes toward feminism. *Representative Research in Social Psychology* 6:51–56.

Smith, P. 1988. *Discerning the Subject*. Minneapolis: University of Minnesota Press.

Smith-Rosenberg, C. 1985. *Disorderly Conduct: Visions of Gender in Victorian America.* New York: Knopf.

Snitow, A. 1990. A Gender Diary. In *Conflicts in Feminism,* 9–43. *See* Hirsch and Keller 1990.

Squire, C. 1989. *Significant Differences: Feminism in Psychology.* London: Routledge & Kegan Paul.

Stacey, J., and B. Thorne. 1985. The missing feminist revolution in sociology. *Social Problems* 32:301–16.

Stanley, L., and S. Wise. 1983. *Breaking Out: Feminist Consciousness and Feminist Research.* London: Routledge & Kegan Paul.

Stevens, G., and S. Gardner. 1982. *The Women of Psychology.* Cambridge, Mass.: Schenkman.

Stewart, A. J., and S. Gold-Steinberg. 1990. Midlife women's political consciousness: Case studies of psychosocial development and political commitment. *Psychology of Women Quarterly* 14:543–66.

Stewart, A. J., and J. E. Malley. 1989. Case studies of agency and communion in women's lives. In *Representations,* 61–76. *See* Unger 1989c.

Stewart, A. J., and J. M. Healey Jr. 1986. The role of personality development and experience in shaping political commitment: An illustrative case. *Journal of Social Issues* 42:11–31.

Striegel-Moore, R. H. 1993. Toward a feminist research agenda in the psychological research of eating disorders. In *Feminist Perspectives on Eating Disorders,* ed. P. Fallon, M. Katzman, and S. Wooley, 438–454. New York: Guilford.

Striegel-Moore, R. H., L. R. Silberstein, and J. Rodin. 1986. Toward an understanding of risk factors for bulimia. *American Psychologist* 41:246–63.

Striegel-Moore, R. H., and J. G. Morawski. 1993. "Should We Define Feminism—or Just Measure it?" Department of Psychology, Wesleyan University, March.

Stringer, P. 1990. Prefacing social psychology: A textbook example. In *Deconstructing Social Psychology,* 17–32. *See* Parker and Shotter 1990.

Suls, J. M., and R. L. Rosnow. 1988. Concerns about artifacts in psychological experiments. In *The Rise of Experimentation,* 163–87. *See* Morawski 1988c.

Tanner, A. 1986. The community of ideas of men and women. *Psychological Review* 3:549–550.

Tedlock, B. 1991. From participant observation to the observation of participation: The emergence of narrative ethnography. *Journal of Anthropological Research* 47(1):69–94.

Terman, L., and C. C. Miles. 1936. *Sex and Personality, Studies in Masculinity and Femininity.* New York: McGraw-Hill.

Terry, J. 1990. Lesbians under the medical gaze: Scientists search for remarkable differences. *The Journal of Sex Research* 27:317–39.

Thorne, B. 1990. Science with a conscience. Review of Ellen Fitzpatrick, *Endless Crusade: Social Scientists and Progressive Reform. Women's Review of Books* 7:22.

Tiefer, L. 1987. Social construction and the study of human sexuality. In *Sex and Gender,* ed. P. Shaver and C. Hendrick, 70–94. Newbury Park: Sage.

———. 1991a. New perspectives in sexology: From rigor(mortis) to richness. *The Journal of Sex Research* 28(4):593–602.

———. 1991b. Commentary on the status of sex research: Feminism, sexuality, and sexology. *Journal of Psychology and Human Sexuality* 4(3):5–42.

———. 1991c. Historical, scientific, clinical, and feminist criticisms of "the human sexual response cycle" model. *Annual Review of Sex Research* 2:1–23.

———. In press. Critique of the DSM-IIIR nosology of sexual dysfunctions. *Psychiatric Medicine.*

Toulmin, S. E. 1975. The Twin Moralities of Science. In *Science and Society: Past, Present, and Future*, ed. N. H. Steneck, 111–24. Ann Arbor: University of Michigan Press.

Toulmin, S., and D. E. Leary. 1985. The cult of empiricism in psychology and beyond. In *A Century of Psychology as Science*, 594–617. *See* Koch and Leary 1985.

Towson, S. M. J., M. P. Zanna, and G. MacDonald. 1989. Self-fulfilling Prophecies: Sex Role Stereotypes for Behavior. In *Representations*, 97–107. *See* Unger 1989c.

Trigg, M. 1987. "The Characterization of Herself: Lorine Pruette on Women, Men, and Marriage in the 1920s." Paper presented at the Seventh Annual Berkshire Conference on the History of Women, June.

Turner, V. 1977. Variations on a theme of liminality. In *Secular Ritual*, ed. S. F. Moore and B. G. Myerhoff, 36–52. Amsterdam: Van Gorcum

Unger, R. K. 1979. Toward a redefinition of sex and gender. *American Psychologist* 34(11):1085–94.

———. 1983. Through the looking glass: No wonderland yet! (The reciprocal relationship between methodology and models of reality). *Psychology of Women Quarterly* 8(1):9-32.

———. 1989a. Explorations in feminist ideology: Surprising consistencies and unexamined conflicts. In *Representations*, 203–11. *See* Unger 1989c.

———. 1989b. Sex, gender, and epistemology. In *Gender and Thought*, 17–35. *See* Crawford and Gentry 1989.

———, ed. 1989c. *Representations: Social Constructions of Gender.* Amityville, N.Y.: Baywood.

———. 1990. Imperfect reflections of reality. In *Making a Difference*, 102–49. *See* Hare-Mustin and Marecek 1990a.

Unger, R. K., and M. Crawford. 1992. *Women and Gender: A Feminist Psychology.* New York: McGraw-Hill.

Venn, C. 1984. The subject of psychology. In *Changing the Subject: Psychology, Social Regulation and Subjectivity*, 119–52. *See* Henriques et al. 1984.

Verhave, T., and W. Van Hoorn. 1984. The temporalization of the self. In *Historical Social Psychology*, ed. K. J. Gergen and M. M. Gergen, 325–46. Hillsdale, N. J.: Lawrence Erlbaum.

Walkerdine, V. 1990. *Schoolgirl Fictions.* New York: Verso.

Wallston, B. S. 1981. What are the questions in psychology of women? A feminist approach to research. *Psychology of Women Quarterly* 5(4):597–617.

Walsh, R. T. 1989. Do research reports in mainstream feminist psychology journals reflect feminist values? *Psychology of Women Quarterly* 13:433–44.

Walsh-Bowers, R. T. 1992. "Democracy in American Psychological Research Practice." Paper presented at the annual meetings of the American Psychological Association, Washington, D.C., August.

Watson, J. B. 1978. The weakness of women. In *These Modern Women: Autobiographical Essays in the Twenties,* 141–43. *See* Showalter 1978.

Wegner, D. M. 1992. The premature demise of the solo experiment. *Personality and Social Psychology Bulletin* 18:504–8.

Weisstein, N. 1971. Psychology constructs the female. In *Women in Sexist Society,* ed. V. Gornick and B. K. Moran, 207–24. New York: American Library.

Wertsch, J. V., and J. Youniss. 1987. Contextualizing the investigator: The case of developmental psychology. *Human Development* 30:18-31.

West, C., and D. H. Zimmerman. 1987. Doing gender. *Gender and Society* 1(2):125–51.

West, S. G., J. T. Newscom, and A. M. Fenaughty. 1992. Publication trends in JPSP: Stability and change in topics, methods, and theories across two decades. *Personality and Social Psychology Bulletin* 18:473–84.

Westkott, M. 1979. Feminist criticism of the social sciences. *Harvard Educational Review* 49:422–30.

White, H. 1980. The value of narrativity in the representation of reality. *Critical Inquiry* 7:5–27.

Wiersma, J. 1988. The press release: Symbolic communication in life history interviewing. In *Psychobiography and Life Narratives,* ed. D. P. McAdams and R. L. Ochberg, 205–38. Durham: Duke University Press.

Wilkinson, S. 1988. The role of reflexivity in feminist psychology. *Women's Studies International Forum* 11(5): 493–502.

Wolf, C. 1986. Legitimation of oppression: Response and reflexivity. *Symbolic Interaction* 9:217–34.

Woolgar, S. 1988a. *Knowledge and Reflexivity.* London: Sage.

———, ed. 1988b. *Science: The Very Idea.* New York: Tavistock.

———. 1989. The ideology of representation and the role of the agent. In *Dismantling Truth: Reality in the Post-modern World,* ed. H. Lawson and L. Appignanesi, 131–44. New York: St. Martin's.

Woolf, V. 1938. *Three Guineas.* New York: Harcourt, Brace and World.

Worell, J. 1990. Feminist frameworks: Retrospect and prospect. *Psychology of Women Quarterly* 14:1–5.

Wright, M. 1989. Personal narratives, dynasties, and women's campaigns: Two examples from Africa. In *Interpreting Women's Lives,* 155–71. *See* Personal Narratives Group 1989.

Yerkes, R. M. 1940. Social behavior of chimpanzees: Dominance between mates, in relation to sexual status. *Journal of Comparative Psychology* 30:147–86.

Yerkes, R. M. 1943. *Chimpanzees, a Laboratory Colony.* New Haven: Yale University Press.

Yllö, K. 1988. Political and methodological debates in wife abuse research. In *Feminist Perspectives on Wife Abuse,* 28–50. *See* Yllö and Bograd 1988.

Yllö, K., and M. Bograd, eds. 1988. *Feminist Perspectives on Wife Abuse.* Newbury Park: Sage.

Young, I. M. 1990. *Throwing Like a Girl and Other Essays in Feminist Philosophy and Social Theory.* Bloomington: Indiana University Press.

Zanna, M. P. 1992. My life as a dog (I mean editor). *Personality and Social Psychology Bulletin* 18:485–92.

Zinn, M. B. 1989. Family, race, and poverty in the eighties. *Signs* 14:856–74.

Zinn, M. B., L. W. Cannon, E. Higginbotham, and B. T. Dill. 1986. The cost of exclusionary practices in women's studies. *Signs* 11:290–303.

Index